DESIGNING FOR AGING   PATTERNS OF USE

DESIGNING FOR AGING

PATTERNS OF USE

Sandra C. Howell

The MIT Press
Cambridge, Massachusetts, and London, England

PUBLISHER'S NOTE

This format is intended to reduce the cost of publishing
certain works in book form and to shorten the gap between
editorial preparation and final publication. Detailed
editing and composition have been avoided by photographing
the text of this book directly from the author's typescript.

Library of Congress Cataloging in Publication Data

Howell, Sandra C
   Designing for aging.

   Bibliography: p.
   Includes index.
   1. Aged--United States--Dwellings. 2. Architecture
and the aged--United States. I. Title.
NA2545.A3H68   728'.0463   80-15977
ISBN 0-262-08107-5

To my parents, Edith and Harry Cooper,
who still invite me home.

CONTENTS

INTRODUCTION AND ACKNOWLEDGMENTS

In perspective, this book represents a first attempt in the field of human development and aging to combine design and social psychological issues in a format that is generative to design methods and, as well, suggestive for extending theory and research in environment and behavior. The literature now available to guide the design of residential settings for the elderly tends to be either quite *prescriptive* or to be an attempt to impute design significance to social psychological response tendencies. The *prescriptive* material, often in the form of Guidelines, presents secondary or tertiary translation of gerontological information in graphics and specifications. It essentially accepts the designed world as it appears to be. The social psychological reports, more often than not, create the unverified impression that most of what has been successfully built for aging people meets their needs in quite satisfactory fashion. Neither approach adequately honors the quality of life potential of Designing for Aging.

The study of Patterns of Use attempt to take an existing set of housing prototypes and explore their implications for *habitability*. Of necessity, issues are raised relative to perceptions of age, life style and culture appropriateness of particular design solutions. As well, the effects of building industry and policy/program practices as they determine design, are questioned.

This is a large personal commitment by the author, but reflects a disinclination to produce simply another set of presumptive recommendations for living environments.

ORGANIZATION OF THE BOOK.

The preparation of Designing for Aging gave the author a valued opportunity to reorganize her thinking about a set of problems related to social science research and its application. In the process, a primary challenge became how to place design issues in a much wider context. A subtler writer might have found a way to tantalize readers into exploring territories unfamiliar to them. The intention here is rather more insistent. In order for the design oriented audience to locate guidelines to placemaking it may be necessary to share the agony of complexity and indeterminacy that are an integral part of both research and practice. For the social science-gerontologist reader, becoming more familiar with concepts and issues in building design and the exercising of a retarded visual mode of thinking may prove to be the more difficult challenge.

Chapter 1 attempts to place the residential aspects of American aging in a framework of broader concern, that of the meaning of *habitat*. It exposes the author's growing awareness that a too determinate building solution is being generated for a sensitive social problem.

Chapter 2 extends the discussion of design and aging into the realm of production, program and practice as these factors influence the shape of new living environments. Subjects which are not, frankly, the academic concern of the author, but absolutely cannot be ignored, are presented briefly, candidly and more as a hoped-for initiation of dialogue than as explanation.

Chapter 3 provides a walk through the multiple facets of research development that preceded the in-depth design behavior studies. The reader may find this methodological chapter somewhat cumbersome, however it may be necessary to plow through this section in order to understand the real complexity of integrating social, psychological and environmental design issues. The research methods chapter takes the reader through a difficult and by no means completed journey, in which a number of gerontologists have devoted considerable time over the past ten years. We now are in some agreement that the role of environmental variables in late life experiences cannot be adequately clarified through survey research instruments or standardized scales dealing globally with morale and satisfaction. We are clearly confronted with an arena in which the behavior-relevant architectural variables themselves have to be identified and made operational.

Chapters 4 and 5 will, hopefully, become a user's manual for programming and design review of housing for some aggregations of aging people. These case studies are primarily to be seen as research documents for the "problem seeking" architect. They were originally developed to test *translation* of behavioral research for design practice.

Chapter 6 consists of a brief summing up and a discussion of future directions for collaborative work in designing for habit-ability across the human life cycle.

Appendix materials provide selected items from the large file of data in the author's research pool. The aim of the selection is to stimulate a reshaping of research in environments for aging and to encourage replications of the case studies in order to verify or refine the hypotheses suggested in the text.

The literature in all of the areas touched upon in this book is enormous. There was no attempt to cover it all in the Reference list. It is considered sufficient to the purpose that a few of the most relevant in a particular area be recalled. Fuller search is up to the reader.

Considerable effort was put into the organization of the Index in order that the expected multi-disciplined audience might be better able to locate subjects of particular interest and to explore concepts unfamiliar to them.

ACKNOWLEDGEMENTS.

To Powell Lawton and our collaborating friend Lucille Nahemow go the credit and appreciation for pushing my own curiosity beyond the realm of "traditional" social gerontology.

For every push toward action there needs to be a complementary pull; this came from my colleagues and friends in architecture who incessantly asked embarrasing questions about the utility of social science to design and the dubious influences of design on human behavior. I am particularly indebted to Louis Gelwicks and Chester Sprague, each in his own way, for not giving up the dialogue.

Many others in the profession have also supported my explorations, most notably Louis Sauer, Tim Anderson, Ezra Ehrenkrantz, Jan Wampler and John Habraken.

Without Gayle Epp the search for modes of design translation would have probably been lost. This was by no means her only contribution to the conduct of the design oriented parts of the research effort. Gayle's ability to organize the activities of an often diverted collection of graduate students, and to encourage their creative performance in the process, was outstanding. Surrounded by a very complex and huge accumulation of data, Gayle Epp superbly managed a retrieval system which will allow a ten year pool of information to provide base-line material for many future studies of elderly housing.

The initial national field research conducted from 1973-75 was jointly coordinated by Pamela Dinkel, out of my Design Evaluation Section at MIT and by Miriam Grimes at the Philadelphia Geriatric Center. In addition to a compulsive attention to detail, these two brought to an extensive survey research effort a necessary warmth and humor which protected the field workers and the rest of us from drowning under the weight of it all.

Jessie Gertman, now at the National Institute on Aging, was our very special grants manager. While all major research activities critically depend upon sustained funding, it is not always the case that the representative of a funding agency is personally committed to the subject matter of the research. Jessie has been consistently concerned with the social and environmental needs of aging people, and helping to improve the quality and useability of research in these areas. The Administration on Aging, Social and Rehabilitation Service, HEW, to which she was attached, generously financed the wide ranging efforts reported here from 1973 to 1977 and continues to provide support for studies which emerged as critical tangential issues to those specific to Federal Housing Programs.

The cast of "characters" which made up our student staff over the study years reads like a log of Santa's helpers. It is not possible to record all their names but I think they understand my appreciation for their contributions. Some performed particularly notable tasks: Christine Albright, Brandt Anderson, Charles Cofield, Donna Duerk, Alfonso Govela, Glynton LaRue, Karen Ouzts, Virginia Peltier, Philip Pipal, Jan Reizenstein, Ingrid Ruberg, Kalev Ruberg.

For Diane Rubin, a recent addition to my staff, typing this manuscript and revising graphics and layout was the hard way to support her architectural education. She deserves a medal (she got a raise).

To the people who allowed us into their homes and shared their daily lives with us... without you there would be no story to tell.

Development of this manuscript was partially supported by a grant from: Administration on Aging, Department of Health, Education & Welfare, Grant #93-P-57584/01-04, 1973-77; and support from: The Albert Farwell Bemis Fund, Department of Architecture, MIT, 1977-78.

1

HABITABILITY AND AGING

This book is about a particular housing type and the varied ways by which it can be measured for *habitability*. *Habitability* is a term which connotes warmth of hearth, closeness of family and containment of domestic activities. In denotation, the word tends to specify safe and sanitary conditions for occupancy, consensually adopted space standards for particular activities, such as sleeping and adequately sound construction to protect residents from weather, fire, floods and earthquakes. While modern housing is achieving ever greater technical capacity to meet the more specific requirements for *habitability*, concern for those habitat conditions which would support psychological and social well being has not kept pace. Part of the responsibility for this knowledge and application gap belongs to behavioral scientists, who have not provided appropriate criteria by which residential building design may be evaluated as meaningful for users.

Housing produced for older people in the United States is the subject of the studies and discussions presented here. "Elderly housing" in the United States has tended to assume prototypic qualities in terms of density and organization. This makes it a particularly valuable field laboratory in which to study *habitability*.

Housing designed for a specific tenant population segregates, by definition, that group from others in a community. In addition, population-specific design may prove to produce buildings which are ill-adapted to changes in use over time. Despite these problems, some groups within a society may still indicate a need for specialized residential settings and such settings probably should exist within the total array of alternatives from which people can choose.

Older people show enormous variability in their interests, capacities and competencies. Part of the rationale for housing programs directed toward this population is to address the need for greater alternatives as it is represented in this variability. The major problem in conceptualizing residential design for older people is in the fact that aging is a process while most building programs assume an essentially static state for users and usage.

IDENTITY AND HOUSING HISTORY.

Where do you want to live when you are old? The answer to that question is probably not as idiosyncratic as you imagine. The factors that enter into an answer reflect your perceptions of what you will be like as an older person and what are appropriate environments for older persons in your society; of your economic status and of what your own personal relationships have been to homes you have known.

Aging is a process of consolidating personal identity. Who am I? becomes a story told in the presentation of surroundings as well as in remembered events and associations. Non-verbal messages come forward in the varied behaviors which older people, like all people, practice. These messages of identity are as often unconscious as conscious. They are messages that can be *read* and systematically interpreted. The messages of *habitability* are reflected in the attitudes, behaviors and physical attributes which aging people exhibit in their home. The cumulative history of the individual, including an environmental history, moves along wherever the late life residence happens to be.

In the United States, personal environmental history has most often been imbedded in a single-family detached home. That home has been the place of nurturance and growth of family, a symbol of success in occupation and a source of pride in assemblage.

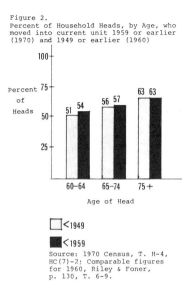

Figure 2.
Percent of Household Heads, by Age, who moved into current unit 1959 or earlier (1970) and 1949 or earlier (1960)

Source: 1970 Census, T. H-4, HC(7)-2; Comparable figures for 1960, Riley & Foner, p. 130, T. 6-9.

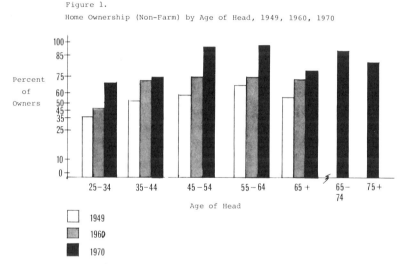

Figure 1.

Home Ownership (Non-Farm) by Age of Head, 1949, 1960, 1970

Source: Survey of Consumer Finances 1960-64 (1949 & 1960)
Census of Population 1970

The majority of older people remain throughout their adult lives in the home in which they raised their children. If you have lived in the same house for 20-40 years, your relationships to that space have become clearly *habituated*. How you enter, use spaces, relate to neighbors and arrange your effects has become a very personal statement of who you are. Your expectations of how you and your living environment should be shaped, in complement, are well established. The rules for perceived *habitability* have been laid down.

Subtle and/or critical events of life change these relationships of person and environment. You become a widow with less of a pension than was expected from your husband's employment; you become less able to afford the taxes and to maintain the property; you find it difficult to shovel snow, mow a lawn or mount stairs; your neighbors and children move away and the

local stores where you shopped and had credit
disappear. In short, you might seek a new
home but with an objective of retaining and
containing major aspects of your self-identity
and life-style. In fact, despite the
commonality of these events, most older
Americans do not move from their owned
homes after age 55.

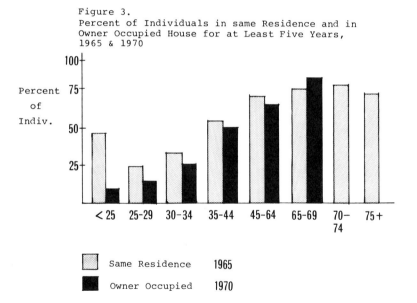

Figure 3.
Percent of Individuals in same Residence and in
Owner Occupied House for at Least Five Years,
1965 & 1970

Source: Census of Population 1970.

As yet, there is little indication in the
United States of a primary shift in the
mobility habits of older people despite the
addition of newer types of alternatives and
conspicuous publicity about "retirement
communities". Projections of future mobility
among people now in their middle years are
difficult to estimate. Such moves will depend
on the availability of suitable alternatives
within the community environments of preference to the aging consumer. The primary
approach that social scientists have used to
study residential mobility among aging groups
is to focus on the destination environments
of the relatively few movers. Among the large
sample of residents of public elderly housing
in the United States that were studied by the
author in 1974 46% had resided in single
family homes, 81% in the same neighborhood.

The factors which govern the decision to move
and the choice of housing among older people
are not now well understood. Certainly
reduced economic circumstances play a role
in these decisions in the United States. That
this is so seems ironical in a society
within which a high value has been placed on
home ownership as a cardinal symbol of the
self-made person. To be sure, some older
individuals and couples voluntarily elect
to trade ownership for renter status in order
to reduce the caretaking burdens. How this
decision is satisfied or not in the rental
market requires specific study. The sample of
former owners who appear in the studies
reported in this book are selective, since
they had to be economically eligible for
subsidy to enter the housing environments
that were observed.

Among older urban renters in this country, who compose only 15% of the total elderly population of 23 million, somewhat more mobility occurs, but it tends to be concentrated within their own neighborhood or immediately adjacent to it.

During the past two decades, a growing number of rental buildings have been expressly constructed to house older Americans. The major earlier demand for units that were being produced was from urban, low-income renters. Such buildings have been required to meet Federal <u>Minimum Property Standards</u>. These standards initially provided few amenities and were predominantly reduced space variants of structurally safe and codeably healthy buildings established under Federal guidelines for low-income families. Increasingly there is evidence that a market exists for apartments for retired singles and couples who are best described as moderate income. This is not, by life style and experience, the same market as the inner city elderly whose needs were seen earlier. This market appears to be more a reflection of growth in absolute numbers than of a clear trend toward mobility, but it may also be an early indication of changing life styles.

SEGREGATION BY AGE.

The primary policy rationale for segregation of lower income elderly Americans by age was security. At a time when the country was beginning to see significant increase in social breakdown and crime in central cities of the United States, the elderly, for whom these locations had been neighborhood for greater portions of their life, became particularly vulnerable. This vulnerability appeared to be further exacerbated as major urban neighborhoods were cleared, in wholesale and inconsiderate fashion, and massive public housing projects were erected. The poorest elderly, single women of racial and ethnic minorities, were rehoused in scattered fashion throughout these new projects or remained dangerously on the fringe, in either case essentially divested of familiar services and admidst a growing population of under-employed and dislocated younger families often with life-styles unfamiliar to them. Political pressure to better safeguard the older poor and to provide more specialized living environments for them led, in the mid-1960s, to the development of age-segregated buildings first directly on the large public housing sites then at scattered sites throughout urban areas. Cities and towns of lower density throughout the country ultimately began to take advantage of the Federal housing programs for older Americans.

MEETING SPECIAL NEEDS.

By the end of the 1960s, special considerations for tenant needs began to appear in standards and to be reflected in buildings for elderly. These were "barrier-free" conditions to support housing needs of the adult disabled, and social or community spaces to encourage the development of new social organization within the housing site. The barrier-free conditions attempted to establish rules for space and hardware that would better support what are known to be sensory-motor incapacities occurring in relatively higher frequency among people as they age. Some of these rules were based upon sound technical information derived from specialists who deal with disability and medical rehabilitation, particularly for those who become wheelchair dependent. Others, such as rules to compensate for reduction in visual or auditory acuity are still not well enough specified in the research literature of either sensory psychology and medicine or of engineering in such ways that translations into performance standards for buildings can be clarified. For example, the characteristics of natural and artificial lighting in residential corridors of varied lengths and in combination with assorted surface materials have yet to be specified in performance terms relative to varied tenant populations and their activities.

The consideration for probable social interaction needs of older residents was met by new space standards which supported the inclusion of non-residential areas within age-segregated sites and buildings. In establishing allowances for communal spaces in housing for elderly, certain behavioral assumptions were overtly or covertly made which will be discussed in later chapters of this book. Although it was concensually acknowledged among gerontologists (researchers and practitioners in human aging), that many older people could benefit from compensatory places within which to replace lost social networks, the patterns by which older individuals might resocialize and the design conditions that might support these behavior patterns was not predicated on research. As a consequence, what is too frequently observed in systematic study is an under-utilization of communal spaces and a relative absence of architectural definition in the design of these spaces.

Because few rental units built expressly for older people in the past ten years have gone unoccupied, it may be assumed by planners and developers that the market for exactly the types of structures that are being produced is likely to grow in direct proportion to the absolute growth of our older population. The use, by private developers, of models for elderly housing constructed under Federal programs is strongly discouraged. Even the Federal Government has had to modify its original space standards which mandated a dominance of efficiency units in elderly housing because of considerable opposition to this residence type from single widows.

DENSITY AND AGING.

In the planning and development of housing for elderly it is often necessary to make decisions about *density*. The number of apartment units put together in a single building on a particular site (units per acre) is the usual way of defining density. This approach to deciding the appropriateness of a concentration of residences is not adequately sensitive to the social and behavioral issues that should be of concern to planners of housing for aging.

Although the density issue was not itself a primary focus of the work to be described, the subject did emerge as we began to identify friendship and neighboring behaviors and to explore uses of common spaces. Eighty-nine percent of the 662 tenants sampled in our national study of elderly in public housing had previously lived at low rise, low density, including those persons from urban metropolitan areas. Most tenants were single women who had lived with a spouse previous to their moves. The move to elderly housing constituted a major environmental and social change. Among the strikingly different experiences facing tenants who move into high density housing are the number of non-related other people who utilize the same entry, corridors and interior common spaces.

Despite the fact that only nine of the 53 housing sites that were studied did not contain any planned social spaces, 57% of the 662 respondents reported never participating in social activities on the site. A mere 11% reported engagement in three or more over a period of one year! The figures for activity and organizational participation off-site is in general equivalently low, with 59% reporting never, 34% reporting one or two, and only 7% who indicated participations greater than three. By contrast, contact with off-site relatives, by phone and in person, was of quite high frequency; for 39% it was daily and for 76% family contact was reported to occur once or more each week. Approximately 40% of our respondents reported that during the week prior to interview they had neither "visited" nor been visited in their apartment by on-site friends. Another 20% experienced no more than one such within-unit social occasion.

The implication of this data is surely that the dominantly important aspects of a prior life-style were retained; a life-style that can best be described by the term *insular*.

To explore the possible contribution that building density might make to this *insularity*, several treatments of the national data were performed. Buildings were arrayed by number of apartment units, height and number of units per corridor and this data correlated with frequency of leaving the building during the past week, activities and friendly visits on site. The associations are suggestively strong, that the higher the building density the less the likelihood that an older tenant will leave the building, visit friends on site or engage in activities.

Do you recognize most people in this building? With this question an attempt was made in a supplemental study of four Massachusetts buildings to understand the interpersonal potentials of elderly housing in relation to the design and number of units in the setting. There was an inverse relation between building density and recognition; the larger the building (300 units) the greater the proportion of negative responses. A companion inquiry into the number of people known, by name, revealed a similar association between size and acquaintanceship. Frequency of visiting within apartment units appeared again to be significantly less in the setting of greatest size.

Many older people seem to behave somewhat reticently in housing that deviates from the accustomed density and form. At least it can be said that if the design of moderate to high density buildings is intended to seduce the elderly into unaccustomed social interactions, it has not been con- spicuously successful. It would seem that, as it is with "senior centers" so too with elderly housing: the more gregarious will always find social opportunities in space; the majority of older people, however, perpetuate their pre-move social *patterns* which dominantly involve kin in their own or relatives' personal residence. The designer and planner needs to understand these *patterns* of response to space among older people by providing variations in density across settings within communities and variations within settings of unit size and in the allocation and configuration of common space.

CHANGE OVER TIME.

In addition to the divergencies among people who are considered by society as older, planners and designers should appreciate the unpredictability, to the tenant, of their changing needs over time. The individual who moves into an age congregate setting as fully *functional* does not plan to be less mobile or depressed by disability and losses five to ten years later. The couple who moves to a retirement setting really does not consciously acknowledge that one of them will become disabled or die.

If the goal of elderly and congregate housing is to support independence and prevent premature institutionalization, the initial programming and design must *build-in* adaptation and flexibility. This may mean that living units have to be spatially interchangeable, extendable or retractable, or that the allocation of residential and nonresidential spaces requires new definition. It also may mean that spaces considered in an original occupancy cycle as adequate for

management and services should provide ambiguities in functional intention that may later be adapted to alternative service use.

Density and design become particularly sensitive issues if a goal in elderly housing is to encourage communal meals. When did you last have dinner in a noncommercial setting with one hundred other people? Probably at an Annual Church Supper. Designing to support the social and psychological meanings of mealtime within the economic and space constraints provided ought to be a primary challenge in settings for aging people.

Given presumed economies of scale in the construction of low cost housing, and particularly since land values in urban areas often dictate density and building type, what can be said to the developer, architect or housing authority to minimize the apparent *anonymity* and *withdrawal* effects of elderly settings of moderate to high density? First, some program mechanisms will need to be developed to provide a wider range of setting densities, particularly in urban areas, in order that natural selection or freer choice of residential environment can be available to the older citizen. Secondly, the standard approaches to arranging spaces (plan) in apartment buildings need to be completely re-evaluated in the case of housing for aging persons. Higher density could be promoting tendencies to withdrawal and preferences for insularity rather than fostering engagement. The spaces of concern are 1) building entry, 2) residential corridors, and 3) communal areas.

The dominant characteristics of these semi-public spaces as they are now designed seem to create a particular problem of dissonance with the past personal experiences of older people in residential settings.

A mental walk through any building would perhaps better convince the reader of the psychological truth of this speculation than would the finest of quantitative data. The comfort felt in traversing a space appears to be related to one's ability to predict what is likely to occur in that space. Predictability is associated with familiarity; the more one frequents a place, the more likely it is that people, their behaviors and the surroundings will become comfortable. But familiarity has meaning beyond frequency; the valence of past occasions of use is also implied.

Building entries in high density elderly housing possess a commercial quality and a consequent absence of residential symbolism. Most hotel entry areas are more inviting, psychologically, than the majority of currently produced residential buildings. There has been no clear and systematic study of people's perceptions of entry areas and the meanings or associations related to them. There is no doubt, however, that building entries have historically been considered important symbolic elements.

The majority of current (and presumably future) older tenants are accustomed to approaching their own house and those of their friends through a gradual transition from public to recognizably private space.

Photodocumentation of American residential neighborhoods affirms the degree of personalization that takes place both immediately outside and just within the entries to single family and low-rise attached homes. Can a multifamily structure replicate that image for the collective? The lobby area that greets a resident or guest to elderly housing is most often bleak, bare and harsh in materials, lighting and furnishings. The cost of programmed attention to these design elements appears to be minute compared to total costs and the probable long-term benefits to tenants and managers.

Corridors on high density residential floors in multi-family housing have been a source of concern to designers and social researchers alike for some time. For reasons mysteriously blamed on the production process, little improvement in corridor ambiance has resulted from this concern. Research on neighboring between residents of high density buildings seems convincing in its reports that the best known neighbor is likely to be the most proximate one, and that the more units there are along an undifferentiated linear corridor, the less likely neighboring will occur. Neighboring is most often operationally defined in terms of reciprocities: exchanges of visits, staples, chores or assistance.

It is instructive, intuitively valid (if you will) albeit of limited statistical reliability that elderly tenants in high density buildings report incidents of error in identifying either their floor from the elevator or their apartment door along the corridor. A low-income tenant advisor to our research efforts indicated that she achieved her greatest sense of comfort in traversing her building only after closing her apartment door behind her.

Brief explorations with a "semantic differential" (a difficult instrument at best, and especially across socio-cultural communities) indicated a strong tendency for elderly to respond that their building corridors were "institutional" as contrasted with "residential", were "bland" as contrasted with "stimulating".

Predictability and comfort are as relevant to corridors as to entry areas. In the case of aging people, there are complicating physiological factors of reduced visual acuity. A long corridor (100-200 feet) tends to distort approaching figures and to be perceived as a tunnel. Locational cueing can be lost in the continuous repetition of shadows and edges.

It would seem considerate for designers to apply the concept of *familiarity gradient* to circulation systems in residential settings. From the approach to the building entry to the door of the most distant apartment units, a path should contain articulation and differentiating cues that can become part of the new residential experience.

The behavioral effects of varied lighting systems in long corridors is an important topic about which we have no good *human factors* research. The standard solution, consistent with industrialized construction

is recessed ceiling lights, equidistantly spaced. The lack of cue value in this solution should be obvious to anyone, but the possible distortion effects created by this solution has not been well documented.

When a group of mixed-age, multi-ethnic tenants in a New York public housing project were permitted to redecorate their own corridor, one of the first modifications they made was to replace the recessed light fixtures with hanging fixtures.

AGING AS PROCESS.

Because aging is a process, change over time is the critical theme by which designers and planners ought to organize their housing programs for aging populations. The demographic data make it clear that more of us are going to grow older and that a larger proportion of us are going to experience the various frailties of older ages. It has already been brought to the author's attention that buildings designed for the more highly mobile, well elderly do not now work to support the changed spatial needs of the frailer tenants. To what extent industrial building practices and operating subsidy programs contribute to this misfit is the subject of Chapter Two.

2

BUILDING PRACTICES AND PROGRAM PERFORMANCE

Elderly housing in the United States is
dominated by a single building type, the
moderate to high-rise block, of concrete
slab construction, with a central utility
core (elevators and plumbing) from which
double-loaded residential corridors radiate.
Such building types are the product of the
application of industrialized building
systems to a public program initiated
as much for social/psychological objectives
as for the purpose of providing economical,
safe and sanitary shelter.

This chapter is devoted to issues related
to the design and production of housing.
Within this context, the older housing
consumer is seen as part of a
much larger picture. The discussion is
included in this book because a behavioral
frame of reference for consideration of
critical programs and policies relative
to the housing industry has not been
clearly represented in the literature.
It is also the author's conviction
that the most vulnerable in a society,
by reason of health, age, political power
or economic status, are typically the
easiest to be manipulated into accepting
the consumer goods that are produced
(e.g., housing) as if there were no options.
The chapter contains unanswered questions
about housing economics and building
technology which, hopefully, will raise
controversy. There is no attempt to imply
special expertise on these questions,
but rather to develop a forum.

BUILDING SYSTEMS AND HOUSING PERFORMANCE

It is unusual for a behavioral scientist to
discuss building systems, although many
architects discuss human behavior. The
word "system" has such a high technology
sound that the non-enlightened may well
shy away from it. The reasons that
building systems are important to understand
is that increasingly the design of large
scale residential environments depend on
them. What is not at all clear is the
extent to which an industrialized building
system or any of its components (e.g.,
windows) is responsive to the varied needs
of a building's residents.

A building system is a set of rules by which
the structuring and the structure (the
process and the products) for a building
are *organized*. If applied to the process
and product of housing construction, a
building system should lead to the *organization* of *habitable* spaces. Building systems
may involve standardized elements (i.e., walls,
floors, doors, framing) which are combined
in coordinated and/or standard ways.
Typically, and particularly in the case of
housing, this results in repetitive space
arrangements and restrictions on the
locations and size of certain types of
spaces (e.g., hallways, kitchens). Even
the preferred location of openings (doors
and windows) are dictated by many building
systems. Standardization is also connected
to the principle of "least effort", i.e., to
minimize "surprises" and maximize routine.

Standardization has two basic means of coordination of elements:

By modular coordination (i.e., dimensional)
By controlling interface (i.e., "fit")

Industrialized building systems, as used for moderate to high density housing, do not necessarily have to result in high rise buildings nor do they necessarily mandate interior uniformity. It is just that they often do. It seems, to an uninitiated observer, that the line of least resistance in the application, as well as the conceptualization, of a building system is more the rule than the exception.

It is doubtful that building systems, as formulated, are based upon particular and articulated assumptions about human activities, *norms* and needs of intended occupants. It is more likely that general precedents of minimally acceptable housing form, reinforced by rigid regulation, have been applied in the design of residential building systems. The precedents do not seem ever to have clearly articulated how the building elements, or the applied system as a whole, will *perform* when the building is occupied. Roger Sherwood probably reflects the pervasive intellectual position relative to housing design, which seems to indicate a primary bypassing of user-needs issues, at least at the basic form-giving stage.

"...housing lends itself readily to systematic, typological study. Most building types, such as theatres, schools, factories, or even office buildings, have to respond to different programs and are rarely consistent and repetitive. Housing, because it consists of repeating units with a constant relation to vertical and horizontal circulation, can more logically be studied in terms of its typological variations. Although housing would seem to embrace almost unlimited possible variations, in fact there are not many basic organizational possibilities and each housing type can be categorized fairly easily."
(Roger Sherwood, Modern Housing Prototypes, p. 2)

Performance is a concept increasingly used in the evaluation of buildings. It is a term earlier used by engineers to specify requirements which a piece of equipment, in operation, is supposed to meet under a set of particular conditions. The requirements involve such measurable outcomes as tolerance to variations in temperature or vibration. The *performance* concept, when applied to whole buildings, sets criteria which range from sway limits in high winds to durability of plumbing systems. That a building constructed for residential use should be required to *perform* in accordance with daily life habits and varying needs of occupants is certainly as important as its long term structural integrity.

Groups concerned with establishing *performance* criteria for *habitability*, such as the United States National Bureau of Standards, occasionally ask behavioral scientists to provide data on human behavior which is translatable into design guidelines. Traditional research approaches relative to individual and social behavior do not directly or easily translate into information specifically appropriate to building design. Two types of social science research, however, have quite direct transferability to design: these are called *Post Occupancy Evaluation* and *Human Factors Research*.

PERFORMANCE BASED INFORMATION

Post Occupancy Evaluation (POE) is a systematic method for assessing the extent to which completed buidings and their site plans perform satisfactorily for tenants. The method involves a preliminary statement of how a setting is expected to meet quite explicit needs of tenants. Once this statement has been particularized, a study protocol is developed which may include

structured interviews, scheduled specific and repeated observation (recorded and mapped) of resident behaviors, supplemental photography, resident diaries and more informal participatory interviews of residents in the course of individual and social activities. Samples of these types of methods can be seen in the case study chapters and in the Appendix of this book.

The cumulative data from *Post Occupancy Evaluation* is only as valuable to the designer as the translation is readable and fits into the information search and processing styles consistent with architectural practice. A preliminary assessment of how behavioral science information from *POE* might be utilized in the planning-design process is suggested in Figure 1. Experimental studies of actual points of use of behavioral information in design have not been systematically conducted and are a critical need.

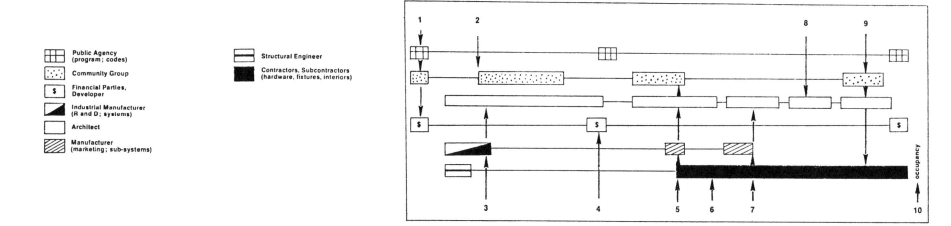

Figure 1. Points of entry for behavioral information into the process of residential development.

Source: Howell, S. "Needed, Preformance Specifications for Using Behavior Science", Industrialization Forum, 1974, 5, 25-29.

Human Factors research most often deals with micro-level interactions between a person and a space (for example, a work station), a set of related fixtures, an environmental stimulus or an individual piece of hardware. Although *human factors* studies had their origins in analyses of operator character- istics relative to such systems as airplane control panels, the method has proven very useful in understanding the minimum turn radii for wheelchair users, translated into Barrier Free Design Standards, and in developing Thermal Comfort Standards. *Human Factors* research is not now required in the manufacture of most fixtures and components incorporated into residential buildings. For example, there is no evidence that measurements of the readibility or accessability of thermostats and heater controls for a range of real residential users have preceded the design of such controls. Windows are another standard housing component which do not now benefit from systematic *human factors* testing prior to design and manufacture, except in relation to safety on breaking. Evaluations conducted with elderly residential occupants provide particular feed-back on the inadequacies, for them, in the design and installation of these window component systems (Figure 2).

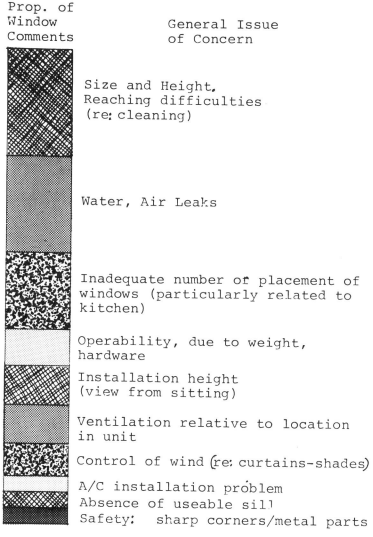

Prop. of Window Comments

General Issue of Concern

100%

Size and Height. Reaching difficulties (re: cleaning)

Water, Air Leaks

Inadequate number or placement of windows (particularly related to kitchen)

Operability, due to weight, hardware

Installation height (view from sitting)

Ventilation relative to location in unit

Control of wind (re: curtains-shades)

A/C installation problem

Absence of useable sill

0%

Safety: sharp corners/metal parts

Figure 2. Relative distribution of free comments from elderly about window-related issues, 53 national sites, MIT Design Evaluation Project, 1974.

Performance criteria developed from information systematically collected from building occupants are possible to develop and translate into design related elements. For a variety of reasons, this user information disappears in the housing production process.

CONSTRAINTS TO INFORMATION USE IN THE HOUSING PRODUCTION PROCESS

The following memorandum from a Contractor to a Project Architect illustrates only one of the problems in assuring that sound behavioral science information is utilized throughout the design-build process.

"Kitchen Cabinets...(he) advised that upper cabinets, for 2, 3 and 4th floors built incorrectly in that quantity of doors and swings are wrong; he added that manufacturer will require 10 weeks to correct problem. (He) also said that if cabinets must be replaced, construction schedule will be affected for painting and other 'critical path' items that follow. (It was) mentioned that cabinets do not meet design intent of architectural drawings and shop drawings; owners must be approached for acceptance of redesign. (They) observed cabinets after meeting and discussed problem further. (He) stated that considering critical time schedule of construction, remanufacture of cabinets may cause substantial delays in construction completion and building occupancy, and the owner must reluctantly accept the incorrect cabinets, but only with substantial credit, since this mistake is solely the manufacturers'". (emphasis Architect's).

The needs of future building residents appear often to be compromised or traded off in the process of production of the setting. Although no systematic studies of *trade-offs*, *change orders*, or decisions along the path from design to building occupancy appear to have been conducted, any developer, architect, contractor or consulting social scientist can report numerous incidents for a single project. The loss, in the building process, of consideration for the ultimate user appears to be related to current accounting practices which focus on production efficiencies (first costs) rather than life-time value and life-cycle costs of a building. Focusing on production time and costs often masks inefficiencies in the manufacturing, delivery, administration or labor relative to the creation of a completed housing project.

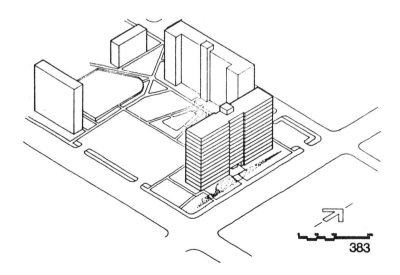

383

Standards Not Based on Performance appear as either too firm or lacking in clarity.

Too Rigid:

● "primary bedrooms shall have at least one uninterrupted wall space of at least 10 ft."

● "kitchen counter top minimum frontage in lineal inches:

Number of Bedrooms				
0	1	2	3	4
21"	30"	36"	36"	42"

Too Loose:

● "The relationship of rooms within the dwelling shall provide a degree of privacy commensurate with desirable living conditions".

● "Provide light and ventilation to achieve a healthful environment within the dwelling and so located as to provide an acceptable degree of comfort".

Source: HUD Minimum Property Standards, 1973 edition.

The *regulatory* process, set in place to guard the public welfare, is known to perform in such a way as to block or override both the better intuitions of the Architect and new knowledge of user needs. Two aspects of the *regulatory* process appear to be primarily at fault:

● The code and regulation format.

● The review process.

The format of codes and regulations for housing construction are, at once, rigidly specific on matters in which new approaches might be tested and excessively loose in relation to potential social and psychological implications of a living environment. An Architect may sense the inappropriateness of 200 ft. corridors, but find no alternatives, given the regulations and review decisions played out in the program development stage. Waivers are often difficult to arrange and severely time constraining. Again, "least effort" is the rule which shapes design decisions.

Regulations and codes are additive and incremental requirements imposed on the construction industry at Federal, State and Local levels. Rarely are they ever reviewed in totality. There is no evidence that they are responses to research-based performance requirements relative to most *habitation* needs of housing users. Even in the concern for fire safety, the evidence of their validity, particularly in the case of aging, disabled or child populations, is totally inadequate.

The *review process* involves a disproportionate focusing on construction and production issues and poor attendance to design responsiveness. Public reviewers are often ill-prepared to assist in interpreting regulations and have a tendency to adhere strictly to the letter of the specifications, as they have read them for all prior projects.

There is virtually no corrective *feedback* in the regulatory system other than the decidedly idiosyncratic experiences that a particular individual has had with a prior project. Neither financing, developing nor regulating agencies provide for evaluation of completed and occupied settings. Thus, no systematically accumulating body of data is available for improving the quality of design through better *performance* statements.

It is the opinion of the author that the ossification of regulations and their application has contributed, in the case of elderly housing, to oversized "egg crate" apartment buildings which, as tenants grow older and frailer, completely disallow interior adaptations to the needs for reduced scale of the social environment and for the incorporation of in-house services.

Public programs inhibit the application of user information. A particularly sensitive Architect for a State Housing Finance Agency recently indicated that the major determinant of building density in elderly housing was the method of allocating units, as provided by Federal legislation, to a particular local jurisdiction. "The *programs* themselves tend to force us into high density solutions and the shortage of available sites directs us to high rise design". Only in the most rural of areas does it appear rational and feasible to construct settings of under 150-200 elderly units. An apparently ignored United States General Accounting Office analysis of differential costs of producing similar numbers of apartment units per elderly building in high-rise versus low-rise form showed surprising results. In seven of ten states studied from 1970-1973, the costs (excluding land) for construction of high-rise buildings for elderly exceeded the per unit cost of low-rise by $216/unit to $2,373/unit. In one state comparison, high rise exceeded low rise costs by 82%, while the largest excess of low over high rise was only 10%. Operating and maintenance costs were also significantly greater in high-rise over low-rise (1-3 story) buildings.

How, then, have the myths of lower cost and greater tenant preference persisted to justify high density, and most regularly, high-rise solutions to the needs of older Americans for subsidized housing?

DESIGNING FOR HOUSING PREFERENCE

When housing planners argue that the prevailing housing types represent the *normative preferences* or needs of a particular resident population, they seem to base these statements on a variety of source materials:

● Marketing information

● Preference and satisfaction surveys

● Estimates of functional space needs

● Recommendations from social planners

Information on housing *preference* is frequently the only basis upon which real estate developers determine what kinds of housing to produce. The information that is used most often is derived either from records of types of housing rented or purchased or from responses to mailed question-naires or personal interviews which have asked preference questions.

Personal *preference*, like satisfaction, is highly dependent upon an individual's past experience and, in the case of housing, perceptions of status and the appropriateness of a place to live. It is a complex psycho-logical variable not clearly keyed to building design issues. In the case of older interview-ees, it is confirmed that housing preference and satisfaction are inherent in wherever the respondent currently resides. The exceptions to this overwhelming tendency to respond positively to an existing setting are among those very few people who are just in the process of changing residence. Preference and satisfaction questions turn out to provide very limited information for the design of residential settings. It is only when questions are posed about specific *activities* in residential space or in relation to a fixed aspect of a building that respondents provide good behavioral data for design. Thus, in the studies reported in this book, a resident of elderly housing would say both that the kitchen cupboards were very satisfactory and that she had to store things on the sink because most shelves were too high. Had the specific question not been asked, the computerized response would only dictate a perpetuation of present storage systems and installation practices.

HIGH RISE LIVING: THE CREATION OF NEW *NORMS*

Since most American older persons have lived their residential lives at low density, in low-rise buildings and in age integrated settings, a change in all three of these residential characteristics should require rather profound readjustment. The planners and architects of age-congregate settings appear to assume easy adaptation and ready restructuring of learned social-spatial rules. It is appropriate for a psychologist to question the assumed smoothness of acquisition of new environmental experiences for most "non-cosmopolitan" older people. If housing design, in the market place, is based upon prevailing social *norms*, what is produced for older, low income consumers actually breaches the accepted rules of marketing and is based, rather, on new *norms* imposed by policy and program directors, not on effective demand. The concept of effective demand assumes a choice in a "free market", relative to supply and price.

The major social arguments used to justify decisions on *density* and scale in housing for the elderly are 1) that older residents prefer and feel more secure in a larger elevator structure, 2) that an individual will have better social opportunities the more other elderly there are, and 3) that as tenants become older and require more services, it is more "efficient" to deliver these services to a single, large scale setting. There is no reliable evidence that any of these arguments are valid, for the majority of eligible elderly, or that the broader implications of these decisions has been studied. A review of high density, high rise residential effects is disturb-ingly inconclusive.

We should be able to determine how, under what circumstances and for whom particular building designs affect human behaviors. It is only when such research carefully controls for the many mediating variables that some impacts of building form, itself, suggestively emerge. One of the critical variables which appears to this author to be relevant to elderly is social and spatial *familiarity*. Chapter 1 addressed the facts of residential *familiarity* for older Americans. The case studies appearing in Chapters 4 and 5 attempt to clarify the psychosocial issues that ought to be fundamental to *performance evaluation* of high-rise, age segregated elderly housing.

PERFORMANCE AS BUILDING-ACTIVITY TRANSACTION.

It is a given that building systems and housing programs which were not specific to the changing needs of an aging population will continue to be applied to that residential use. Since that is so, how can they become accommodating to *habitability*? It has been argued that part of the problem falls within the arena of responsibility of the behavioral scientist to state the criteria for *habitability*. In order to perform this task, a revision is required in the methods by which we, as behavioral scientists, currently conduct our research. This is the subject of Chapter Three, which follows the process of reorganization and refinement of methods for studying environments as they are used. The

prototype buildings are moderate to high density elderly housing. The *activities* are the social and private daily lives of aging people.

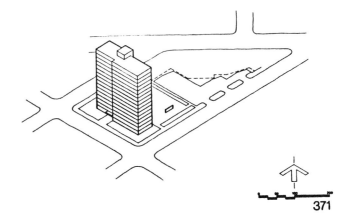

371

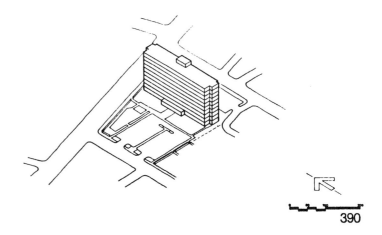

390

3

STUDYING ENVIRONMENTS IN USE

INTRODUCTION

The process of systematically exploring the built environment in use required quite different methods than are employed for most other social science research. Transfer of results from more traditional techniques, which include probability sampling, pre-structured interviews and standardized scales, have proven relatively uninforming to design. In addition, formal modes of inquiry have disappointed our expectations for understanding the subtle interplays between people and the places they inhabit.

The purpose of formal rules of scientific exploration is to assure, in the research community, that a study can be replicated. In order to be able precisely to reproduce a research process, and thereby validate a set of results, all conditions within which the research was conducted need to be stipulated. The researcher must be able to specify, in some understandable way, what it was that was being looked at and how, specifically, the looking procedure was organized and conducted. In design behavior research we want to look at the physical features of built place, consequently one set of study materials needs to be *readable* descriptions of places. To *read* a building architecturally is not equivalent to understanding it behaviorally but only to comprehend its formal structural principles.

The clinker in design-behavior research, at this point in history, is that we have not yet found explicit ways to describe, behaviorally, the physical environment that we wish to study. The converse is also true, our research languages for describing human behavior have excluded attributes of environment from behavior descriptors. The closest approximation to a system for environment-behavior study has been the *Behavior Setting* analytic method as most recently described by Bechtel in Enclosing Behavior.

Behavior setting studies are extremely complex in that they require extensive periods of observation and recording and the handling of large quantities of quite diverse pieces of information. In addition, the results of most such studies do not yet adequately inform the design community about the *performance goals* to be sought in the production of buildings of a particular type and purpose.

The task of developing behavior-contingent building typologies, that is to say, a classification system for buildings and their elements which reflects human use (actual and potential) is at the core of the explorations described in this book. In order to perform this task, original inform-ation gathered about a particular "species" of building, elderly housing, which utilized very traditional survey research methods, had to be disassembled and re-assembled in a variety of experimental ways. It is this process of reassembly and the development of supplemental pilot studies which followed, that will be described in this Chapter.

ORIGINS OF RESEARCH.

In 1971, a national study headed by M. Powell Lawton sampled 104 Federally funded housing sites and 2000 elderly tenants. This research provided an abundance of descriptive information relative to the social and physical characteristics of the settings which included records and descriptions of the types of communal spaces inside and outside of buildings, as well as reports, from tenants and managers, of the uses of the various areas in and around the buildings. In addition, measures were made of features of private living units. Much of this file material remained unanalyzed, since primary attention in that study was focused on the measures of well-being and social activities of residents, only roughly related to design issues. When, in 1973, a restudy was mounted by Howell and Lawton, the earlier file material became available for re-analysis and expansion.

1974 Sample.

For the 1974 national study of elderly residential environments, a sample of 53 of the original 104 sites was chosen. Only public housing sites were included (excluding 202 sites). These 53 sites provided approximately 5,700 target elderly designated units for study and further sampling. Two-thirds of the sites were age-segregated. Geographical distribution of the sample reflected a concentration of elderly housed in subsidized buildings on the east coast. 18 of the 53 sites were located in the East; 14 sites were on the West coast. Approximately 75 percent of the sites were in towns with a population greater than 50,000 and were located outside of the downtown area in residential and commercial neighborhoods. Most of the sites were within walking distance of some shopping area and had access to public transportation as well. As for recreation facilities on site, almost all had outdoor areas for passive and/or active activities and only 9 sites did not have common spaces (lounges, recreation rooms. etc.) on the grounds. The target buildings ranged from one story duplexes in small towns to 20 story apartment buildings in New York City. Approximately 60% of all the buildings were apartments over 6 stories in height (and of these buildings, more than half were taller than 10 stories). Of the target 5,700 elderly designated units in the sample from which 662 interviews were collected, 30 percent were efficiencies, 58 percent one bedroom units, and 12 percent had two bedrooms.

Table 1. Size of Community by Height of Sampled Buildings, Design Evaluation Project, 1974.

LOCSIZE (Pop.)	NUMBER OF STORIES				
	1-2	3-5	6-10	11-15	15+
Less than 1,000	-	-	-	-	-
1,000-4,999	6	-	-	-	-
5,000-9,999	4	-	1	-	-
10,000-49,999	-	1	2	-	-
50,000-99,999	3	1	4	2	-
100,000-499,999	6	-	4	4	-
500,000+ except NYC	-	-	3	4	2
New York City	-	-	-	2	4
TOTAL	19	2	14	12	6

SETTINGS FOR RESEARCH.

The reprocessing of primary information from a 1974 study of fifty-three national elderly housing sites conducted by Howell and Lawton constituted the framework upon which the specifically design-relevant research was formulated.

The reprocessing of data required architectural and planning skills not typically included in social research. Five particular research methods issues will be discussed here, since their clarification should assist the reader in understanding the evolution of the two case studies included in this volume. In addition, the chapter should serve as an example of general modes for developing hypotheses about *habitability*.

The topics to be discussed include:

1. Defining a population and a sample;

2. Defining a use-neighborhood relative to a housing site;

3. Classifying site characteristics and building attributes appropriate to behavioral analysis;

4. Defining the interior characteristics of residential buildings in relation to density - behavior propositions;

5. Comprehending the living unit in relation to plan and relative to user activity.

It should be evident from this array of selected issues, that our "secondary data analysis" of the architecture of planned elderly housing proceded in accordance with accepted concepts of *scale*, from the level of macro and micro neighborhood to that of private living quarters. In fact, this is probably a total reversal of the ways in which residential scale is psychologically perceived by residents, particularly those inhabiting elderly housing, where the living unit assumes a primary, hierarchical importance relative to other levels of space.

Defining a Population and a Sample. Ideally, research wants to tell us enough about a studied individual, group and situation that we feel reasonably comfortable in making generalizations to other similar situations and persons. The best way of assuring that kind of *reliability* is to develop a representative sample. A sample is a group of people whose characteristics are typical of the total population which they represent, OR environments that are also representative of a known population of settings which these types of people inhabit. We call the characteristics of any population from which we choose a sample, the *parameters*.

Population parameters, in social science research, typically focus upon demographic and personal characteristics of the people to be studied (e.g., age or marital status). Except for gross community size variables, few parameters ever allude to the physical attributes of settings within which environmental users function. It is probably just because we have not sampled from a

population of describable environments that
our ability to understand and to predict
behavior in environments is weak.

The population from which samples were
selected in our 1974 study of elderly housing
consisted of all elderly in the United States,
who resided in public housing as of 1968.
Although this represented a particular
housing-subsidized population of elderly
persons of that time, it did not necessarily
represent the population of settings provided
for this user group and thus did not allow
for representative sampling of setting
locations or building types.

In order to understand the environments that
incidentally fell into our study by reason
of sampling people, it was appropriate
to develop detailed descriptions of each
neighborhood site and building.

It is necessary for the reader to understand
that this body of information does not
consitute a set of population *parameters*
but only a descriptive collection with
which a classification scheme for sites and
buildings might begin. A uniform descriptive
method for future analysis of elderly
housing was required. Two approaches to the
description of incidentally sampled national
sites were used:

> 1) Analysis of *land use* maps of the
> proximate neighborhood surround-
> ing a housing site, collected in
> the 1974 field study;

> 2) Uniform *axonomic* representation
> of all sampled sites and
> buildings based upon photographic
> and descriptive data, collected
> in the national study and
> partially provided by HUD forms.

Defining a Use Neighborhood Relative to a
Housing Site. No residence is describable
independent of a *context*. *Contexts* for
residential settings are simultaneously
social, functional and physical. Especially
for an aging residential population, the
context outside the residential perimeter can
facilitate or inhibit independent mobility.
An ideal building or set of living units may
be so isolated from daily service needs or
so physically barriered by hills, highways
or uncongenial land uses (building vacancies)
that tenants become totally dependent upon
services provided within the setting itself
or on specially scheduled mobile transport
services to distant resources (Table 2, 3).

The research process used in developing the
basis for neighborhood understanding involved
data collection and analysis of several
sorts:

● Detailed land use mapping within a
variable area (approximately 600 ft.)
surrounding a sampled building. This
procedure took an average of 1-1/2 days
and involved coding each building by
use, using a uniform notation system,
on uniformly scaled maps of the area,
prepared for the field in advance.

- Detailed interviewing of sampled tenants on their use of resources within and beyond the land mapped area, Table 4 (see interview and summary of results in Appendix A).

- Codification and graphic representation of site-specific resources and characteristics (see Brandt program in Appendix A).

- Graphic representation and overlay of site-specific tenant uses of available resources, as recorded (Figs. 1&2).

Data resulting from the mapping, interviewing and graphic development make it possible to better understand any given neighborhood selected for an elderly housing site in terms of its absolute contribution to the well-being and activity level of the aging tenant at a given point in time. Such information, if utilized as base-line data, could also provide a monitor function for changes over time which might guide service delivery and neighborhood assistance programs.

Comparisons of land use and resident use in neighborhood settings should support a wider focus analysis of neighborhood resource structures and lead to *habitability* criteria. We are currently attempting to develop a continuous scale relative to resource richness that might better assist future planners of elderly housing to evaluate alternative sites.

Table 2 and 3. Neighborhood Characteristics 53 National Sites, Design Evaluation Project, 1974.

Type of locale	N Sites	%	N E.D.Us*	%
city-main downtown area, large business area	9	17.0	1,260	22.1
city-but not the downtown area	40	75.5	4,271	74.9
suburbs-well built-up suburban area	1	1.9	84	1.5
rural-open country, scattered housing	3	5.6	85	1.5
TOTAL	53	100.0	5,700	100.0

Local Land Use	N Sites	%	N E.D.Us	%
mainly residential	16	30.2	1,658	29.1
residential and commercial	19	35.8	1,709	30.0
residential and industrial	1	1.9	20	0.4
commercial and industrial	1	1.9	99	1.7
residential, commercial and industrial	9	17.0	1,488	26.1
mixed**	7	13.2	726	12.7
TOTAL	53	100.0	5,700	100.0

* Elderly Dwelling Units

** any combination of at least 4 of the following: residential, commercial, industrial, open space, playground, vacant lots, forested areas

Table 4. Location of Resources Actually Utilized
Percent of Respondents

	Food #1	Food #2	Clothing	Physician	Check Cashing	Barber/ Beauty	Drug Store	Church/ Synag.	Snack	Public Transp.	Outside Friend #1	Outside Friend #2	Go for walk
site	2	1	1	3	14	4	1	9	18	29	-	-	40
ne 1	38	31	9	10	28	26	23	18	15	63	12	17	35
cality ot Zone 1)	50	57	58	59	49	56	65	50	44	8	55	52	24
t of cality	10	11	32	28	9	14	11	23	23	-	33	31	2
	100	100	100	100	100	100	100	100	100	100	100	100	101
arest source?	61	48	51	58	72	56	60	59	51	98	-	-	-
	525	286	420	589	509	307	460	427	248	271	233	114	350

Source: 53 National Sites, Design Evaluation Project, MIT, 1974.

Resources Available and Intensity of Use

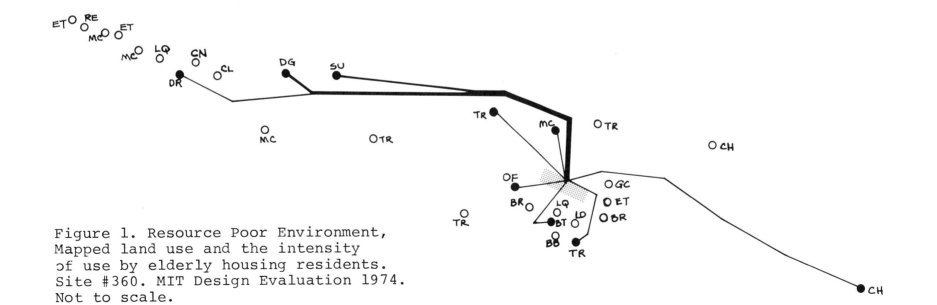

Figure 1. Resource Poor Environment,
Mapped land use and the intensity
of use by elderly housing residents.
Site #360. MIT Design Evaluation 1974.
Not to scale.

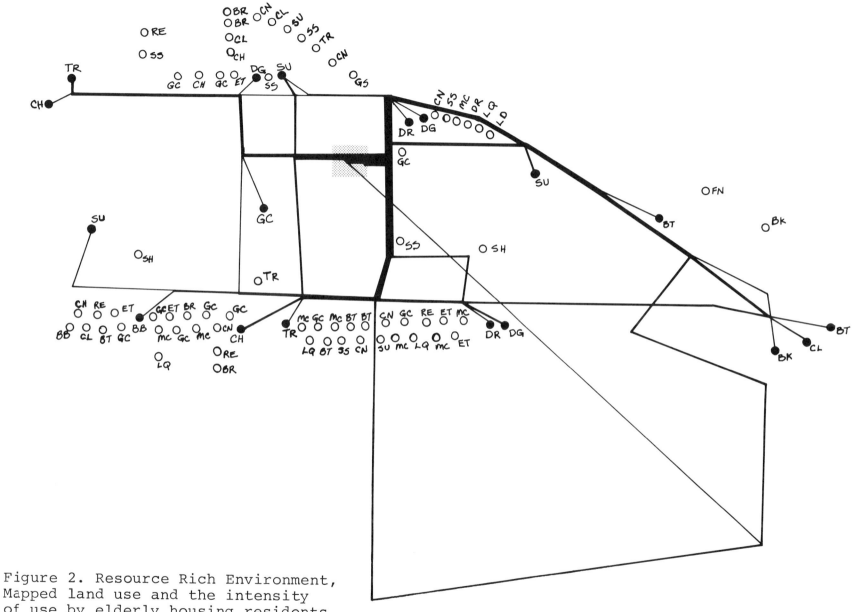

Figure 2. Resource Rich Environment,
Mapped land use and the intensity
of use by elderly housing residents.
Site #365. MIT Design Evaluation 1974.
Not to scale.

Classifying Site and Building Characteristics.
In order to develop a classification of
building types, the first task was to reorganize the sample of 53 settings in terms of
physical attributes. The global hypothesis
which shaped the new research methods was
that design characteristics do affect the
spatial behaviors of older people. In what
ways these associations might emerge
depended upon the clarity of descriptive
variables which the research team could
produce. Tables 5 and 6 describe the
height of neighborhood and sampled buildings.
This information was supplemented in the
1974 field research by photographs of the
buildings, sites and the immediate neighborhood. Information gathered on the
fifty-three study sites was treated
statistically and architecturally, in a
number of ways, most of which were not
clearly relevant to our search for design-
behavior variables. The preliminary
variables chosen became *scale* in relation
to neighborhood, *massing* (the organization
of the building on the site), *orientation*
of entry relative to the street (Fig. 3).
All of these terms are specifically
architectural but appeared to have underlying implications for how a residential
environment might be perceived or used.
For each of the 53 sites, standardized
axonomic drawings were composed.
On a selective pilot basis, interior space
photographs were produced with the objective
of exploring the role of photodocumentation
in design-behavior research. The effectiveness of photography in generating design
awareness of human use can be judged in
Chapters 4 and 5.

Table 5. Scale of Immediately Surrounding
Neighborhood, 53 National Sites, Design
Evaluation Project, MIT, 1974.

Stories	N Sites	%	N E.D.Us	%
1-2	34	64.1	3,045	53.4
3-5	17	32.1	2,310	40.5
6+	2	3.8	345	6.1
TOTAL	53	100.0	5,700	100.0

Table 6. Scale of Sampled Buildings, 53
National Sites, Design Evaluation Project,
MIT, 1974.

Stories	N Sites	%	N E.D.Us	%
1-2	19	35.9	903	15.8
3-5	2	3.8	80	1.4
6-10	14	26.4	1,043	24.6
11-15	12	22.6	2,342	41.1
greater than 15	6	11.3	972	17.1
TOTAL	53	100.0	5,700	100.0

Figure 3.

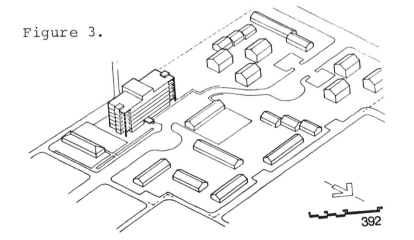

392

Building Interior as a Social Space.
Information on the use of common spaces by
residents was gathered in interviews with
tenants and managers in the national sample.
Questions referred to frequency of use and
general nature of activities within these
spaces.

Interviews about the use of a built environment often do not adequately reflect the day
to day engagements with space by the user.
Respondents do not consistently attend, unless
trained to do so, to their spatial movements,
sensitivities or activity patterns. More
importantly, interviews need to be synchron-
ized with the actual physical configurations
of a space, groups of spaces or total
setting.

If "every building is a hypothesis", then
the environmental researcher, as directed
by the architectural plan, needs to specify
what it is about the design that is
hypothetical relative to human use.

Preparation for Behavior Mapping.
Recording the use to which a space is put
seems to be an obvious way of determining
if design matches need. In fact, the
process and the result of such data
collection can be very ambiguous. Commonly
this kind of design-behavior information is
gathered by architects incidentally in the
course of one or two observations of a
built space plus casual conversation with
users and managers of the space. The problem
with that approach is that it produces
distorted information.

Systematic analysis of space use involves
diagrammatic recording of activities over a
sample of times, supplemented by both
structured and informal interviews. If an
observer is not aware that his/her convenience
times are irrelevant to the life of a setting,
the incidental observations will certainly not
reflect the space in use.

Behavior maps allow precise accounting of the
types and frequencies of use of a space,
in graphic as well as quantitative form.
(Appendix B-1).

The *behavior map* is a necessary, but by no
means sufficient, data gathering device
by which understanding can be gained on the
human uses of space. Mapping requires
substantiation and supplementation via interview, observational notes and photography.
The counting of people, by their characteristics (e.g., man or woman) and nature of
activities and locations in space only
exhibits what people are doing, not how they
might behave in an architecturally different
space. Ideally, a behavioral scientist would
prefer to conduct architecturally relevant
intervention experiments. An *intervention*
paradigm requires that the same people be
given an opportunity, over a naturally
appropriate span of time, to explore a
variant space to the one in which they were
initially observed and interviewed. In our
research of both shared and private space
we were only able to compare spatial use by
similar people in defineably different
spaces.

Variables in Use of Common Space.

Although a structured interview might include
questions about the frequency of individual
tenant use of communal space in a particular
housing setting, an understanding of the
relationships between the designed communal
space and the frequency or character of that
use requires a) geometric or architectural
description of the communal space within
the building, b) systematic mapping of
the particular spaces as used over time,
c) systematic photographic documentation of
the spaces in-use and d) purposive sampling
of potential users of the communal space
(by residential locational or other
speculative variables.

When this type of effort was mounted in our
1976 supplemental studies it was found
that the following *variables* probably
affect residents' use of communal spaces
in elderly housing:

- a) building density
- b) building height
- c) location of the communal space in
     relation to the primary path between
     building entry and tenant's apartment
- d) location of tenant's apartment unit
     within the building and on a floor
- e) configurations of the communal space
- f) past residential experiences of
     tenant
- g) history of social activity level of
     the tenant
- h) current outside (non-residential)
     social activities of the tenant in
     terms of friendship, relatives
     and organizational activities in the
     community

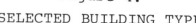

Figure 4.

SELECTED BUILDING TYPES
ENTRY CIRCULATION PATTERNS

CRITERIA:

% visibility of
community Room
from entry to
elevator path

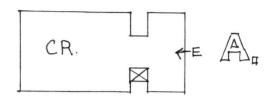

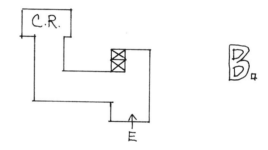

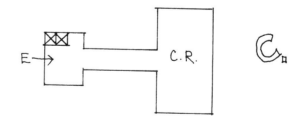

In all good methods of inquiry, it is necessary to get the bugs out of the system. One of the ways that we attempted verification of our mapping methods was to enlist several researchers elsewhere in the United States to test our procedure in settings similar to the prototypic common spaces we had defined (e.g., ground floor) with varied spatial relationships to a *common path* (Figures 4&5). Comments from this field *reliability* study indicate methodological problems in behavior mapping which still need to be resolved, particularly difficulties in coding activities and locating observer.

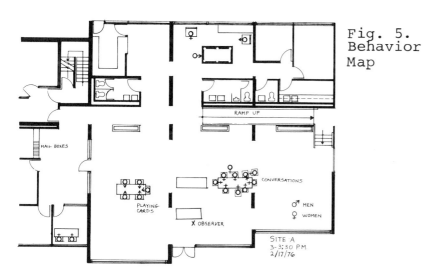

Fig. 5. Behavior Map

Living Unit as Private Activity Space.
How much can we learn about residential *life-styles* from analyses of activities and furnishings in private residential·space? That was the focusing question that governed our quite open-ended exploration of the daily life and its accompanying physical props of the elderly in Cambridge, Massachusetts age-segregated housing in 1976.

The importance of this type of study becomes relevant to design because *furnishability* is now considered an alternative design review justification to square footage, within the Federal Minimum Property Standards.

A major pilot question presented in our 1974 national elderly housing survey asked about furniture left behind by older people moving to subsidized apartment units. The responses focused on bedroom and dining furniture and suggested a strong psychological need to retain the ambiance of sleeping and dining environments, not necessarily the explicit furniture. To our curiosity and amusement, selected pieces of furniture representing this ambiance reappeared continuously in the apartment unit mapping and photographing. These pieces, not now allowed according to United States standards, were the china cabinet (as symbol of gracious entertaining?) and "high-boy" bedroom dresser (as symbol of male partner presence for widows?)

A major methodological problem in furniture mapping was dimensional parameters for furniture pieces. What size and shape ought the designer use to test the *habitability* of the designed unit? Interestingly, for the current generations of older people, the dimensions and shapes provided by the Sears Roebuck Catalogues appeared to best match their life styles. This realization happens to be consistent with *photodocumentations* of residential interiors of working class middle-aged and older people in the United States.

Interviewing tenants within their apartment units also resulted in some interesting insights with regard to structured questions. For example, the question "What is the most important piece of furniture to you?" turned out in some cases to be a piece that in itself was insignificant (a straight dining chair) but allowed *reminiscence* of times past, through viewing the china cabinet, or was *functional* in some regard to spatial *orientation* or hobby *activities*.

The Nature of Interviews.

The personally administered interview is a standard procedure in social science research. It is promised that the *reliability* of the results is dependent upon
a) the propriety and adequacy of the sample of respondents and
b) the appropriateness of the questions to the subject matter under study (*validity*).

In the case of people's relationships to their physical environment, surveys have rarely sampled respondents by their location within a physical setting, as well as by their particular personal characteristics. In addition, environmental surveys have been dominated by questions which address user satisfaction with aspects of the environment or reports of the frequency of use of the environment in general.

A part of our search for information more discriminating to design was to identify the particular locational or experiential characteristics of the elderly housing environments and to pinpoint interview items to particular places and activities or environmental elements.

As our questions moved from the more global (How satisfied are you with this apartment?) to the more specific (Can you comfortably reach dishes in your cupboards? Is the distance from the building entrance to your apartment too far or all right when you are carrying groceries?) the responses became increasingly refined. The specific questions, of course, mean little to design if the attributes of the environment to which the respondent is referring are not also specified (the height and depth of kitchen cupboards; the length of corridors).

The most instructive information gleaned from environment-behavior surveys are the non-structured and open ended questions which allow a resident to show and tell their experiences in daily living.

In both of the following case studies the clusters of resident comments are used with graphic data, to illustrate the issue of environment-behavior interaction. These free comments will reshape prior structured questions and contribute to the development of new ones (Appendix B-4).

In summary, the predominant research efforts required for *performance* focused analysis of the private living unit involved detailed descriptive drawings of furnishings and photography of comparable settings, complemented by interviews with elderly residents concerning their daily life and their use of their apartment spaces. This work constitutes what is traditionally required in the development of *base-line* data. Future researchers only need to compare our data on spaces, furnishings and their placement, and responses to interviews with their own case studies at different sites.

PATTERNS OF USE.

Studies of both the semi-public and private
spaces within existing elderly housing, as
used, constitute the *message* of Chapters
Four and Five. The results of these case
studies point to *patterns* of generationally
specific behaviors which require further
exploration. In the meantime, there is no
reason why our preliminary studies cannot
be used to better inform the design and
program planning community on the environmental needs of the aging residents of
moderate to high density settings. The
ancient admonition of medical practice,
"at least do no harm" is appropriate to the
production of Guidelines for designing
environments for living and aging.

4

SHARED SPACES:
A CASE STUDY

PURPOSE

The major purpose of this case study is to illustrate the methods by which residential settings may be analyzed in relation to the behavioral needs of occupants.

How will a built environment perform in use? This is a core question to be posed during the design process. Performance is always an underlying issue relative to a building structure and its components. Laboratory and field tests have cumulatively provided data which allow moderately good engineering prediction. Now it is also desirable that similar predictions be developed for user performance from cumulative post-occupancy evaluations.

The Guidelines provided with this case study are to be interpreted as <u>performance review statements</u>, not as explicit design recommendations. The distinction may seem subtle, but what it says to a designer is: bounce the <u>user-need issue</u> into your team reviews at <u>early design development</u> stages, rather than adopt, uncritically, the exemplified solution. Many solutions may respond to the behavioral issue. That is creative design. On the other hand, premature selection of a building system tends to preclude or compromise most considerations of user-appropriate design solutions.

The case study, founded on a substantial knowledge about aging Americans, suggests ways in which residential settings may better enhance daily life for this particular segment of our population. Engineers must continually retest combinations of new mater-ials; just so should designers and social scientists, together, continue to evaluate new spatial relationships for potential conflict with user needs and for innovative solutions which may better support or delight daily life.

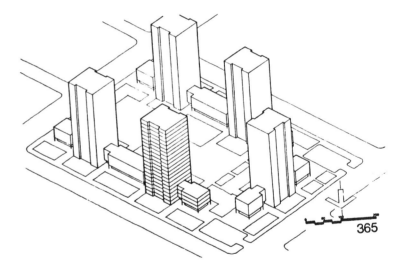

365

Methodological Issues

This case study and associated guidelines represent an effort to particularize a single set of design issues related to a specific housing type and tenant population. In developing the study, a sequence of methodologic issues required attention. Primary to all research is problem definition. The clarity of this statement effects all other methods issues and determines the ultimate validity of the research. Following problem definition, the work sequence consisted of selection of study settings, formulation of spatial concepts and definitions, data collection, which began with concept and instrument development and pre-tests, and data treatment, which organized the information accumulated. The preparation of data into reports and guidelines in order to test their utility in program and design review was a goal of this research. Applied research should also propose further issues for study. The formulation of hypotheses concerning the behaviors of older people in moderate to high density living environments constituted a final intellectual challenge.

PROBLEM DEFINITION. At the beginning of the study, the research team met with an advisory committee composed of housing officials, architects and elderly residents. During monthly meetings this group repeatedly expressed a need for more information about shared spaces. Some of the major questions they asked included:

What role do shared spaces play in initial encounters and in the development of friendships within the building?

What is the range of activities that needs to be accommodated in buildings of different sizes?

What types and sizes of social spaces are needed? Does this need change with varying population sizes?

How do alternative design decisions about shared spaces impact social behavior and resident interaction?

Floor plans from nationally studied elderly housing sites as well as Massachusetts elderly projects were reviewed in order to classify design characteristics that might have impact on resident social behavior. In addition, resident behavior in shared spaces at local sites in Massachusetts was observed. This pilot data was mapped on floor plans and used to generate preliminary hypotheses about resident behavior in different types of shared spaces.

Three elderly housing projects in Cambridge, Massachusetts were selected as case studies. Each building was viewed as a complex system of interrelationships between social behavior and design characteristics. To facilitate cross-site analysis, the same design variables were explored at each site. These design variables cover such issues as the location, differentiation, and size of social spaces as well as the visual connections between various spaces. By looking at each design issue and associated behavioral implications at three sites, patterns of resident use were developed. Design guidelines were then formulated based on these patterns of use as well as on residents' comments.

SELECTION OF STUDY SETTINGS. Design evaluation research often suffers from the limitation of a single site or from comparisons of settings in which either tenant or building characteristics are significantly different. The three settings selected for this research allowed control of certain key variables which might bias conclusions. Most of these variables could be specified in all such research. The sites were chosen for the following characteristics:

1. Comparable length of resident occupancy. All three buildings had been occupied for two years. A minimum occupancy period of one to two years allows patterns of spatial use to develop which may differ from the patterns residents show in exploring a new environment.

2. Demographic similarities in the resident populations. Residents came from the same applicant pool, a local housing authority list, and were preponderantly long time residents of the same city. Single women comprised the majority of the population at each site. Men represented approximately ten to fifteen percent of the populations while only five to ten percent were couples. Blacks comprised approximately ten percent of the population at each site.

3. Similarities in management policies and practices. All sites were managed by the same local housing authority so were guided by the same management directives. Each site had a manager who was available several days a week. He was responsible for the renting and maintenance of the building but was not involved with any social programming as all activities were resident-generated.

4. Location in areas with low crime rates. Residents from all sites perceived their neighborhoods as safe during daylight hours and felt comfortable walking in the general vicinity of their site. Those who wanted to socialize at night, however, preferred to do so within their own building and, like most older people, only a few ventured out alone after dark.

5. Location of social spaces on ground level. This study is concerned with the alternative locations of the social spaces at the entry level relative to other areas within a building. Field observations and the literature suggest that social spaces located in the basement or on upper floors are underutilized because of their isolation.

6. An unusual fringe benefit of the sampled sites was that they were all designed by the same architectural firm according to the program of a single development agent during the same period of time. Although all of these conditions might not be able to be met in future evaluation research, certainly comparing purpose-specific settings produced by a single firm or developer, during a specified time period, is feasible.

By reducing variability in those characteristics that could affect the use of shared spaces, behavioral patterns can be attributed more directly to design differences in shared spaces. (Figure 1).

Figure 1. DESIGN SIMILARITIES AND DIFFERENCES ACROSS SITES

Design Variable \ Site	A	B		C
Massing				
Ground floor plan	social spaces	East	West	
Number of apartment units	181	122	77	305
Number of floors	12/5	6	6	19
Apartment units per floor	13/9	26	13	18
Relationship of social spaces to primary path	Branch	Street	Branch	Branch
Secondary spaces in addition to community room	pool room club room kitchen	sitting room pool room crafts room vending machine room kitchen		crafts room game room library kitchen
Location of laundry	5th floor	ground floor	basement	ground floor
Present population	220	245		360
Population at full occupancy	220	245		360
Community room: Total square feet Sq. ft. per resident	1,869 8.5	1,988 8.1		2,760 7.7
Secondary social spaces: Total square feet Sq. ft. per resident	1,071 4.9	1,940 7.9		1,450 4.0

SPATIAL CONCEPTS AND DEFINITIONS

Spatial concepts describe the different types of spaces in the residential environment according to the activities they accommodate. The interior spaces at each site can be thought of in terms of four zones which differ according to access and activity. These four zones are defined as *public, semi-public, semi-private, and private* (Figure 2).

PUBLIC ZONE - area in the building where the daily coming and going activities occur. It is the focal point of all circulation and includes the pathway from the front entrance to the elevators. All visitors to the building, staff, and residents typically pass through this zone.

SEMI-PUBLIC ZONE - designated area for social and recreational activities of the elderly residents. It is the focal point for resident gatherings, both formal and informal. Other users of this zone, in addition to the residents, include their invited guests, the manager, and other support staff (e.g., custodians, recreational directors, arts and crafts teachers).

SEMI-PRIVATE ZONE - spaces on residential floors shared by tenants who live on that floor. These include corridors, elevator lobbies, and lounges. Activities associated with this zone include circulation and socializing with neighbors.

PRIVATE ZONE - apartment unit to which each resident controls access. In this zone residents can avoid encountering others if they so desire.

These four zones should be used as conceptual guidelines and not as rigid divisions between spaces. The activities within and between each zone are fluid and dynamic and not static.

Table 1 further elaborates a zonal typology based upon patterns of use in existing elderly housing.

Figures 3, 4 and 5 depict the interior spaces and zones for each studied site.

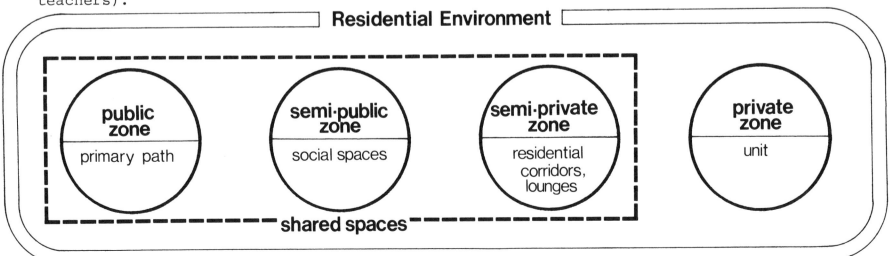

Table 1.　ZONAL TYPOLOGY[*]　

ZONE	SPACES AND ROOMS	USERS	ACTIVITIES
Public	Vestibule Lobby Manager's office Mail area Elevators Circulation area 　between main 　entrance and 　elevators	Visitors Manager and support 　staff Service personnel Residents	Orientation to people and 　places within building Arrival and departure Mail pick-up and delivery Business affairs Waiting Watching others come and go
Semi-Public	Community room Kitchen Library Crafts room TV room Sitting room Game room Laundry Circulation area	Residents and their 　guests Manager and support 　staff	Resident social activities 　such as watching TV, 　playing bingo, arts and 　crafts, reading, parties Doing laundry Entertaining large family 　gatherings Tenant meetings Hot lunch program
Semi-Private	On residential 　floors: 　Elevator lobby 　Lounge 　Corridors	Floor residents 　and their guests	Small group activities such 　as birthday parties, 　cards, talking Casual interaction with neighbors
Private	Apartment unit	Individual resident(s) 　and guests	Personal activities Entertaining small groups 　of friends and relatives

[*]This typology deals specifically with interior spaces.
 Outdoor spaces can be similarly classfied but they are
 not included as part of this study.

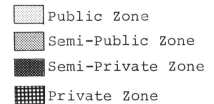

Public Zone

Semi-Public Zone

Semi-Private Zone

Private Zone

Site A
zones

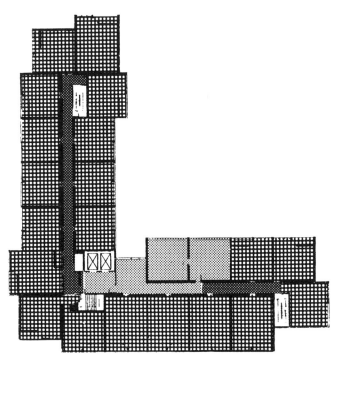

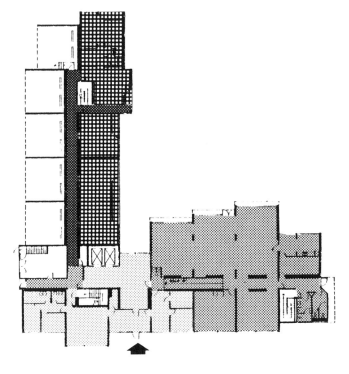

fifth floor   10   20

ground floor   10   20

Figure 3.

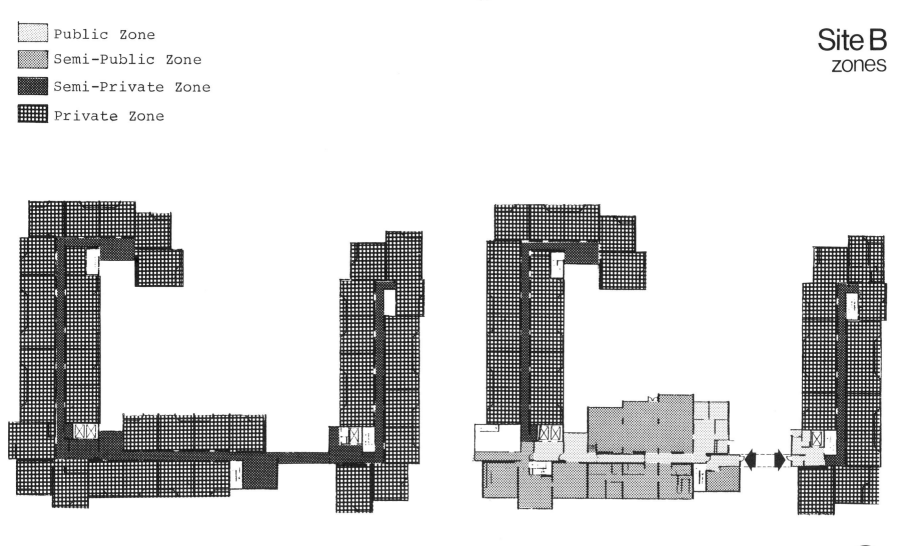

Public Zone
Semi-Public Zone
Semi-Private Zone
Private Zone

Site B
zones

residential floor ___ 10 20

ground floor ___ 10 20

Figure 4.

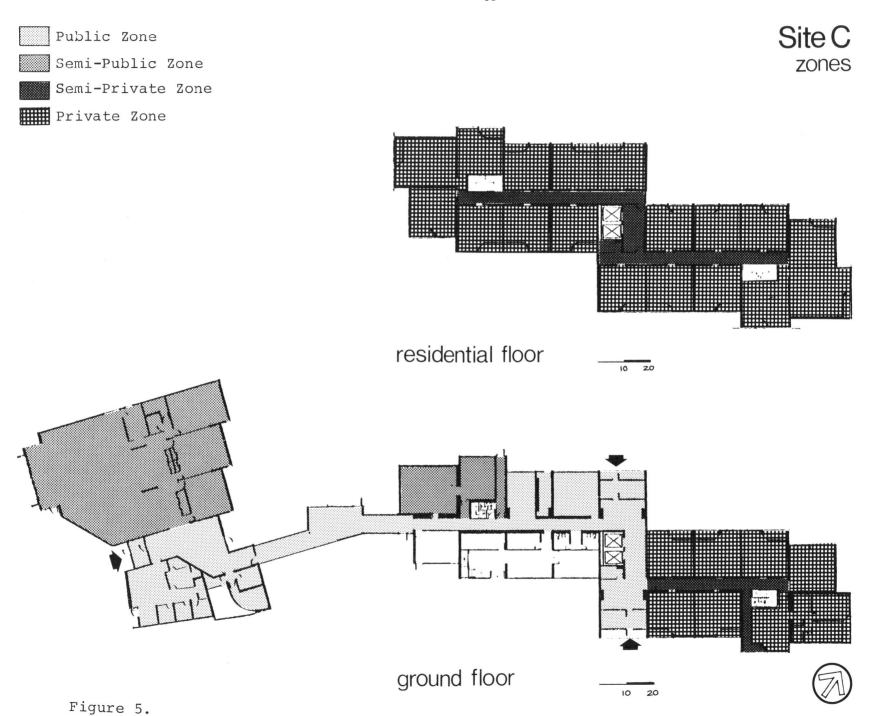

Public Zone
Semi-Public Zone
Semi-Private Zone
Private Zone

Site C
zones

residential floor

10 20

ground floor

10 20

Figure 5.

SPATIAL DEFINITIONS

Residential environment - all indoor and out-door spaces found within the legal boundaries of the project site. This includes the four zones found within the interior of the building(s).

Shared spaces - all areas within the buildings other than apartment units and mechanical and maintenance areas. They include any space used by residents for social or functional purposes. The public, semi-public, and semi-private zones comprise the shared spaces.

Social spaces - areas specifically designed for resident social and recreational activities. This term is used inter-changeably with semi-public zone.

Community room - typically the largest area in semi-public zones designed for resident gatherings such as meetings, bingo games, lunch programs, and parties. Other terms frequently associated with this area include: multi-purpose room, recreation room and meeting room.

Secondary spaces - areas in semi-public zone which are designed to accommodate small groups and specific activities such as pool, crafts, or reading. Secondary spaces plus the community room comprise the social spaces (semi-public zone).

Primary path - circulation area between the main entrance and elevators. It is the route travelled most by residents as they go in and out of the building. This path is in the public zone.

Secondary path - optional route through the semi-public zone which residents can use when entering or leaving the building. This allows them to pass by the social spaces on their way to other destinations.

DATA COLLECTION. A variety of methods was used to study resident behavior in different types of shared spaces. A single trained researcher studied each building over a four month period. The methods used in data collection included resident interview, behavior observation, photography, manager interview, and researcher diaries. A brief description of each method follows. A more detailed description of the methodological approach that includes the specific instruments used in this study appears in the appendix.

Resident interview. Selected residents were interviewed about their attitudes toward, and uses of, shared spaces in their building. Specific questions about frequency of use of social spaces, participation in formal and informal activities, and friendship patterns were included. Questions were both forced choice and open-ended. The 55 residents interviewed at the three sites received $5.00 for their information and time.

The interviewed residents were sampled from specific, pre-designated apartment locations in each building. This differs from the usual procedure of random sampling of residents. The preliminary hypotheses about elderly behavior in shared spaces were used to select the apartment locations. For example, residents in units at different distances from the elevator were interviewed to see if this distance influenced friendship formation or frequency of space use.

Behavior observation. Resident behavior in selected social spaces was recorded according to a time sampled schedule. From this information, population concentrations in various social spaces were calculated for different times of the day. These figures give an indication of the percentage of the resident population at each site that used these spaces on an informal, drop-in basis.

In addition, resident behavior was mapped on floor plans and generalized behavioral patterns for the social spaces at various time of the day were compiled. These maps of resident behavior provide information about the range of activities occurring in shared spaces, the participants (male vs. female, large gathering vs. small groups) and their location, furniture that is used, as well as time and duration of each activity. Interaction between residents engaged in different activities in different parts of the social spaces was also recorded. This data is used to establish need for differentiation and circulation between social spaces.

Photographic documentation. As different issues emerged in each building from the interviews and observations, photographs were taken to visually document the relationship between resident behavior and the design features of shared space.

Manager interview. The manager in each building was interviewed about management policies and practices that might have some impact on resident use of shared spaces. This information was helpful in understanding the extent to which residents control and manage their environment.

Researcher diaries. Researchers recorded information pertinent to the study after each building visit. This included relevant information not elicited as part of the scheduled interview or observation such as information generated from informal conversation with residents.

The combination of these methods provides information on actual use patterns in the shared spaces, resident participation in formal and informal activities, resident-reported needs for different types of activities and spaces, and the extent to which the resident population is a *social community* which shares values, perceptions, and responsibilities regarding their residential environment.

DATA TREATMENT AND PREPARATION FOR USE.

Data resulting from this multi-method approach to post-occupancy evaluation was treated in direct relation to the translation goal. While tabulations of interview responses, activity and time observations were made, the focus of the treatment was on graphic representation of central tendencies. The small size of the sample as well as the varied nature of the data disallowed use of formal statistical procedures.

Interview material was integrated into a preliminary organization of the total case study narrative and particularly used to clarify photographs.

Photographs for each site and across sites were compared for content consistency and validity in representing other data forms.

A number of passes were made in the organization of the varied materials for publication. The primary objective of the initial 1976 monograph was to test the usefulness of the research information for programming and design. In this text, that transfer objective is secondary to explanation of research process and generation of future research issues.

HYPOTHETICAL CONCEPTS.

Several important concepts have emerged from this study which may describe the relationship between resident activity and various spaces within the residential environment. Behavioral concepts describe recurring social and psychological phenomena across elderly housing sites. These concepts, the basis for future hypothesis construction, include *social community*, *offensive sur - veillance*, *commitment*, *group privacy*, *personalization and orientation*.

Social community, which is similar in concept to a neighborhood, is defined as people sharing physical space and boundaries who also share social ties, provide support to group members, exchange information, and often become self-managing. An underlying assumption of this research is that a *social community* should develop which encourages interaction while supporting individual privacy and control. Indicators of an active *social community* include high participation rates in formal activities like tenant meetings and parties; frequent use of the social spaces on a casual drop-in basis; visiting between apartment units; existence of a resident organization that establishes regulations and policies within the building; and a communal concern for shared spaces as evidenced by personal touches and resident maintenance of these spaces.

Offensive surveillance is a situation not uncommon to dense residential environments where some individuals experience resentment or displeasure at being closely watched by others. It is particularly a problem in settings for the elderly as one popular activity of older persons is sitting and watching others. Some do not have the energy, interest, or agility for more active participation in their surroundings; for others social engagement is neither comfortable nor a familiar experience. As most of the continuous activity in any building is associated with the comings and goings of residents and visitors, those who like to sit and observe are attracted to lobby areas.

Some passers-by enjoy interacting with these watchers, but there are also residents who find this situation offensive because they view it as an invasion of privacy. They feel uncomfortable having to walk near these watchers, particularly if direct eye contact cannot be avoided. The desires of both groups, those who wish to watch activities and interact with others or those who want to circulate with minimum surveillance, should be accommodated in elderly residential settings.

Commitment refers to the degree of psychological and physical effort that must be expended to reach a particular destination like the social spaces. Before going to such areas, an individual may weigh the costs involved against the expected benefits and rewards. For some residents the cost of going to the social spaces may only be the time and exercise it takes to travel the distance from their unit to these spaces. For others, such as disabled residents, the costs may be higher if walking any distance requires much physical effort or is painful.

There are also psychological costs that must be weighed such as a fear of passing through a space where a clique hangs out, risking rejection by other residents, or finding the social spaces empty. To compensate for such risks, residents measure rewards in the social spaces that outweigh the costs involved in getting there. Sought after rewards may include interacting with friends, participating in activities, having a view of outdoor activity, or just being in a different environment. A high degree of *commitment* is necessary to go to an area in the building if the known costs (i.e., negotiating long distances or physical barriers) are high relative to the expected rewards.

Group privacy is a need that is often overlooked in shared residential environments. Individuals can seek privacy in their apartment units but some groups need other spaces where they can control observation by others, outside distractions, and unwanted intrusions. Small groups that desire privacy at a variety of levels might include the men's club, a card playing group requiring focused attention, and an intimate family gathering that is too large to be comfortably accommodated in the apartment unit. Areas within the shared spaces should be able to meet the privacy needs of such groups.

Personalization is the changing of one's environment to accommodate and reflect personal tastes and lifestyles. An individual typically feels a great need to influence his surroundings in the residential environment. Within the private living unit *personalization* can be intense as reflected in choice of furnishings and decoration.

For residents of a multi-family building, the issue of *personalization* is collectivized. They have an extended residential environment created by their living units' relationship to such shared areas as lobbies, corridors, elevators, and social spaces. If these areas are to function effectively as extensions of an elderly person's home environment, they must encourage and accept resident *personalization*. Elderly persons will often contribute furniture, pictures for walls, and plants to shared areas they frequent or are attached to.

Orientation is the process by which individuals seek to comprehend their environment. It includes understanding which paths lead to desired destinations within the building. To orient themselves to new environments people use various cues, some of which are explicit like a sign with arrows, and some that are implicit such as varied light intensities along corridors. In more familiar environments, *orientation* is an issue of reinforcing people with cues they have seen before and have come to associate with a particular area or path. These cues might include any signs that distinguish one area from another such as different furnishings, colors, surface textures, and plants. People also need to have a sense of their location with respect to their immediate neighborhood surroundings. This is provided most readily by visual connections to the outdoors. Orientations to outdoors also reinforce, for older people, a sense of time and changing weather.

INTRODUCTION TO EVALUATIONS

Each of the three selected buildings (sites A, B, and C) is discussed separately. These sites are located in Cambridge, Massachusetts and are managed by the Cambridge Housing Authority. The sites (A, B, and C) were designed by the architectural firm of Benjamin Thompson & Associates, and were constructed in the fall of 1973. The buildings are made of pre-cast concrete slab and the finishing materials and details at all three are identical. The unit designs are also identical, with each unit having a small recessed balcony. Three-fourths of the units at each site are efficiencies and one-fourth have one bedroom. Major design variations at the three sites occur in the massing and in the location and configuration of social spaces and circulation paths.

Support staff at each site includes a part-time manager and several custodians during weekdays. There are no security guards. Each site is entered through a vestibule where an intercom/buzzer system is located. Residents enter the interior locked door with a key and visitors gain access through the buzzer system connected to each unit. There is an additional security device of a closed-circuit television monitoring system.

Each building presentation includes a site description, site and floor plans, a discussion of the social community, a series of maps summarizing resident behavioral patterns in the social spaces at various times of the day. and a discussion of seven design related issues. These issues deal with the spatial definition and organization of individual rooms and zones. The issues emerged during the analysis as the design variables appearing to have the most influence on resident behavior and on the subsequend development of a *social community*. These seven issues are:

① Public Zone

② Location of Semi-Public Zone

③ Differentiation of Semi-Public Zone

④ Square Footage of Semi-Public Zone

⑤ Visual Connections

⑥ Semi-Private Zone

⑦ Laundry Room

Site A

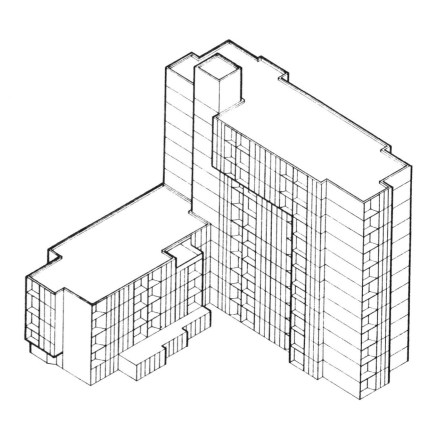

Site Description

Site A is located in a working-class neighborhood on the edge of a warehouse area. There are small corner stores within a few blocks of the site and public transportation connects residents with the major shopping district eight blocks away. The streets that bound the front and back of the site are quiet with little traffic. A small warehouse is adjacent to one side while the other side is bounded by three and four story multi-family residences of wood construction about 40 to 60 years old. Resident parking along both sides provides a buffer between the building and these adjacent structures. A wooden fence around the back of the site encloses a landscaped area which is seldom used because there is no protection from the hot summer sun. Several of the residents plant and tend flowers and bushes in the backyard.

The front portion of the L-shaped building that parallels the street is five stories tall while the section at right angles to the street is twelve stories tall. There are 181 units of which 141 are efficiencies, 39 are one bedroom, and one unit is two bedroom. Although a neighborhood health clinic is physically part of the structure at ground level, clinic patients have no access to the inside of the building as the main lobby door is locked. Residents enter with a key while visitors gain entrance through the intercom/buzzer system connected to each apartment.

Site A

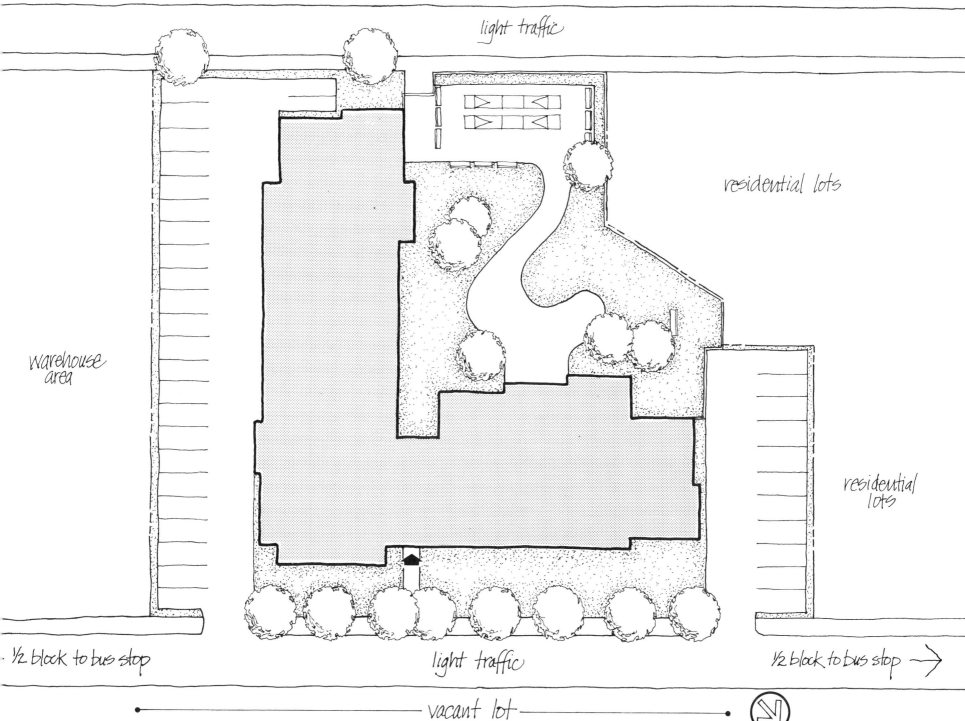

residential lots

light traffic

Site A

warehouse
area

residential lots

residential
lots

½ block to bus stop

light traffic

½ block to bus stop →

vacant lot

Site A
ground floor

Covered Parking

Unit with Balcony

Half level change

Community Room

Kitchen

Custodian's Area

Side Door

Maintenance

Lobby

RAMP UP

Mailboxes

Neighborhood Health Clinic

Vestibule

Manager's Office

Pool Room

Club Room

0   10   20

Site A
residential floor

This section of building is 12 stories

This section of building is 5 stories

Unit with balcony

Terrace (5th floor only)

Laundry

Unfurnished lounge

Lobby

0   10   20

Social Community

There is a very active *social community* at Site A as indicated by high participation rates in organized activities, casual get-togethers, and apartment visiting. Most of the 220 residents know one another at least by sight and exchange greetings when they encounter one another throughout the building.

There is an active tenants' club that meets once a month in the community room. Attendance at these meetings ranges from 50 to 75 residents. Almost all policies that affect residents and their use of the building are discussed and voted on by those present. As a result, this organized and committed tenants' group exercises some control over their residential environment. Such self-management leads to the development of a more cohesive social structure within the building. There is also a social club to which half of the residents pay dues. This allows them to participate in a variety of planned events ranging from parties and pot luck dinners to bus excursions into the countryside. As many as 100 residents will attend some of these gatherings. Bingo games which attract between 50 to 70 residents are scheduled for every Friday night; whist card parties, which draw over 20 residents, are held every other Tuesday. In addition, there is a newsletter that is distributed every month.

Many residents also participate in daily drop-in activities in the social spaces. Approximately half of them visit these spaces at least once a day. If they see or hear someone they know when passing by, the majority will go into the social spaces to say hello. Many residents also visit one another in the apartment units.

During an average day, residents in the social spaces can be observed watching and waiting for friends, reading the newspaper, chatting, sewing, playing cards, shooting pool, or watching others engaged in these activities. Most of these informal get-togethers take place in the pool room or club room or around the table under the window in the community room. A group of residents can usually be found at this

The front table in the community room attracts many residents throughout the day. It is typically the first stop for those entering the social spaces from the lobby.

Site A

front table because the location offers views of coming and going activities in the lobby as well as of activities in other areas of the semi-public zone.

The pool room was originally designed for arts and crafts activities but eventually became the location of the library which doubled as a card room at night. When a new pool table was acquired, the residents chose to put it in this room so the equipment could be locked at night. The club room next door is used as a sitting area for talking and sewing during the day and for playing cards at night. The residents intend to furnish this room with several upholstered chairs and sofas to suggest a more club-like atmosphere.

The male residents who represent only 10 to 15 percent of the building's population, group together for camaraderie and use the pool room as their gathering place. The wives of the men hanging out in this room will wander in and out of this area to talk with them and will occasionally shoot a game of pool when the men are not using the room. Some single women, however, expressed being intimidated by this male gathering and avoid the "men's room".

In general, Site A is large enough (in terms of resident population) to generate an active *social community*. There is no pressure to participate. It is not too large so as to create a general sense of anonymity and isolation among the residents.

The desire of the small group of men to be together has led them to establishing a place that they can call their own (the pool room).

Residents, particularly women, use the club room for sewing, talking, playing cards, and watching activity along the street in front of the building.

Site A

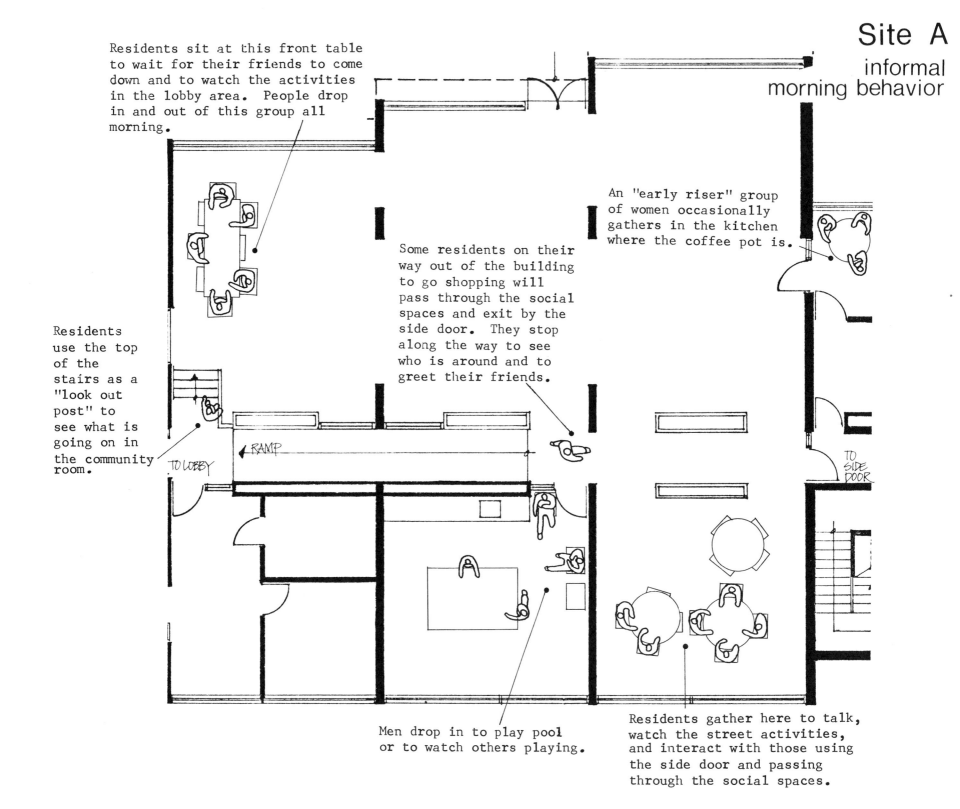

Site A
informal
morning behavior

Residents sit at this front table to wait for their friends to come down and to watch the activities in the lobby area. People drop in and out of this group all morning.

An "early riser" group of women occasionally gathers in the kitchen where the coffee pot is.

Some residents on their way out of the building to go shopping will pass through the social spaces and exit by the side door. They stop along the way to see who is around and to greet their friends.

Residents use the top of the stairs as a "look out post" to see what is going on in the community room.

TO LOBBY

RAMP

TO SIDE DOOR

Men drop in to play pool or to watch others playing.

Residents gather here to talk, watch the street activities, and interact with those using the side door and passing through the social spaces.

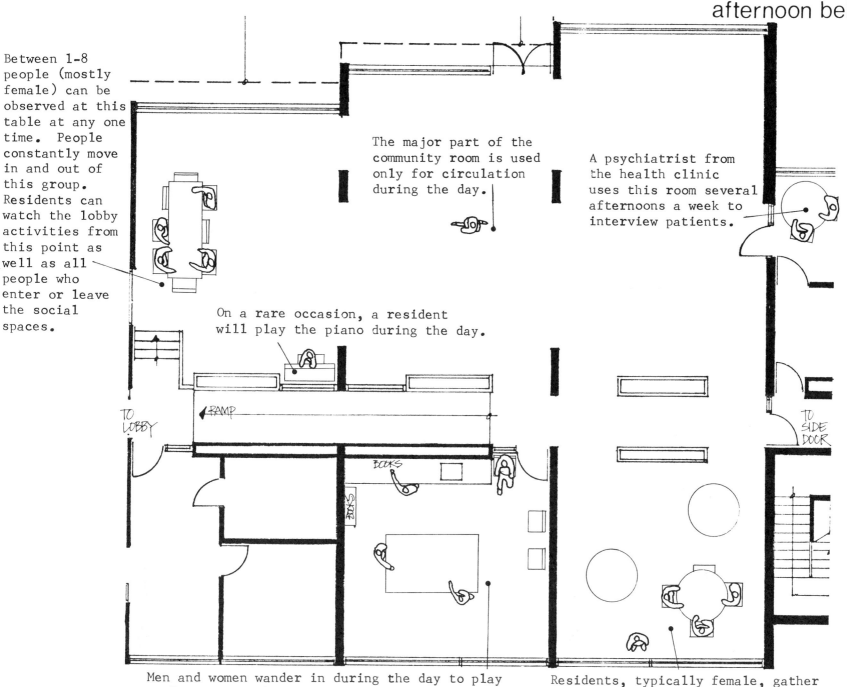

Between 1-8 people (mostly female) can be observed at this table at any one time. People constantly move in and out of this group. Residents can watch the lobby activities from this point as well as all people who enter or leave the social spaces.

The major part of the community room is used only for circulation during the day.

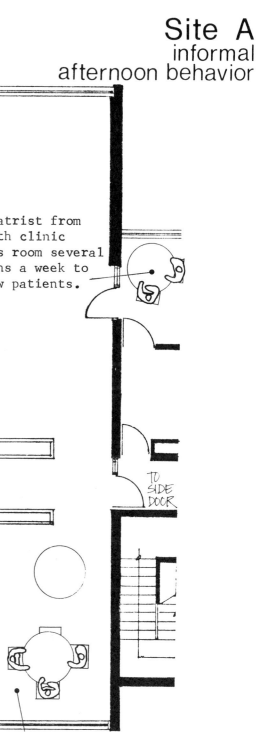

A psychiatrist from the health clinic uses this room several afternoons a week to interview patients.

On a rare occasion, a resident will play the piano during the day.

TO LOBBY

←RAMP

BOOKS

BOOKS

TO SIDE DOOR

Men and women wander in during the day to play pool or to watch others playing. Others will drop in to get a book from the library which they bring back to their apartments to read.

Residents, typically female, gather in the club room to sew, talk, or watch the activity along the street.

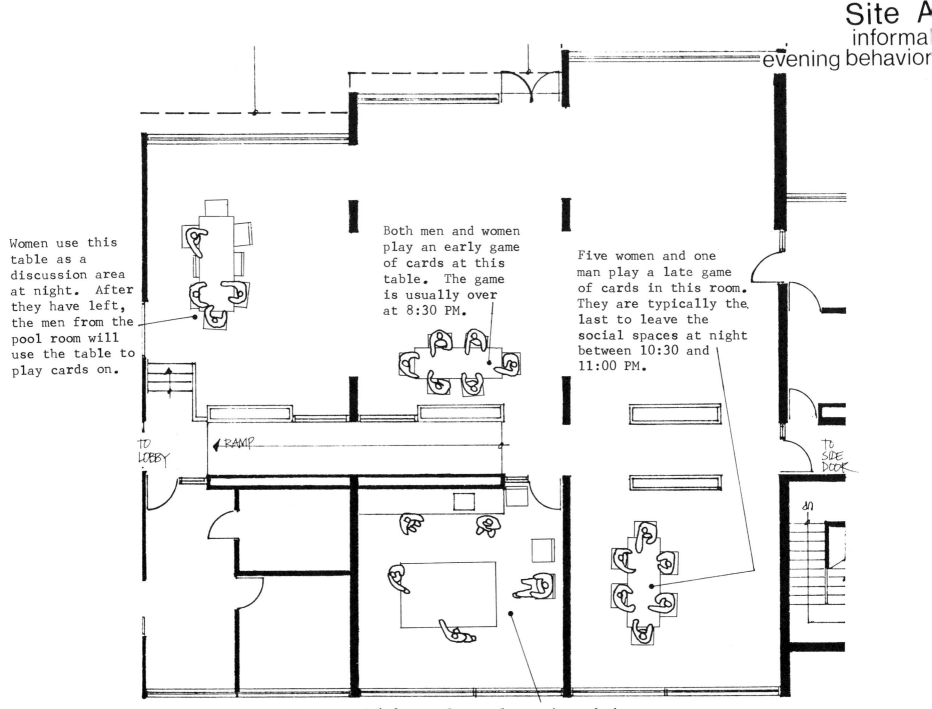

Women use this table as a discussion area at night. After they have left, the men from the pool room will use the table to play cards on.

Both men and women play an early game of cards at this table. The game is usually over at 8:30 PM.

Five women and one man play a late game of cards in this room. They are typically the last to leave the social spaces at night between 10:30 and 11:00 PM.

TO LOBBY

RAMP

TO SIDE DOOR

A group of 4-8 men play pool, watch, and chat with one another every night. After the pool room is closed, some of these men will stay to play cards in the community room.

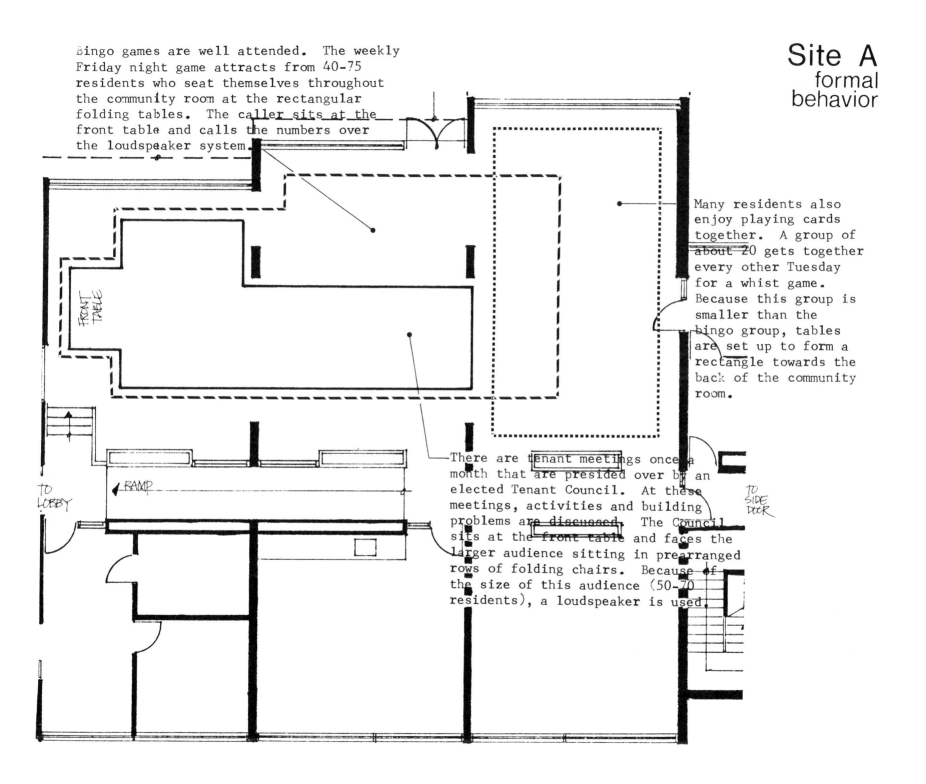

Bingo games are well attended. The weekly Friday night game attracts from 40-75 residents who seat themselves throughout the community room at the rectangular folding tables. The caller sits at the front table and calls the numbers over the loudspeaker system.

FRONT TABLE

Many residents also enjoy playing cards together. A group of about 20 gets together every other Tuesday for a whist game. Because this group is smaller than the bingo group, tables are set up to form a rectangle towards the back of the community room.

TO LOBBY

RAMP

There are tenant meetings once a month that are presided over by an elected Tenant Council. At these meetings, activities and building problems are discussed. The Council sits at the front table and faces the larger audience sitting in prearranged rows of folding chairs. Because of the size of this audience (50-70 residents), a loudspeaker is used.

TO SIDE DOOR

Design Issues

① The Public Zone

The primary path between the main entrance to Site A and the elevators is short (45 feet) and direct. Residents appreciate the quick and easy access to the elevators, particularly when returning from shopping trips with packages. The mailboxes, bulletin board, and newspaper stands are conveniently located along this major circulation route and are frequent stopping points for residents entering or leaving the building.

This public zone is defined by a series of doors, windows, and walls which separate it from other zones in the building. As a result, the daily comings and goings of residents and visitors do not interfere with activities in other areas. Glazed areas provide views of these other zones, however.

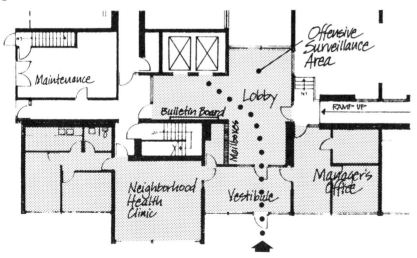

A waiting area for vehicular arrival has not been provided. Lobby sitting is not allowed because some residents feel that it creates a situation of *offensive surveillance*. The zone is too small to provide the necessary separation between circulation and lounging activities. Some residents, however, occasionally stand in the lobby by the glazed front entrance either watching people come and go or waiting for a ride.

When entering or leaving the building through the main entrance, residents can view activity in the community room.

② Location of Semi-Public Zone

The social spaces "branch" off the primary path and are separated from the public zone by a glass door. A secondary path leads through this semi-public zone to a side door that residents can use for both entering and

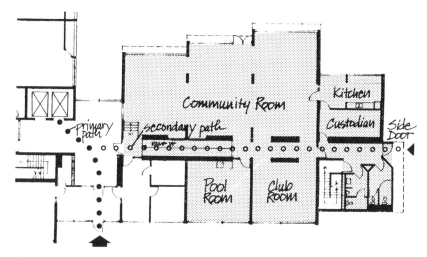

leaving the building. This door is
conveniently located in the direction that
they move off site to go shopping.

There are some advantages to the physical
separation of the two zones and to the
creation of a secondary path. First,
residents do not have to encounter others
when entering or leaving the building
because the primary path does not take them
through socially active areas. Second,
those residents who want to become more
socially involved can use the secondary path
through the social spaces. Residents
observed using this route always stop to
chat with their friends in the semi-public
zone.

Very little effort is required to check out
activities in the semi-public zone because
of the immediate adjacency to the primary
path. Residents who want to survey
activities and people in these spaces
before committing themselves to participating need only deviate 10 feet, at most,
from the primary path. Those who are

*One-third of the residents occasionally use
this ramped hallway and side door (in the
background) when entering or leaving the
building. While walking along this secondary
path they can check on the activities in the
semi-public zone.*

willing to make more of a *commitment* can
follow the secondary path into the social
spaces.

③ Differentiation of Semi-Public Zone

The semi-public zone includes the community
room, kitchen, club room, and pool room.
Their clustering contributes to almost
continual use of this zone by the residents
on a casual and informal basis. There is a
great deal of interaction between the
activities in the different areas because
the distance between rooms is minimal and
residents can move from one area to another
with little effort.

Site A

The three major social spaces differ in size, degree of enclosure, and furnishings and therefore offer a range of settings for resident activities. The community room is a large open space that can be entered at several points. The club room is open to the community room across the hallway but is more isolated from the activities in the public zone because of its location. The pool room with its glazed door is the only social space that can be closed off and therefore offers more *group privacy*. But because this room is furnished with only a pool table and a few folding chairs, it cannot be used for more private activities like reading, writing letters, or entertaining family or friends. Several residents have suggested that the pool table be moved into the club room but others

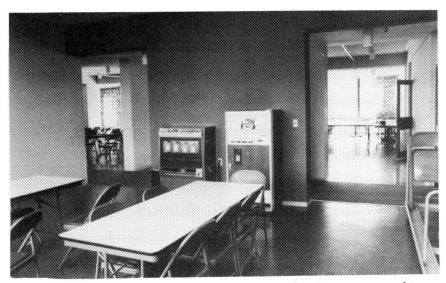

Views of the secondary path and the community room (in the background) from the club room encourage resident interaction.

want it to remain where it is to protect the equipment at night by locking the door.

The pool room and club room are separated from the community room by a secondary path that leads to a side door. Because this hallway is only partially enclosed, residents can still move easily between the spaces during the day. When large formal gatherings are held at night in the community room, however, residents not participating can walk down this ramped hallway and out the side door or into the secondary social spaces without disturbing the meetings.

(4) Square Footage of Semi-Public Zone

The community room at Site A contains 1,869 square feet, averaging 8.5 square feet per resident. The room easily accommodates the largest resident gatherings and is rarely filled to its limits. For the majority of meetings and bingo games, only two-thirds of the room is used. In terms of area, the room is slightly oversized for the resident population that gathers in it. Two columns sub-divide the room into thirds so it does not appear to be as large as it really is. These columns, however, become visual barriers in large gatherings.

Secondary social spaces include the pool room, club room, and kitchen. These rooms total 1,071 square feet, or 4.9 square feet per resident. The activities that take place in these secondary social spaces are easily accommodated within the area allotted among the three rooms. Overcrowding in any room has never been a problem and all rooms are frequently used by the residents.

Site A

Chairs for tenant meetings must be set up around the columns so everyone has a view of the speaker at the front of the room. This forces a long and narrow furniture arrangement that puts too much distance between the speaker and the audience in the back which creates visual and aural difficulties.

⑤ Visual Connections

Visual connections between spaces play an important role in the successful operation of areas used for social interaction. A window and glazed areas in and around the door between the public and semi-public zones provide visual connections between the primary path and the community room. Residents passing by can catch glimpses of what is happening in this social space and possibly be drawn in to participate. In addition, those in the community room can watch the coming and going activities in the public zone through the window. This window is located at floor level in the lobby

and at eye level in the community room so direct eye contact is typically not made between people on either side. This visual access does not lead to *offensive surveillance* because residents going in and out of the building are not conscious of being observed.

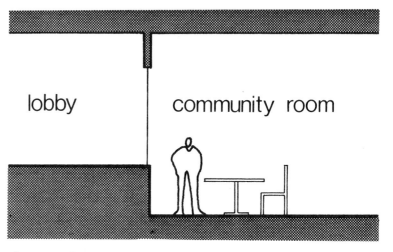

The pool room and club room do not benefit from visual connection with activities generated by the primary path. To find out what is happening in these secondary spaces residents must open the glazed door and walk down the ramp. Drop-in activity in these spaces is generated primarily from community room activity and circulation activities along the secondary path.

Visibility among the social spaces and circulation areas in the semi-public zone increases the interaction between activities in different areas. Both the club room and pool room are visible from the community room and residents freely move from one space to the next. The ramped hallway (secondary path) which separates the community room and secondary social spaces is

Site A

formed by a series of large openings that permit views of activities in different areas of the semi-public zone. Openings along the ramp and hallway allow for greetings between those in the social spaces and those walking by.

Visual connections between outdoor areas and the semi-public zone are important at this site. Visibility between the pool and club rooms and the street has two beneficial results: those walking by can look in to see what is going on and those inside can watch the street activity. The distance between the sidewalk and the glazing in the rooms is great enough (25 feet) so the visual connection is more informative and

While walking down the ramp, residents will stop at these visual openings to look into the community room. Contacts which may lead to further social participation are frequently initiated here.

interesting than offensive. The privacy of those both walking by outside and in the semi-public zone is protected by this distancing. Visual connections between the community room and backyard provide a quiet view of landscaped areas. Backyard activities are often extensions of community room activities, so visibility between inside and outside areas is important.

6 Semi-Private Zone

Areas included in this zone are corridors, elevator lobbies, and lounges on residential floors. The elevator, because of its central location at the juncture of the L-shaped building, equally serves the two corridors on the first five floors. On floors 2-5, a lounge area adjacent to the elevator lobby is unfurnished and unused. Some residents reported wanting sitting areas on residential floors that can be used for visiting with neighbors or more quiet activities like reading and sewing. They find the existing lounges "too public" and want areas that are visually protected from the elevator lobby.

Residents did not find the corridor lengths (84 and 105 feet) to be too long. They did, however, comment on their institutional appearance. Descriptions of the corridors included: "like a cell block"; "cold and uninviting"; "stark and drab because there are no signs of hominess like paintings hanging on the wall." The wall surfaces and narrow hallways do not invite any resident *personalization* outside of an occasional doormat or door decoration.

Site A

While standing in the elevator lobby on a residential floor one has a complete view of the adjacent lounge area. Lacking any visual privacy from circulation activities, this area remains unfurnished and unused by the residents.

All hallways and doors look alike and there are no graphics to distinguish one floor from another. Most residents have gotten off of the elevator on the wrong floor at least once. Several have even gone so far as to try to open an apartment door before noticing they were on the wrong floor. Many would like to see the floor number painted on the wall directly across from the elevator opening to aid in *orientation*.

(7) Laundry Room

The laundry room is located on the fifth floor off a residential corridor and adjacent to apartment units. There is a

terrace directly off the laundry but since it faces west and has no protection from the sun, it is often too hot in the summer to use for socializing or just sitting.

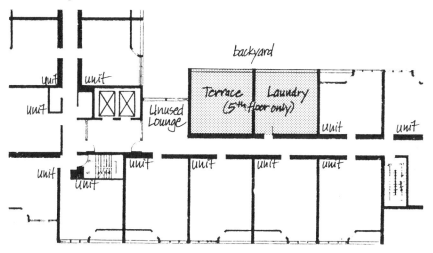

Because of the elevators residents do not think the laundry room is too far from their own apartment. Most do object to its location on the fifth floor, however, because the activity it generates intrudes on the privacy of surrounding residents. The drains occasionally back up and flood the bathroom of an adjacent unit. Those who live across the hall have to put rugs and towels under their apartment doors to keep the noise from machines and residents from disturbing them. Some residents suggested that the laundry would be better located in the basement or on the first floor away from the apartment units. Some would like to wait in the social spaces while their laundry is washing and drying. Due to the noise and heat in this laundry room, it is a functional space and not a social gathering area.

Site A

The ratios of one washer for 45 residents
and one dryer for 55 residents create
occasional waiting periods for machines.
Some residents suggested adding another
washer and dryer to minimize the waiting
problem. Many would prefer to dry their
clothes on an outside line and would like
lines put up on the terrace to allow for
this.

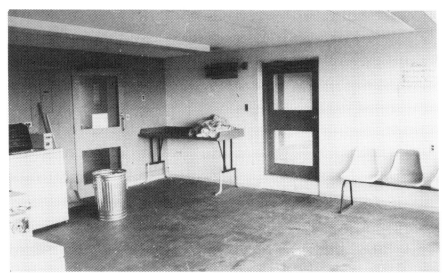

*The laundry room is minimally furnished with
machines, four banked chairs, and a single
table for folding clothes.*

Site A

Site B

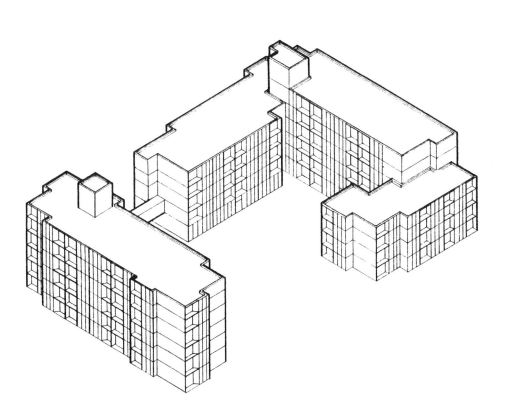

Site Description

Site B is located one block from a heavily trafficked avenue. This is a commercial strip oriented to the car and has many gas stations and quick food outlets. In the immediate area of the site there is only one small variety store. Residents must travel one mile for major shopping. However, a bus route with a stop one block from the site provides regular and frequent service to this shopping center.

The immediate neighborhood is primarily residential with a mix of two and three story multi-family houses of wood construction. Teenagers attending high school one block away pass by the building everyday. Some residents enjoy watching this activity on an otherwise quiet residential street.

Two buildings, East and West, comprise Site B. They are entered by a covered walkway which leads to two separate main entrances. On the second level only there is an enclosed bridge which connects the two buildings. Together they partially define a courtyard which has benches and shuffleboard courts. The six story West Building contains 77 units (61 efficiencies, 15 one bedroom units, and 1 two bedroom unit). The East Building is larger with 122 units (93 efficiencies and 29 one bedrooms). Its massing varies from four to six stories. All of the social spaces for the site are located in the East Building.

Site B as viewed from the front. The social spaces at ground level look directly out on the sidewalk and street.

The enclosed bridge connects the two buildings at the second level and covers the main entrance.

Site B

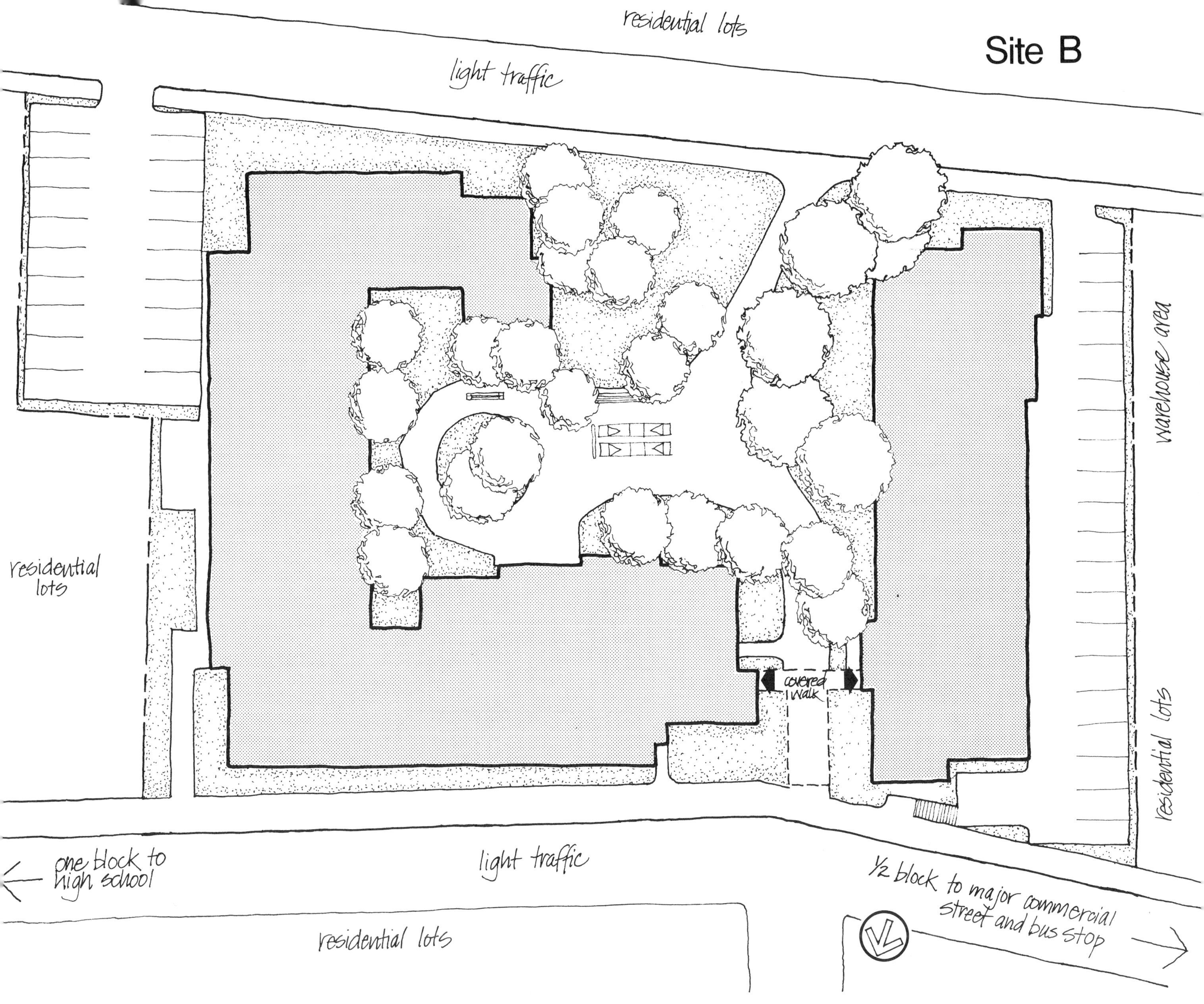

Site B

residential lots

light traffic

residential lots

one block to
high school

light traffic

residential lots

½ block to major commercial
street and bus stop

residential lots

warehouse area

covered
walk

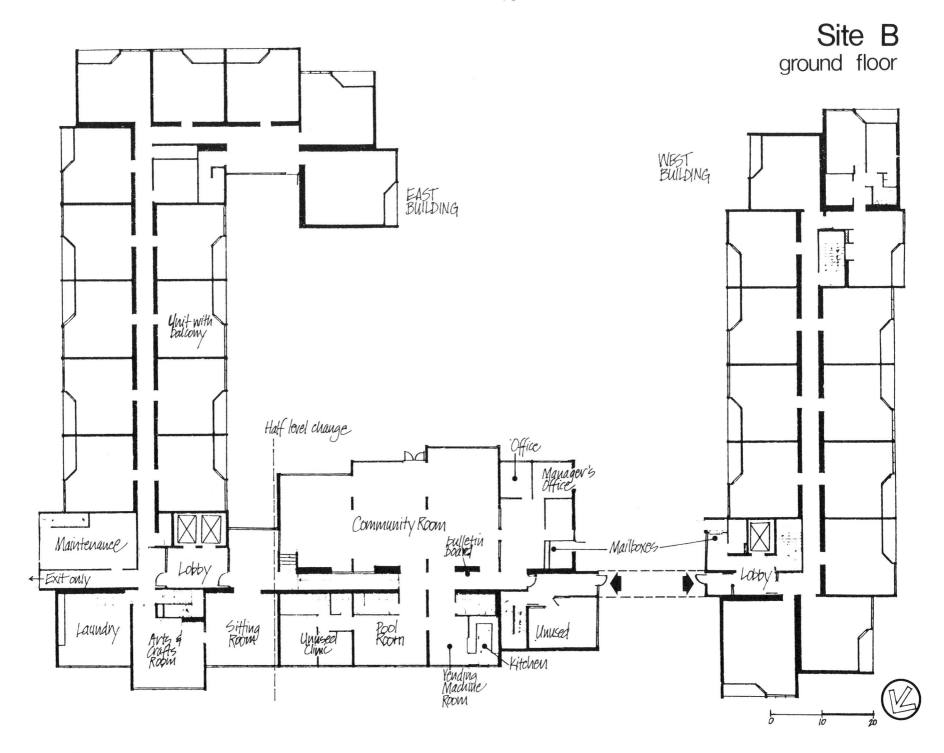

Site B
ground floor

EAST BUILDING

WEST BUILDING

Unit with balcony

Half level change

Office

Manager's Office

Community Room

Maintenance

Mailboxes

bulletin Board

Lobby

Lobby

Exit only

Laundry

Arts & Crafts Room

Sitting Room

Unused Clinic

Pool Room

Unused

Kitchen

Vending Machine Room

0   10   20

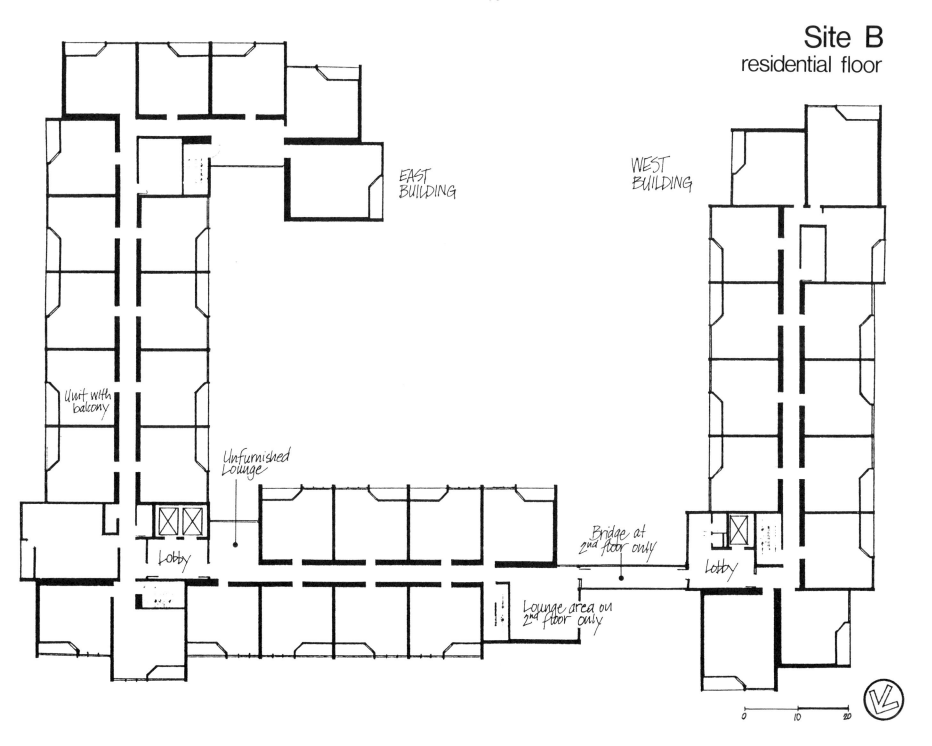

Site B
residential floor

EAST BUILDING

WEST BUILDING

Unit with balcony

Unfurnished Lounge

Lobby

Bridge at 2nd floor only

Lobby

Lounge area on 2nd floor only

0   10   20

Social Community

The *social community* at Site B has few active participants and is somewhat divided. Only one-third of the 245 residents attend the monthly tenant meetings and a smaller percentage participate in other social events. Weekly bingo games attract 30 women and anywhere from 15 to 45 residents participate in the hot lunch program in the community room. Art and exercise classes led by teachers from the city were offered for a few months but these programs were discontinued because of insufficient interest.

Only a small group of residents numbering between 10 to 15 uses the social spaces on a regular basis. Members of this group can be observed playing cards, shooting pool, and chatting during a typical day. They are also instrumental in the organization of bingo games, monthly parties, and the lunch program. Some residents refer to this group as the "community room clique" and feel unwelcome by them. Others passing by the social spaces dislike the feeling that this clique is watching them. As a result, many residents avoid using the social spaces on an informal basis. However, three-fourths of the interviewed population visited in each other's apartments, and could distinguish visitors from residents.

During the day the most active time in the social spaces is an hour before the sub-sidized lunch is served. Residents wander

The same group of men gathers every weekday afternoon to play cards and talk.

A group of women collects around one table in the community room every afternoon to talk.

Site B

between the pool room, community room, and
mail area to check on mail, talk with
friends, and wait for lunch. In the afternoon and evening a few small groups gather
to play cards, shoot pool, and talk.
Although these activities are informal and
unscheduled, they often have a specific time,
place, and group of residents associated
with them. For example, the men's afternoon card game begins at 2 PM every weekday
at the same table in the community room. By
late afternoon the social spaces are usually
empty. At this time those residents who
wish to avoid contact with the "community
room clique" will come down to check their
mail.

There is some tension between the residents
of the East and West Buildings. Residents
in the West Building where there are no
social spaces feel unwelcome in the semi-
public zone in the East Building and
consequently rarely use this area on an
informal basis. There is also some ill-
feeling among residents over the use of
the East Building's laundry room by those
in the West Building who dislike their
cold, dark, basement laundry facility.

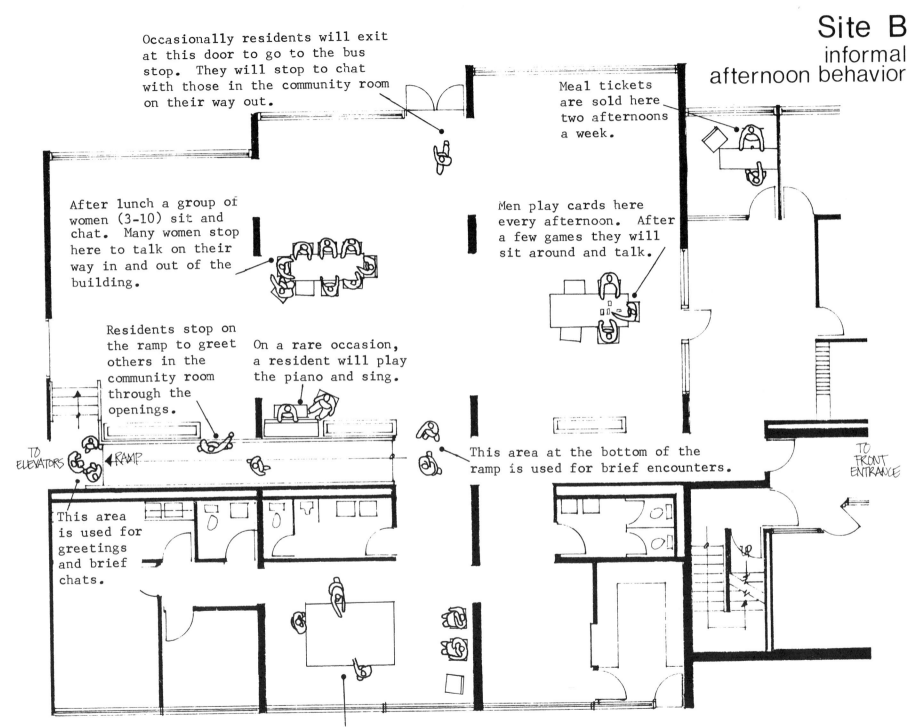

Site B
informal
afternoon behavior

Occasionally residents will exit at this door to go to the bus stop. They will stop to chat with those in the community room on their way out.

Meal tickets are sold here two afternoons a week.

After lunch a group of women (3-10) sit and chat. Many women stop here to talk on their way in and out of the building.

Men play cards here every afternoon. After a few games they will sit around and talk.

Residents stop on the ramp to greet others in the community room through the openings.

On a rare occasion, a resident will play the piano and sing.

TO ELEVATORS

←RAMP

This area at the bottom of the ramp is used for brief encounters.

TO FRONT ENTRANCE

This area is used for greetings and brief chats.

Between 3 to 8 women can be found shooting pool, sitting, and chatting during the afternoon hours.

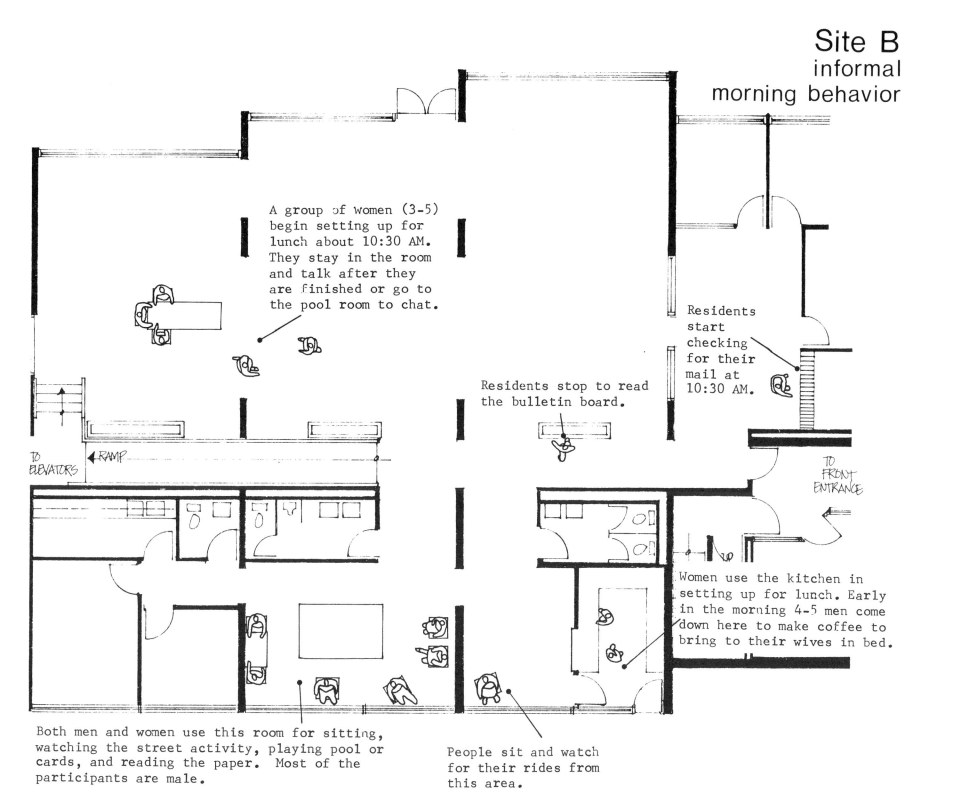

A group of women (3-5) begin setting up for lunch about 10:30 AM. They stay in the room and talk after they are finished or go to the pool room to chat.

Residents start checking for their mail at 10:30 AM.

Residents stop to read the bulletin board.

TO ELEVATORS

← RAMP

TO FRONT ENTRANCE

Women use the kitchen in setting up for lunch. Early in the morning 4-5 men come down here to make coffee to bring to their wives in bed.

Both men and women use this room for sitting, watching the street activity, playing pool or cards, and reading the paper. Most of the participants are male.

People sit and watch for their rides from this area.

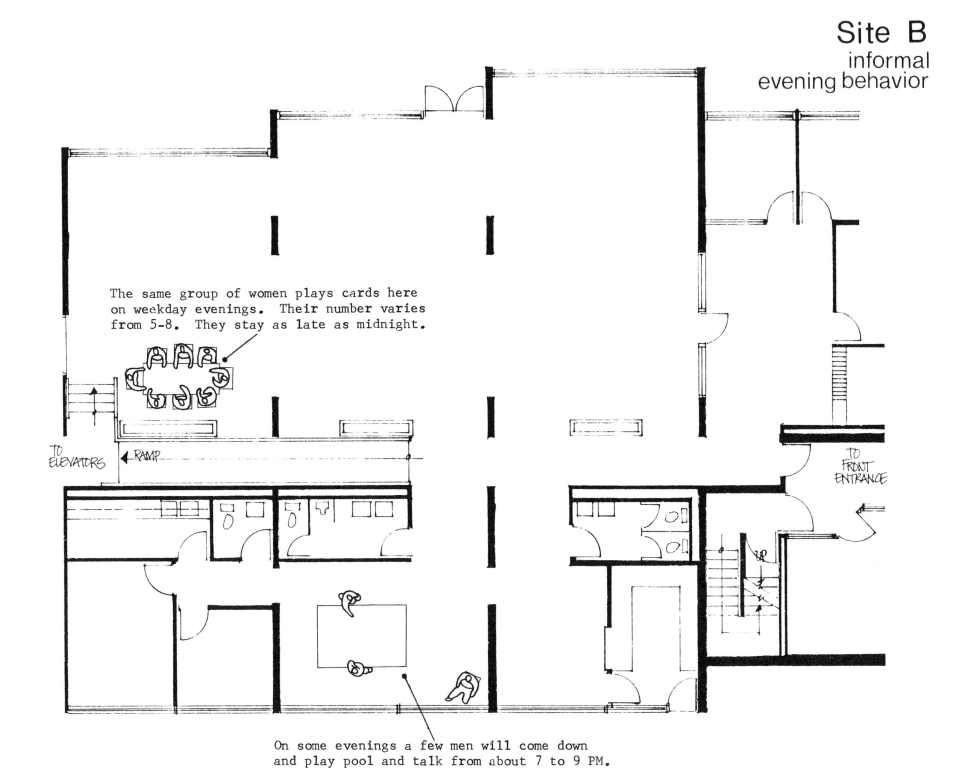

The same group of women plays cards here
on weekday evenings. Their number varies
from 5-8. They stay as late as midnight.

TO
ELEVATORS

RAMP

TO
FRONT
ENTRANCE

On some evenings a few men will come down
and play pool and talk from about 7 to 9 PM.

Site B
formal behavior

This area is used for the lunch program
program which is available every
weekday. Anywhere from 15 to 45
residents participate. The same
area serves as the setting for
bingo one night a week. 30-35
women attend.

Tenant meetings are held in this area
once a month. Folding chairs are lined
up to face the front along the ramp.
Over 80 residents usually attend and
some entertainment typically follows.

FRONT

TO
ELEVATORS   ← RAMP

This space is used as the food
area for the parties which follow
tenant meetings.

TO
FRONT
ENTRANCE

UP

DN

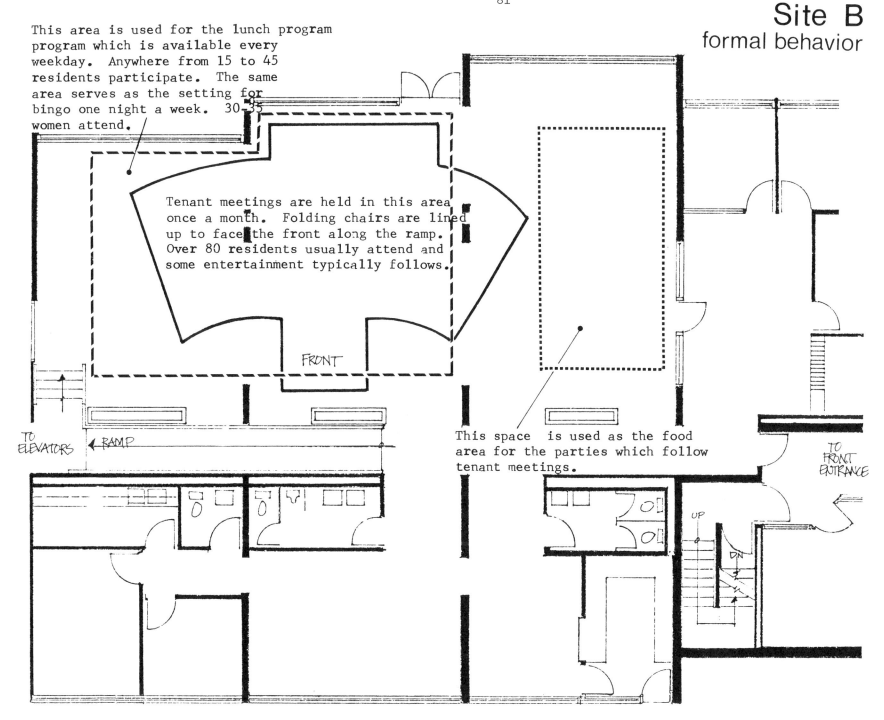

Design Issues

(1) Public Zone

The primary path in the East Building runs directly through the social spaces. *Offensive surveillance* is almost unavoidable along this path as a major pastime of those sitting in the social spaces is watching passersby. Although all residents entering the building must use the primary path, some choose to leave the building through side doors to avoid this situation.

The primary path is 120 feet in length and is considered by some residents to be too long to walk, particularly when carrying packages. This distance also causes *orientation* problems for visitors who have difficulty locating the elevators after they enter the East Building. The narrowness of the path leads to congestion, particularly around the bulletin board. However, the length and location of the primary path does give ample opportunity for resident surveillance of unwanted visitors.

The mail room is conveniently located just off the primary path near the front entrance in the East Building. It is easily reached and is large enough to accommodate the small groups which occasionally gather there. This public zone does lack a waiting area for vehicular arrival, however. The vending machine room is used for this activity, but it is too far from the front entrance and has inadequate seating.

The primary path leads through the semi-public zone and up a ramp to the elevator lobby. Some residents find this long walk uncomfortable.

Site B

The public zone in the West Building is comprised of a small elevator lobby and an alcove with mailboxes and a bulletin board. Congestion is a problem in this alcove where no more than two people at a time can easily move around. The primary path is short so residents with packages do not have to carry them long distances and visitors have no *orientation* problems. The public zone in the West Building has no waiting area either.

(2) Location of Semi-Public Zone

The semi-public zone in the East Building was designed to serve all residents on site. The West Building residents, however, do not feel welcome in this zone and some have expressed the need for social spaces in the West Building. A high level of *commitment* is needed on their part to either go out-doors at ground level or use the bridge connection at the second level to reach

the social spaces. Several residents also feel they are entering someone else's territory because they do not live in the building where the semi-public zone is located.

The public zone runs through the semi-public zone in the East Building creating an active pedestrian "street". This arrangement has created areas of zonal overlap. This is most evident at the base of the ramp where visitors and residents often deviate from the primary path and disrupt on-going activities in the social spaces.

The lack of physical separation between the public and semi-public zones maximizes *offensive surveillance* opportunities. This situation is accentuated by the absence of a secondary path providing an option for entering and leaving the building with little risk of encountering other residents. The unavoidable contact between residents in both zones has not led to any extensive use of the social spaces from drop-in socializing. These spaces are underutilized despite the minimal *commitment* necessary to enter them. Social encounters forced upon the population because of the semi-public zone appear to contribute to residential tension and underuse.

(3) Differentiation of Semi-Public Zone

Although the social spaces are adjacent to one another, a half level change in the semi-public zone has created two separate clusters of spaces. One cluster is located at the base of the ramp and includes the pool room, vending machine room, kitchen, and community room. The active nature of this cluster is often a result of the overflow of activities

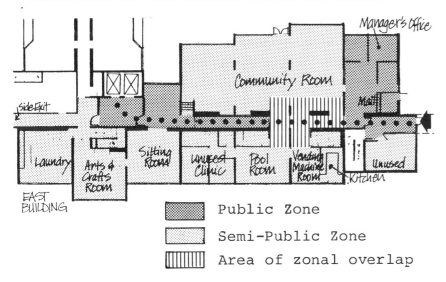

Manager's Office

Community Room

Mail

side Exit

Laundry Arts & Crafts Room Sitting Rooms Unused Clinic Pool Room Vending Machine Room Kitchen Unused

EAST BUILDING

▓▓▓ Public Zone

☐ Semi-Public Zone

▒▒▒ Area of zonal overlap

from the community room which diversify into the smaller social spaces. Most of the activities in this more active cluster are unfocused in nature such as watching others, circulating, and talking. It is difficult for more focused activities like card playing, sewing, and reading to take place because of the distractions generated by activity along the primary path. No provisions for *group privacy* have been made in this lower level cluster. A group of male residents that frequents the pool room and community room has had discussions with the manager about finding a room exclusively for their use.

The other cluster of social spaces is situated at the top of the ramp across from

There is much circulation between the social spaces at the base of the ramp (to the right) because there is very little physical separation.

the elevators and consists of the crafts, sitting, and laundry rooms. With the exception of the laundry room, this cluster is rarely used by the residents. Its location along the primary path is convenient for most residents, yet that alone has not been sufficient for developing an active area for socializing. The doors to these rooms are always shut so it is difficult to see inside them when walking by. This factor plus distance from the community room may contribute to their underutilization.

④ Square Footage of Semi-Public Zone

The 1,988 square feet (8.1 square feet per resident) in the community room easily accommodates large gatherings like tenant meetings, bingo games, parties, and the hot lunch program. Columns divide the room into three bays of different sizes. At any one time only two of these bays are fully utilized suggesting that the room is slightly over-sized. The columns create visual barriers during the large tenant meetings. During informal activities, small groups of residents tend to gravitate toward the edges of the community room or near a column in an effort to find some definition of place within the larger space.

The secondary spaces, consisting of the sitting, crafts, pool, and vending machine rooms plus the kitchen and clinic area, total 1,940 square feet (7.9 square feet per resident). Of these spaces, the clinic and crafts room are never used; the vending machine and sitting rooms are occasionally used; and the pool room is used frequently. There is also an unused room near the main entrance to the East Building which was

Site B

supposed to be a small variety store.
Although the underutilization of these
secondary spaces depends on other variables
like clustering, relationship to primary
path, and extent of visual connections,
another contributing factor is the
allocation of too much space for a resident
population of this size.

⑤ Visual Connections

Views between the primary path and the semi-
public zone are available for the entire
length of the path. Many residents have
complained of invasion of privacy while
entering or leaving the building.
Residents using the social spaces, particularly those clustered at the bottom of the
ramp, also complain because they are
constantly under observation by others
around them. Some residents try to avoid
this area of the building as much as
possible. These visual connections do
facilitate drop-in socializing, however,
for it is difficult not to be aware of
activities in the community and pool rooms
when passing by. There are limited views
between the primary path and the social
spaces across from the elevator which
contribute to their underutilization.

Visual connections between the pool, vending
machine, and community rooms are strong.
Residents can sit in one room and see some
of what is happening in the others.
Circulation between these rooms during the
day is constant.

All social spaces have generous views to
the outside. The community room looks
out on the courtyard which is a pleasant

but passive setting. Residents do not use
this room to sit and watch outdoor
activities because the courtyard is a quiet
area and the primary path serves as a
pedestrian street which is far more
interesting to watch. Residents do use the
secondary spaces, particularly the pool
room, for outdoor viewing because these

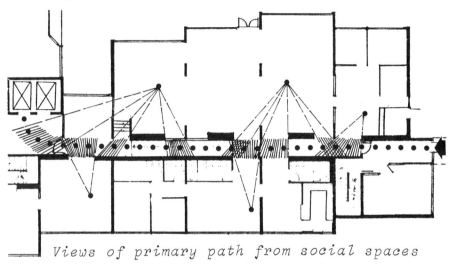

Views of primary path from social spaces

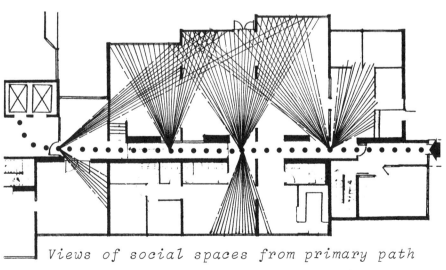

Views of social spaces from primary path

Site B

Some residents dislike being observed by others in the social spaces when walking along the ramped primary path. They sometimes exit by side doors to avoid this very public path.

rooms are located on the street side and have views of pedestrian activity. The distance between the glazing and the sidewalk is only 10 feet and is viewed by some as being uncomfortably close. Drapes are closed at night to protect the privacy of those using the social spaces.

(6) Semi-Private Zone

The semi-private zone in the East Building consists of an elevator lobby and corridors on each floor, a lounge area adjacent to the elevators on floors 2-5, and a lounge area on the second floor next to the bridge connection. The West Building has small

elevator lobbies and corridors. The windows next to the elevators on each floor provide natural lighting, visual relief from the monotomy of long, narrow corridors, and *orientation* to the outdoors.

The lounges near the elevators in the East Building are unfurnished and unused. Residents have shown no interest in extending their apartment unit into this lounge to create a social area. Several residents did mention a desire for floor lounges located away from the elevators in order to maintain some privacy for those using it.

The second floor lounge in the East Building near the bridge was used for several months

Resident personalization is more evident in the enlarged, naturally lit corridor space in the small wing at the back of the East Building.

Site B

by residents in the West Building. These residents wanted a social space for playing cards and chatting which was closer to their own building than the semi-public zone. Locating the lounge at the end of the corridor provided the desired privacy for those using the space as well as for those coming and going from their apartments. The folding tables and chairs have since been moved down into the community room so the lounge is presently unfurnished and unused.

The corridors at Site B vary in length from 100 feet to over 180 feet. Many residents who live at the end of these corridors and have to walk more than 100 feet feel that they are too long. These corridors are also very narrow. Examples of resident *personalization* in this area are sporadic and sparse, limited to mats outside the unit and door hangings. In the small wing at the back of the East Building the corridors increase in width at the end and are glazed on the courtyard side. After walking the preceding tunnel-like corridors, these windows provide orientation and much needed visual relief.

(7) Laundry Room

There is a laundry room in each of the two buildings at Site B. The laundry room in the East Building is on the first floor adjacent to the crafts room. Its location beyond the main elevator lobby off of the primary path limits the visual connection between the major circulation area and the laundry room. Residents are able to use the room without being observed by others coming and going in the building. When carrying

heavy bundles of laundry, residents have a short distance to travel from the elevator and have minimal contact with the public zone.

Although this laundry room is furnished with a few chairs and has an excellent view of the street, residents rarely wait here because of the noise. As the active social spaces are separated from this area by a long ramp, most residents go back to their apartment unit to wait for their laundry.

The laundry in the West Building is located in the basement in a windowless, gloomy area. It is reached by going down a dark and, for some, frightening corridor. The

The laundry room in the West Building is windowless and gloomy. Some residents prefer to use the first floor laundry room in the other building even though it is much farther away.

Site B

walls, floor, and ceiling are concrete. In
the winter the room is cold; in the summer
it is often stuffy. A significant majority
of those interviewed in the West Building
dislike the location. They think it is too
far from their apartments, too isolated, and
"scary." They would prefer a laundry room
with sunlight and a view of the outdoors.

The residents in both buildings would like
to see an additional washer and dryer in
each laundry room. This would change the
existing ratios of washer and dryer per
resident from 1:50 (East Building) and 1:45
(West Building) to 1:35 and 1:31,
respectively. The majority of residents
would like to have the option of drying
their clothes outdoors. No outside lines
are presently available.

Site C

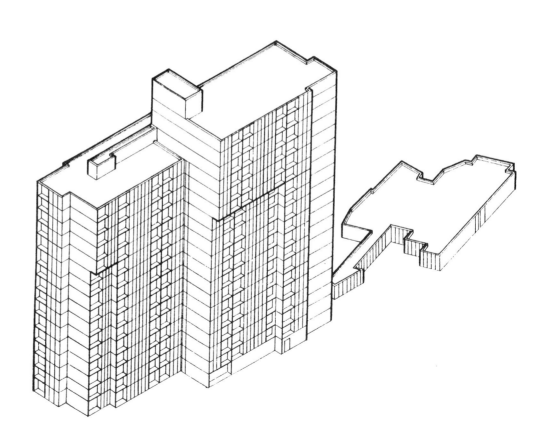

Site Description

Site C is in an area of mixed commercial, residential, and industrial use. The site is bordered on one side by a major commercial avenue along which can be found a bus line and a variety of small commercial establishments such as small grocery and liquor stores, bars, and restaurants. At the opposite end of the site, factories and warehouses are set back from a busy street that is often blocked with large trucks. The commercial avenue and the industrial street are linked by a lightly trafficked road that is lined with two and three story multi-family structures about 50 years old. The site is enclosed on its fourth side by a high timber fence which separates a landscaped backyard from a railroad track along which several trains run daily.

Site C consists of a residential tower and a one story social spaces annex which was built two years after tenant occupancy. The tower is 19 stories tall and accommodates approximately 360 residents. There are 305 units: 245 efficiencies; 58 one bedrooms; and 2 two bedrooms. Two double-loaded corridors of nine units comprise each apartment floor. The residential tower is connected to the annex at ground level by a long enclosed corridor. The annex houses the social spaces and a health clinic. Although the clinic is open to neighborhood residents, a separate entrance has been provided for them, and they are not allowed to use any other part of the building.

Site C's nineteen story residential tower contrasts with surrounding two and three story buildings.

Site C

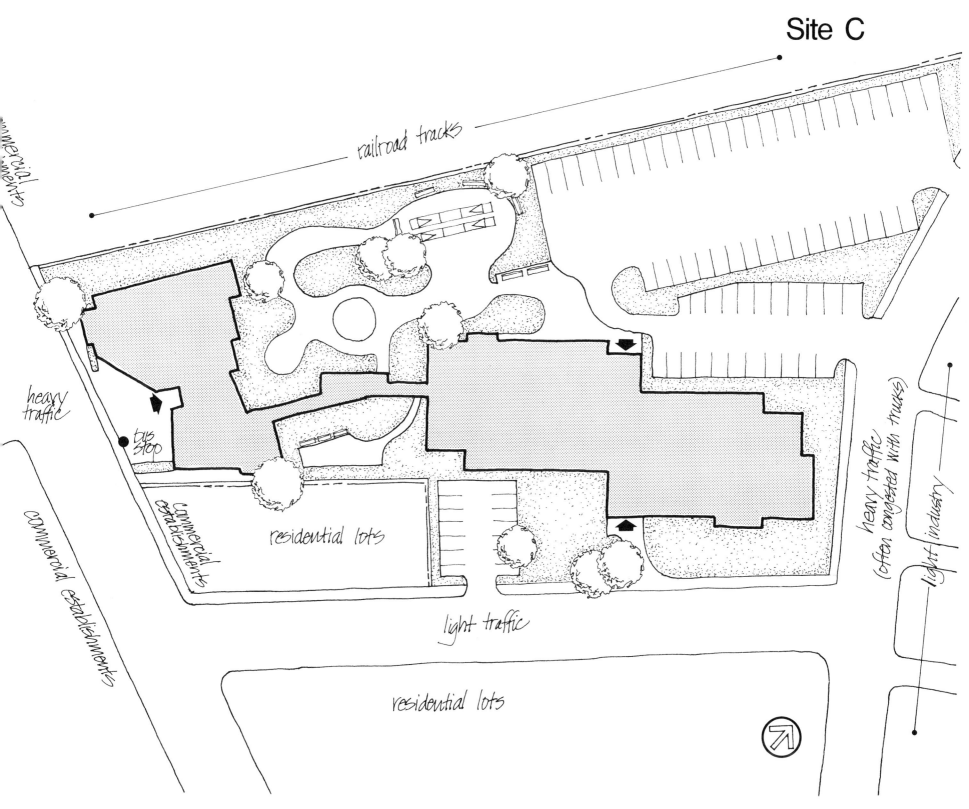

Site C

railroad tracks

commercial establishments

heavy traffic

bus stop

commercial establishments

commercial establishments

residential lots

heavy traffic (often congested with trucks)

light industry

light traffic

residential lots

Site C

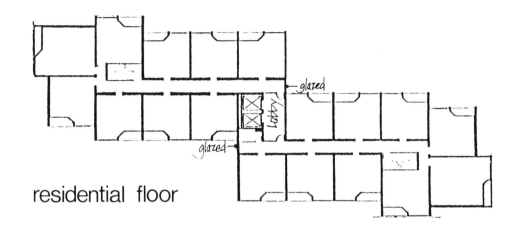

residential floor

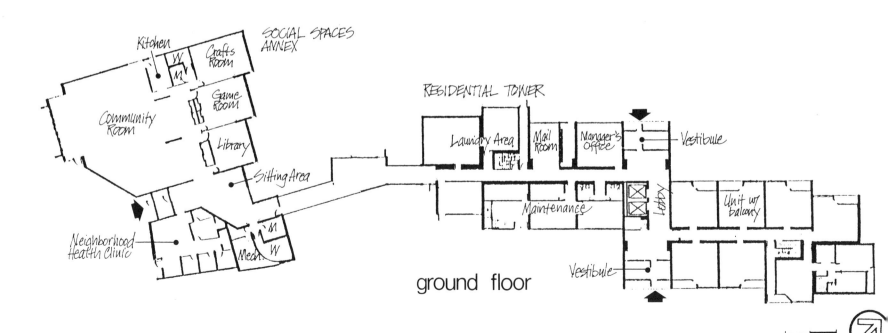

SOCIAL SPACES ANNEX

Kitchen

Crafts Room

Community Room

Game Room

Library

Sitting Area

Neighborhood Health Clinic

Mech.

RESIDENTIAL TOWER

Laundry Area

Mail Room

Manager's Office

Vestibule

Maintenance

Unit w/ balcony

Vestibule

ground floor

0   10   20

Social Community

There is little evidence of a developing *social community* at Site C. The majority of residents do not use the social spaces on a regualr basis, do not visit in others' apartments, and cannot distinguish residents from visitors in the building.

A majority of the 360 residents at Site C do not participate in the building's formal activities. There are tenant council meetings once a month but only 100 to 150 residents attend. The social club which organizes dances, parties, and trips has a membership of only 120 residents. About 50 residents play bingo twice a week in the community room. This group is small but enthusiastic and many of them go to local churches and schools in order to play more frequently. The hot lunch program attracts between 50 and 60 residents each weekday and generates most of the daytime activity in the community room. A few volunteer residents start setting up the tables and equipment around 10:00 AM, lunch is served at noon, and some residents stay on into the afternoon to talk, watch others, or play cards. Of those who do participate in the social life of the building, there is a core group of approximately ten men and women who are "social leaders" and another ten to fifteen who spend a fair amount of time in the social spaces.

With the exception of the sitting area and the kitchen, the secondary spaces are used infrequently. One or two residents will sometimes work on puzzles in the game room. Other individuals may select a book from the library but will return to their

apartments to read. A self-selected group of men uses the crafts room as an informal club room. Here they sit and talk and occasionally do some crafts work. Although there is a tendency for men and women to form separate groups in the social spaces, some mixed groups will gather to talk or play cards.

A major problem in the development of Site C's *social community* is the fact that the social spaces annex was not completed until two years after resident occupancy. Until then the elevator lobby was a favorite gathering place to talk and watch others come and go. Some individuals complained about this *offensive surveillance*, while others felt the "lobby standers" served a function as unofficial security guards. After the annex was opened, the manager instituted a policy of "no hanging out" in the lobby. This has cut down on, but not

The seclusion of the crafts room has encouraged its selective use as an informal men'e club room.

Site C

eliminated, the lobby watching. Although
a sitting area in the annex is a place
where residents typically watch others
passing by, it is not as centrally
trafficied as is the lobby and therefore
seems less offensive.

Other factors that appear to inhibit the development
of a *social community* at Site C may be the
sheer size and number of units in the
building (19 stories, 305 dwelling units),
the distance of the social spaces from the
apartment units, and the lack of alternative
socializing spaces on residential floors.

*About 50 residents participate in the hot
lunch program every weekday.*

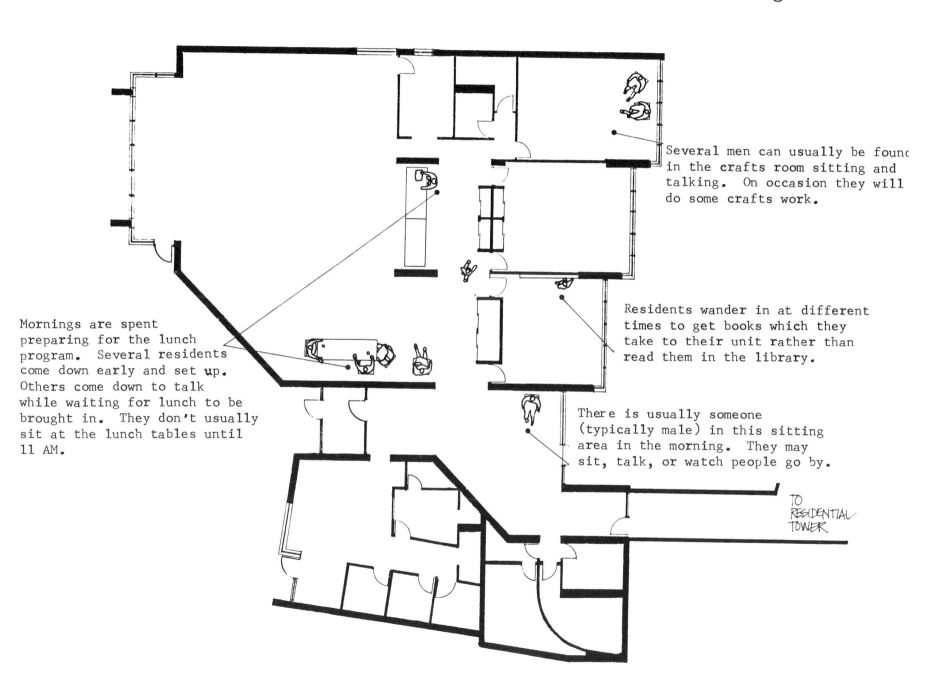

Several men can usually be found in the **crafts room** sitting and talking. On occasion they will do some **crafts work**.

Residents **wander** in at different times to get books which they take to their unit **rather** than read them in the library.

Mornings are spent preparing for the lunch program. Several residents come down early and set up. Others come down to talk while waiting for lunch to be brought in. They don't usually sit at the lunch tables until 11 AM.

There is usually someone (typically male) in this sitting area in the morning. They may sit, talk, or watch people go by.

TO RESIDENTIAL TOWER

Site C
informal
afternoon behavior

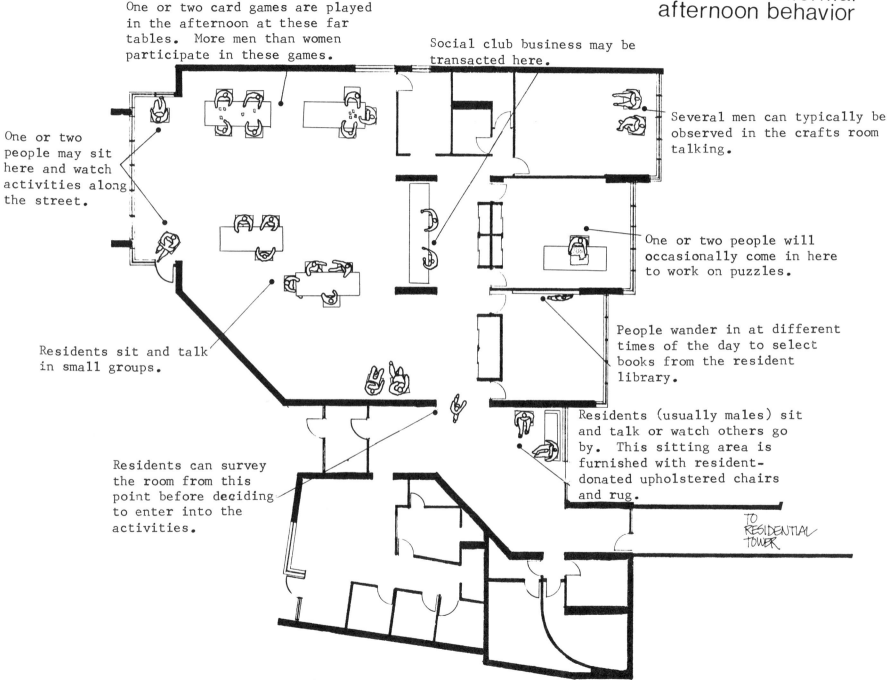

One or two card games are played in the afternoon at these far tables. More men than women participate in these games.

Social club business may be transacted here.

Several men can typically be observed in the crafts room talking.

One or two people may sit here and watch activities along the street.

One or two people will occasionally come in here to work on puzzles.

Residents sit and talk in small groups.

People wander in at different times of the day to select books from the resident library.

Residents (usually males) sit and talk or watch others go by. This sitting area is furnished with resident-donated upholstered chairs and rug.

Residents can survey the room from this point before deciding to enter into the activities.

TO RESIDENTIAL TOWER

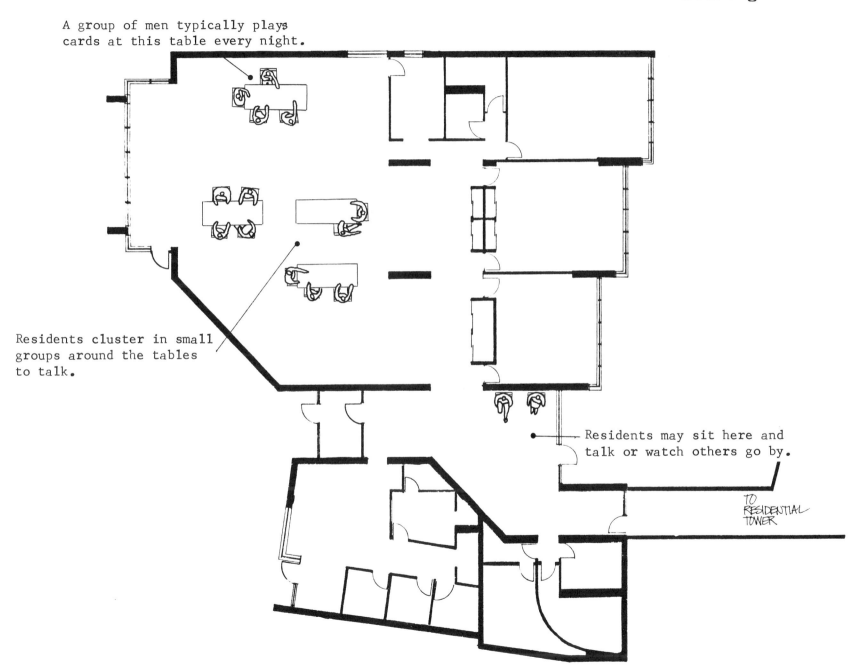

A group of men typically plays
cards at this table every night.

Residents cluster in small
groups around the tables
to talk.

Residents may sit here and
talk or watch others go by.

TO
RESIDENTIAL
TOWER

Site C
formal behavior

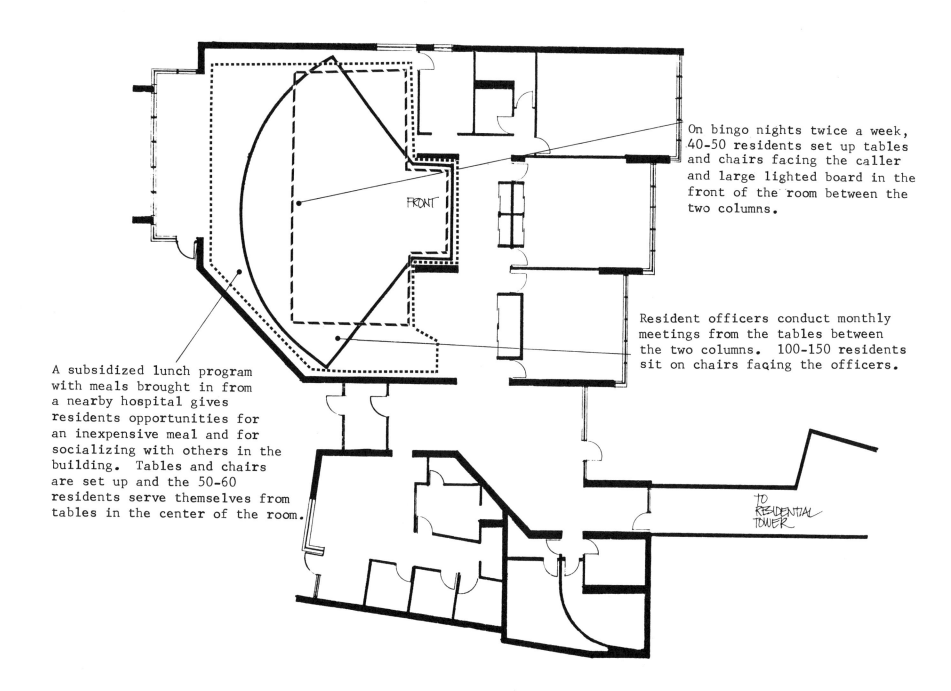

On bingo nights twice a week, 40-50 residents set up tables and chairs facing the caller and large lighted board in the front of the room between the two columns.

FRONT

Resident officers conduct monthly meetings from the tables between the two columns. 100-150 residents sit on chairs facing the officers.

A subsidized lunch program with meals brought in from a nearby hospital gives residents opportunities for an inexpensive meal and for socializing with others in the building. Tables and chairs are set up and the 50-60 residents serve themselves from tables in the center of the room.

TO RESIDENTIAL TOWER

Design Issues

(1) Public Zone

Site C is unique in that it has three main entrances with vestibules and intercom/buzzer systems. These doors create three primary paths and an extensive public zone. The two doors opposite one another in the residential tower provide direct and easy access (40 feet) to the elevators. Although the third entrance in the social spaces annex is located 250 feet from the elevators, it provides the most frequently used primary path. Its popularity can be attributed to the fact that it is the most direct enclosed route to a major commercial street and it passes the social spaces.

A separate room for mail dispersal has been provided for the large resident population.

Although this diminishes congestion in the public zone, individuals still cluster around the elevator to chat, wait for rides, and watch others. Some residents feel uncomfortable waiting for the slow elevator in this small lobby because they are forced into close contact with these people for extended periods of time.

Any resident moving from the apartment unit to the social spaces must follow a very public route along the primary path where encounters with visitors and other residents are inevitable. This tends to have an inhibiting affect on some individuals' use of the social spaces as suggested by the fact that only one third of the population frequents these areas once a week or more.

The only lounge in the public zone is a sitting area opposite the annex door. Because it is 33 feet from the entrance it

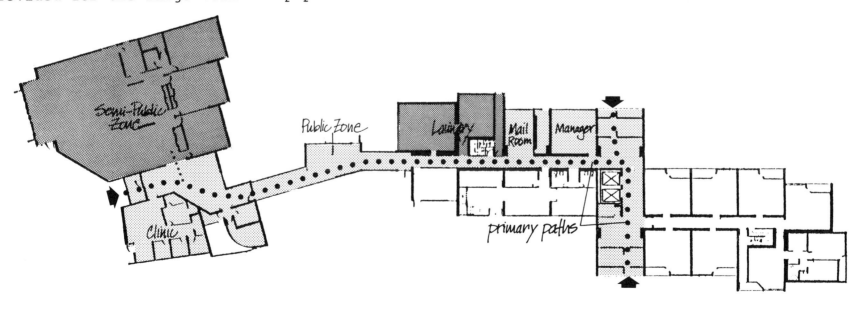

Site C

Despite "No Loitering" signs, there are still a few residents who hang out in the lobby as it is the focal point of circulation within the building.

is not used as a waiting area but rather as a place to sit and talk and watch passing activity. Although the sitting area creates an *offensive surveillance* problem for some residents, they have found this situation easier to accept than in the elevator lobby. This may be because they can pass the sitting area at a distance comfortable enough to acknowledge those seated and yet not so close that they are forced into extended interaction. Also residents who do not want their movements observed have the option of using one of the other two main doors to arrive at the elevators.

② Location of Semi-Public Zone

The social spaces "branch" off the primary path that runs between the elevators and the annex door. When entering or leaving the building by this path residents are provided with views of activity in the community room. The distance of the primary path from the community room allows a resident to see activity without joining or interrupting it. However, residents cannot see social activity in the secondary spaces from the primary path. If a secondary path existed that allowed residents to pass by the smaller social spaces on the way to other destinations, they would be provided with glimpses of activity within and opportunities for drop-in socializing.

As residents pass by the sitting area near the annex door, views of community room activities are readily available.

Site C

For residents who use the annex door the location of the semi-public zone facilitates drop-in socializing in the community room. However, residents using the entrance doors nearest the elevators and those coming from their apartments must walk 250 feet to the social spaces to check on activities. For some individuals this requires too high a level of *commitment* and limits their use of the social spaces. This hinders the development of an active *social community*.

(3) Differentiation of Semi-Public Zone

The clustering of the social spaces at Site C generates some flow of activity between individual spaces, but this is hindered by limited physical access and the variety of settings available.

A circulation area between the secondary space and the community room is defined by column placement, lowered ceiling height, and a dimmer lighting level. This allows a resident entering the social spaces to go into the secondary spaces without disrupting activities in the community room. However, a physical barrier created by two large columns and tables placed between them by residents inhibits circulation between the community room and the secondary spaces.

The three secondary spaces are all approximately the same size with similar interior finishes, ceiling heights, lighting, and view to the outdoors. As a result, a wide range of settings for different activities is not available. Of these three rooms only the crafts room is used with any regularity. Due to its location at the far

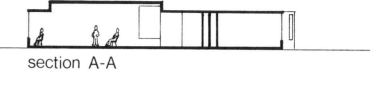

section A-A

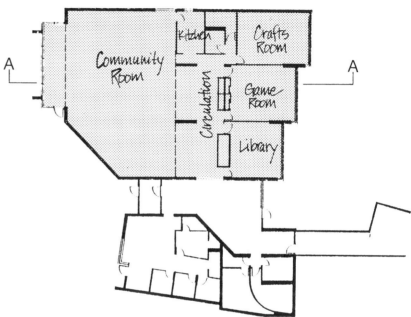

end of the community room and its single entrance, it is distinguished from the other two rooms by its increased ability to provide more *group privacy*. This specialized setting is taken advantage of by a small group of men who use it as a club room.

(4) Square Footage of Semi-Public Zone

The 2,760 square feet in the community room (7.7 square feet per resident) is fully utilized during formal activities such as meetings, parties, and the lunch program.

Site C

These large gatherings are adequately accommodated in the area provided without circulation problems. Smaller groups that use this space for informal activities like playing cards and talking look for locations that offer some definition of a smaller area. As there are no smaller settings differentiated within the larger space, these groups typically look for tables along the edge of the community room. In this way they use the outer walls to define at least one side of their gathering area.

The secondary spaces which include the library, crafts room, game room, and kitchen total 1,450 square feet (4.0 square feet per resident). Only the kitchen and crafts room are used with any regularity. The number of

Within the large community room, no smaller areas are defined which would invite use by small informal groups.

small groups that form and use the community room rather than the secondary spaces suggests that there is a demand for these smaller spaces. The underutilization of the secondary spaces is related more to the lack of differentiation within the spaces and the inadequacy of visual connections to surrounding areas than to any over supply of space.

⑤ Visual Connections

For those residents who use the primary path between the annex door and the elevators, views of the community room are available. At the entrance to the semi-public zone many residents pause briefly to survey the activities and are rewarded with an unobstructed view of over half of the community room. Individuals can also find locations in the community room from which to watch the activities along the primary path.

Visual connections between the community room and secondary spaces are limited. Since opened doors at either side of the smaller rooms provide the only line of sight, residents must actually enter these spaces to discover what is happening within. This can both disrupt ongoing activities and be embarrassing if those entering choose to walk out again. To avoid these awkward situations many residents do not use the secondary spaces.

The view to the outdoors from the secondary spaces is of a landscaped backyard where little activity takes place. As a result residents do not use these spaces to watch

Wooden storage units form walls that limit visual connections between the community room and secondary spaces (in the background).

Elevator lobbies on residential floors have no identifying characteristics.

outdoor activity even when waiting for other people to gather for a game of cards or conversation. Residents prefer to wait for others in the community room where watching the activity around them can be an interesting way to pass the time. Some residents pull folding chairs up to the glazed wall of the community room where the building faces the commercial avenue. Here they can sit and watch pedestrian activity or wait for a bus or cab. However, only a few residents can use this area at any one time because it is quite small.

(6) Semi-Public Zone

The lobbies on each residential floor are so similar that residents report occasionally getting off the elevator on the wrong floor. There are no floor numbers, furnishings, or other decorations in these areas to distinguish one floor from another. There is also no signage to indicate to residents or visitors on which corridor a particular unit is located.

Site C

Long, narrow corridors that lack any sign of personalization remind residents of institutional settings.

As individuals enter either corridor the window to their right provides good *orientation* to the exterior and illuminates the hall with natural light. Residents found no difficulty with the length of the corridors (88 feet).

The corridors lack any signs of resident *personalization*. This is partly due to the hard architectural finishes which do not lend themselves to picture hanging or other decoration. *Personalization* is also inhibited spatially by the narrowness of the hallway and the lack of any indentation at the doorway to provide an entry area.

Although there are eighteen apartment units per floor, there are no lounges in the semi-private zone. Lounges would facilitate residents meeting one another and would provide them with alternatives to the distant ground floor social spaces.

(7) Laundry Room

The location of the laundry poses problems for some residents. The route from the ground floor elevator to the laundry is 105 feet along the primary path. This distance causes difficulties for some residents carrying heavy loads. Some do not like this amount of contact with the public zone during what they consider to be a private task.

Two adjoining rooms, both of which contain machines, comprise the laundry area. The laundry rooms are typically not used by residents for socializing while waiting for their wash because of problems with

heat, noise, and the lack of a comfortable
sitting area. The laundry rooms' distance
from the social spaces minimizes the use
of the latter as an alternative waiting
area.

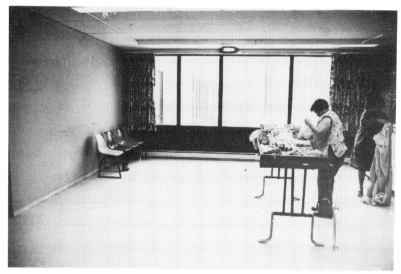

*Many residents return to their apartments
to wait for their wash rather than remain
in the laundry area.*

Site C

SUMMARY OF THE EVALUATIONS

The preceding research suggests that the extent to which a *social community* develops within an elderly housing project is related to several design features of the shared spaces. Those design variables thought to have the greatest impact on social behavior include the location and length of the primary path from the front entrance to the elevators; location, differentiation, and size of the social spaces; and visual connections between shared spaces. The differences between the sites in these design variables have resulted in three different social environments.

SITE A. The *social community* at Site A is the most active and cohesive of those studied. Residents at Site A have high participation rates in both formal (e.g., meetings, bingo games, parties, travel excursions) and informal activities (e.g., discussion groups, card games, pool playing, sewing, reading); are frequently visited in their own apartments by other residents; and play an active role in the management of the shared spaces. Because the social spaces "branch" off the primary path and there are adequate visual connections between these two areas, social encounters are encouraged but not forced upon the resident population. It is possible to see into the community room without going in and disrupting the ongoing social activities. The pool room and club room provide alternative settings for small groups. A side door at the far end of the hallway leading through the social spaces creates a secondary path that many residents use if they are looking for social encounters

on the way in or out of the building. In addition to these spatial features, the size of the resident population provides enough people to have a "critical mass" of social-izers and yet not too many people so as to encourage anonymity. The social spaces at Aite A are used by a higher percentage of the total population on a more continuous basis than at the other two sites.

SITE B. Site B and Site A have similar ground floor plans but differ in two major design variables which contribute to a less cohesive social environment at Site B. First, where Site A is a single building, Site B has two buildings which are connected by a bridge at the second level only. Tension exists between the two resident populations. All social spaces for the site are located in the East Building, but some of the West Building residents do not feel welcome using these spaces on a casual, drop-in basis. They would prefer to have at least one social space in their own building for gathering. In addition, the laundry room in the West Building is in an undesirable location in the basement and some of the residents use the laundry room on the first floor in the East Building. Again this creates tension because some of the East Building residents think the residents in the other building should use their own facilities.

The other major difference between the two site occurs in the location of the front entrance. Although Site A and the East Building at Site B have essentially the same ground floor plan, the relationship between the primary path and the social spaces is different. At Site B, the front entrance is at the far end of the social spaces and residents entering or leaving the building must pass through these spaces. As a result the primary path becomes an active pedestrian "street" through the semi-public zone. As there are few physical barriers to separate these two areas, there are many encounters between those people walking along the circulation path and those using the social spaces. But these forced encounters have not led to higher rates of extended interaction at this site. Many residents find this forced walk through the social spaces when entering and leaving annoying and an invasion of personal privacy. In addition, ongoing activities in the social spaces are frequently disrupted by these circulation activities. This location of the primary path and too much visual access to the semi-public zone plus dissociate clustering of some secondary spaces contribute to the underutilization of social spaces for informal socializing and the creation of tension among residents from forced encounters.

SITE C. Only a small percentage of the 360 residents at this site actively participate in the social environment on an informal or formal basis. The building's large size (19 stories, 305 units) and the lack of social spaces during the first two years of occupancy contribute to a sense of anonymity among residents. Only one-fourth of the sampled population can distinguish visitors from other residents in the building. The new social spaces annex is located quite a distance from the elevators in the residential tower and a high level of *commitment* is required by residents to travel this distance to check on activities. As a result, a considerably smaller percentage of

the total population visits the social spaces at this site as compared to the other sites. Lack of floor lounges in the semi-private zone further aggravates the problem of not having space for socializing closer to the apartment unit. Certain design features of the social spaces such as the large size of the community room and the lack of visual connections between the community room and secondary spaces also inhibit a high level of resident activity and interaction. All these factors contribute to the inability of the resident population at this site to develop a sense of community.

Although the *social community* may vary from one site to the next, there are certain behavioral phenomena that recur across sites. These phenomena are often characteristic of residential settings, elderly populations, or, more specifically, of elderly in residential settings. In all instances, design variables have an impact on the resultant behavioral patterns. A list of the recurring behavioral phenomena across elderly housing sites includes the following:

In these environments, *social encounters and interaction can be encouraged but not forced*. The elderly are a varied population and should be provided with different options for fulfilling social needs. Some prefer to minimize contact with others in their residential environment while others are more willing to develop new friendships. And this willingness can occur at different times. Friendship formation starts with brief, passive encounters within the shared areas. These contacts become more frequent and nodding acquaintances develop which can lead to speaking relationships. If the psychological factors are right, friendships can develop. The number of encounters can be manipulated by the architectural design of circulation paths and shared spaces. But research suggests that at a certain level high encounter rates lead to lower levels of extended interaction and forced encounters can lead to stressful relations among residents.

Many elderly residents enjoy sitting and watching the activities of others on site and are attracted to entrance and lobby areas at ground level. Many do not have the interest or agility for more active participation in their surroundings and find this activity very satisfying. At the same time, there are others in the environment, including residents, visitors, and management, who view such "hanging out" activity as a form of idleness. If lobby or waiting areas are designed specifically to accommodate sitting and watching, this activity will be observed as more legitimate and tolerable in this residential setting. Another problem associated with sitting and watching in entrance lobbies is *offensive surveillance*. Some residents entering and leaving the building are uncomfortable passing by this area if they feel their movements are being closely scrutinized by others.

A men's group typically forms at each site and seeks out social space for gathering in. Men are a minority in elderly housing projects, where they represent anywhere from 10 to 30 percent of a total site population.

These men often feel intimidated by the large number of women in their environment and will seek out other men for socializing. This group will look for a space to gather in (or "retreat" to). If the men use this space on a frequent or continual basis, the women will typically accept this space as "belonging" to the male population and will avoid intruding on their territory.

Some groups have privacy needs in shared spaces. Small groups frequently form at elderly sites in response to a need for social interaction and sense of belonging that cannot be satisfied within a larger residents' organization. Examples of these small groups include a diet club, coffee clatches, card players, and a sewing group. These activities are often more focused in nature and require settings with few outside distractions but yet not so isolated that participants do not sense the larger social environment around them. In addition, some residents entertain large gatherings of family or friends in the shared spaces because their apartment units are too small. These are typically more intimate gatherings which require some visual and aural privacy from others in the residential environment.

The greater the commitment needed by residents to go to a social space, the greater the likelihood that such spaces will be underutilized by a large proportion of the resident population. Using the social spaces involves some risk-taking and residents must feel assured of rewards in these spaces that outweigh the costs in getting there. The social and physical environment as well as the route taken to

get there must be attractive. If the route
to the social spaces is long, involves
traversing barriers (e.g., steps, ramps) or
passes by areas where a clique may hang out.
residents will be less likely to make the
physical and psychological effort needed to
get to the social spaces.

These behavioral phenomena and patterns were
observed at each site to varying degrees and
are likely to be present in other
residential environments for the elderly.

Design Guidelines

Shared Spaces in Housing for the Elderly

Introduction to Guidelines

A design GUIDELINE should direct the architects' attention to critical variables which require exploration of <u>alternative</u> solutions, in order that an <u>environment</u> provide the best match to the expected users. The difference between a *guideline* and a *specification* is in the explicitness of the statement. *Specifications* provide precise directives with respect to engineering or design solutions based, presumably, on substantial research on structure and current information on the *performance* of manufactured products. *Guidelines* provide parameters within which the designer can create <u>probably</u> more useable spaces or select <u>probably</u> better fitted components and fixtures. *Guidelines* suggest the criteria that might govern the *performance* of a setting.

The guidelines which follow are to be used as performance criteria by those involved in the design of shared spaces. These guidelines apply primarily to medium and high rise public housing for the elderly in urban settings, yet may be appropriate for other residential settings for older persons. The social spaces discussed here are assumed to be within the main residential structure rather than in a separate building accessed by going outdoors. The guidelines correspond to the listed *issues* described in our studies which explored the behavioral implications of the design of entry-level communal spaces.

Guidelines, by their nature, should allow reformulations based upon new research and the evaluations, by architects, of their own designs in use. Space is provided, at each Guideline, for such notations.

Guidelines

1. Public Zone
2. Location of Semi-Public Zone
3. Differentiation of Semi-Public Zone
4. Square Footage of Semi-Public Zone
5. Visual Connection
6. Semi-Private Zone
7. Laundry Room

Public Zone Guideline 1

The public zone is that area in the building where the daily coming and going activities occur. It includes the primary path from the main entrance(s) to the elevators and is the major circulation route within the building. Other activities typically associated with this public zone are distributing mail, orienting visitors, and waiting for vehicular arrival.

● THE PRIMARY PATH FROM THE MAIN ENTRANCE TO ELEVATORS APPEARS OPTIMUM WHEN IT IS 30 FEET TO 80 FEET IN LENGTH.

This path should be long enough to accommodate the activities associated with the comings and goings of residents without creating congested areas. The mail area should be located near this path so residents can check the mailboxes on the way in and out of the building. A small area off of the path is recommended so that several residents checking for mail at the same time will not interfere with the flow of daily traffic. A wall space for announcements should also be provided along the primary path in order to be seen by as many residents as possible. These announcements, if located by the elevators, will be readily seen by those waiting to ride up to their apartment floor.

Elevators located directly inside the main entrance are disliked by some residents. They think unwanted visitors can too easily slip inside and go directly to the apartment floors without being seen by the manager or residents. However, residents want easy and direct access to the elevators, particularly when coming home with packages after shopping.

● A WAITING AREA SHOULD BE PROVIDED NEAR THE FRONT ENTRANCE.

Many elderly residents do not own cars and must rely on others for transportation. While waiting for rides, they prefer to be as close as possible to the entrance so they can exit quickly. This waiting area should be provided with seating and a view of arriving vehicles.

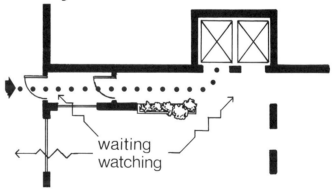

waiting
watching

● AN AREA SHOULD BE PROVIDED WHERE RESIDENTS CAN OBSERVE COMING AND GOING ACTIVITIES BUT OPPORTUNITIES FOR OFFENSIVE SURVEILLANCE SHOULD BE MINIMIZED.

Congregating near the front entrance is an enjoyable pastime for many elderly residents because of the variety of people and

Public Zone

activities that are available for watching.
A space near the entrance should be provided
for these observation activities. However,
there are some residents who dislike being
watched as they enter or leave the building.
It is recommended that partial visual blocks
(e.g. planters or columns) separate this
sitting area from the primary path in an
effort to minimize offensive surveillance
opportunities. If properly designed, this
area can also be used by residents waiting
for rides.

Reader's Insights, Comments and References:

Location of Semi-Public Zone

The semi-public zone includes those spaces designed to accommodate the social and recreational activities of elderly residents. Spaces and rooms typically associated with this zone are the community room, pool room, arts and crafts area, library, TV lounge, sitting room or parlor, and the kitchen. The proper location of this semi-public zone relative to the other zones within the building is essential to the development of an active social community where interaction is encouraged but not forced.

●   THE SEMI-PUBLIC ZONE SHOULD BE LOCATED AT GROUND LEVEL WHERE RESIDENT MOVEMENT IS GREATEST.

Much of the activity in the semi-public zone results from residents stopping by on their way in or out of the building. In addition, some residents like to sit in this zone and watch the activities of others both inside the building and outdoors. Location of this zone on the ground floor allows residents to be close to these activities. A semi-public zone isolated in the basement or on an upper floor will typically be under-utilized by the resident population.

●   THE DISTANCE BETWEEN THE PRIMARY PATH AND THE SEMI-PUBLIC ZONE SHOULD BE MINIMIZED.

The semi-public zone should be located close enough to the primary path so residents passing by can see or hear others in this social zone. This may attract them toward areas nearby to further investigate the ongoing activities without demanding excessive commitment of time or effort. A location of the semi-public zone closer to the primary path increases the likelihood of frequent resident use of the social areas.

●   THE PRIMARY PATH SHOULD NOT LEAD DIRECTLY THROUGH THE SEMI-PUBLIC ZONE.

Opportunities for social interaction should be made available to, but not forced upon, the resident population. A resident should have the option to come and go in the building with little risk of unwanted encounters with others. In addition, social activities in the semi-public zone should be protected from interruptions and distractions associated with circulation activities. A physical distinction between the semi-public zone and primary path provides this protection.

●   WHERE POSSIBLE, THE SEMI-PUBLIC ZONE SHOULD HAVE A SECONDARY PATH.

A secondary path through the semi-public zone provides residents with the option of walking by social spaces on their way to other destinations. Residents who use this path then have the possibility of seeing friends and joining activities, thus facilitating drop-in socializing. However, the primary path must enable others, if they so desire, to enter and exit the building with little social contact.

Differentiation of Semi-Public Zone

The semi-public zone must spatially accommodate a variety of events. Typical group events include tenant meetings and dining and games in which 50-80% of the resident population participates. At other times small, informal groups may play cards or just gather to talk. Some residents might give private birthday parties or entertain family in this zone. Men often gravitate toward one particular area just to be together. Other people may frequent the social spaces to play pool, work on puzzles, or do crafts. Thus a large community room to accommodate group activities is necessary as are secondary social spaces that provide settings for smaller groups and private gatherings.

With this variety of activities differentiation of scale, mood, and furnishings is necessary for the spaces in the semi-public zone. Successful interaction among these social spaces depends on their *clustering*, on *circulation*, and on their *location* within the building.

● CLUSTERING MAIN COMMUNITY ROOM AND SECONDARY SPACES

Space arrangement plays an important role in encouraging the flow of activities and people from one place to another. Clustering generates increased activity by providing more options for residents who find themselves in the semi-public zone. Clustering also promotes a greater sense of togetherness by having residents engage

in activities with the knowledge that others are close by, doing different things, but sharing in the overall sense of community. The cluster of interior social spaces should include an outdoor extension for use in nice weather.

● CIRCULATION BETWEEN THE SOCIAL SPACES

Circulation to secondary spaces should be well-defined and not require passage directly through the community room. Activities can then occur simultaneously in various social spaces without distractions from circulation. However, to encourage social interaction in this clustered semi-public zone, easy physical access should exist among the social spaces.

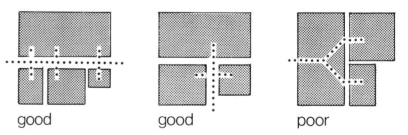

good   good   poor

● SECONDARY SPACES SHOULD PROVIDE A VARIETY OF SETTINGS TO ACCOMMODATE RESIDENT ACTIVITIES.

Providing several similar rooms for small group activities often does not meet the different needs associated with each activity. Residents may use these

Differentiation of Semi-Public Zone   cont.

secondary spaces on an individual basis and
in groups ranging in size from two to more
than twenty. Some activities invite and profit
from interaction with passersby and other
groups in the social spaces. Other activities are more focused in nature (i.e. reading or family gatherings) and seek to
minimize outside distractions. These
varying privacy needs should be reflected
in the degree to which the secondary spaces
are open to surrounding areas.

Reader's Insights, Comments and References:

Square Footage of Semi-Public Zone

Square footage needs for the semi-public zone vary according to the size of the resident population and current and anticipated program requirements. At some sites social spaces may be made available to the surrounding neighborhood for recreational activities and meetings or to the elderly community at large for such activities as a hot lunch program. At other sites meeting spaces for residents may be provided in existing neighborhood structures like a church or recreation hall. As a result less social space is needed at these sites. The following recommendations are appropriate to sites where the semi-public zone is used primarily by building residents only and where neighborhood facilities are not available. Other programming requirements should be reflected in an increase or decrease in area allotments.

The community room and secondary social spaces comprising the semi-public zone typically accommodate different activities and therefore should be considered separately when calculating total area needs. Since other factors such as room proportions and column spacing influence the appropriateness of spaces for certain activities, the suggested square footage allotments should be used only as approximations.

● THERE SHOULD BE SEVEN (7) SQUARE FEET OF COMMUNITY ROOM SPACE PER RESIDENT.

The community room is used primarily for large gatherings of people engaged in more formal and structured activities like meetings, dances, parties, bingo games, and hot meals programs. Insufficient space for these large gatherings will make circulation difficult and result in overcrowding. This may deter some residents from participating in these activities. When not in use for these gatherings, this larger space is often used for more informal socializing by smaller groups. A community room that is too large may create problems if residents feel that it does not permit any differentiation of places within the larger space for small groups. Thus, a community room should be flexible enough to accommodate both large and small gatherings. Some architectural methods for differentiation include ceiling height changes, variation in surface materials, column placement, movable partitions and continuity with adjacent space.

● THERE SHOULD BE FIVE (5) SQUARE FEET OF ADDITIONAL SOCIAL SPACE PER RESIDENT.

Secondary social space accommodates a variety of small group activities and can take the form of several rooms such as a sitting area, TV lounge, crafts room, pool room, and library. Too little secondary space can lead to overcrowding which may

inhibit some residents' participation. The
lack of defined secondary spaces may also
mean that certain activities are pre-
cluded and that particular tenant
interests and changes over time will
not be able to be accommodated.
However, too much secondary space
will result in its underutilization.
The location of secondary spaces may
determine the frequency of their use.

Semi-public zones become semi-private
when they appear as occasional use
spaces on residential floors. In
general, unless a building is very
high density, distributing group
activity spaces at floors does
not appear useful. However, on
residential floors of eight or more
units, potential loose space might be
well considered.

Reader's Insights, Comments and References:

Visual Connections

Visual connections between social spaces can promote interaction among residents. These connections allow those passing by and those within the social spaces to see what is happening around them with minimal commitment. This visibility increases the probability that residents will drop in and join activities.

Visual connections can be achieved with a variety of glazed and unglazed openings. However, such connections must be complemented by other design elements to encourage resident interaction.

● VISUAL CONNECTIONS BETWEEN THE PRIMARY PATH AND THE SEMI-PUBLIC ZONE.

These connections provide visual access to the semi-public zone without requiring residents to enter the zone to find out what is going on. Too much exposure of the semi-public zone to the primary path may invade the privacy of residents using the social spaces.

● VISUAL CONNECTIONS BETWEEN SOCIAL SPACES.

Visual access between social spaces encourages interaction. Once residents are aware of the activities in other areas they are likely to circulate within the cluster of social spaces.

● VISUAL CONNECTIONS BETWEEN SECONDARY SPACES AND OUTDOOR ACTIVITY.

These visual connections allow those passing by outside and those within the spaces to see what is happening around them. Sometimes a resident wants to go to a social space to be near other people or away from the apartment but does not want to engage in a specific activity like cards or pool. Location of secondary spaces with a view of outdoor activity allows for sitting and watching. Windows on the exterior wall should be low enough for seated individuals to see out. Residents walking by can also survey the activities inside. However, to maintain some privacy in the secondary social spaces, a visual *buffer* from pedestrian activity should be provided. This *buffer* can take the form of distancing, trees and shrubbery, or an overhang.

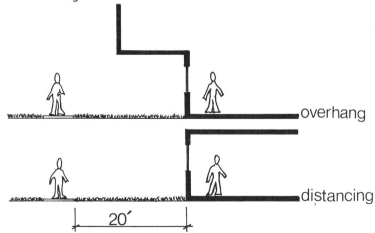

overhang

distancing

20´

Visual Connections   cont.

●   TOO MUCH VISUAL CONNECTION CAN CREATE
OFFENSIVE SURVEILLANCE PROBLEMS.

Some individuals dislike the feeling that
others are watching their movements in or
around the building. Within the social
spaces, certain group activities require
some visual privacy to minimize the distractions of others around them. Too much visual
connection can lead to uncomfortable
tensions between residents and underutilization of some areas in the building.

Reader's Insights, Comments and References:

Location of Semi-Public Zone

A critique of several options for the location of the semi-public zone follows.

Option 1.   The "Branch"

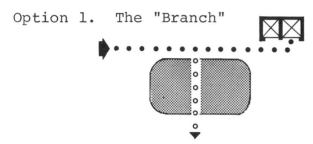

- residents can come and go without interrupting social activities

- drop-in activity is possible if the semi-public zone is located near the primary path

- a secondary path would provide residents with an opportunity to go through the social spaces on their way to other destinations

Option 2.   The "Street"

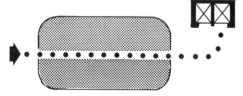

- chance social encounters between circulating residents and those in the semi-public zone are increased and compelled

- the primary path separates zone into two areas thereby inhibiting flow of activities between social spaces

- social gatherings may be easily distracted by circulation activities

- some residents may dislike passing through socially active areas and thus seek more private routes in and out of the building

Option 3.   The "Cul-de-sac"

- residents and visitors entering or leaving the building do not pass by the semi-public zone

- the setting for social activities is more secluded and private

- the absence of a secondary path would increase the "dead end" nature of the semi-public zone

- residents have minimal contact with the public zone when going from their apartment to social spaces

Semi-Private Zone

The semi-private zone includes lobbies, lounges, and corridors on each residential floor. This zone is used for access to units and occasionally as socializing space. As this area marks the beginning of "home", residents often want to personalize it, particularly that area immediately outside of the apartment door. Related design issues for the semi-private zone include corridor length, articulation of doorways, orientation and floor lounges.

● RESIDENTIAL CORRIDORS IN EXCESS OF 100 FEET IN LENGTH ARE NOT RECOMMENDED.

Long corridors are not residential and should be avoided for two reasons. First, some elderly people have difficulty walking long distances. Also residents frequently comment on the institutional character of long hallways because they remind them of motels or office buildings.

● A TRANSITION AREA SHOULD BE CONSIDERED BETWEEN THE SEMI-PRIVATE ZONE OF THE CORRIDOR AND THE PRIVATE ZONE OF THE UNIT.

The narrow width of corridors contributes to an institutional appearance. Most hall-ways are wide enough for circulation only and leave no transition area between the corridor and the apartment unit. When this transitional space is absent, there is little personalization of unit entries. This area is similar to the front porch in individual homes which residents often decorate to indicate personal territory. Examples of possible resident furnishings in this area include wall decorations, rugs, plant stands, and furniture for sitting or setting packages on when searching for keys. Widening corridors or articulating unit entries can provide this transition area as well as lessen the tunnel effect of an otherwise straight, narrow corridor. Consider wall lighting to substitute for or augment ceiling fixtures and provide cues.

● SIGNS AND GRAPHICS TO IDENTIFY BOTH FLOOR AND UNIT LOCATIONS.

Confusion about floor numbers and unit location can be disturbing for residents and visitors. They should be visible from the elevators on each floor. After leaving the elevator, visitors often have difficulty identifying the corridor which contains the unit they are seeking. In buildings with similar looking floors, residents may inadvertently go to the right unit location on the wrong floor and be bewildered by their inability to get in or embarrassed at their attempt to open someone else's door. Orientation by means of readily visible numerals and color coding can alleviate these problems.

● WINDOWS OR OTHER SOURCES OF NATURAL LIGHT SHOULD BE PLACED NEAR THE ELEVATOR ON EACH FLOOR AND ON RESIDENTIAL CORRIDORS.

When getting off the elevator, people are often confused about where they are in relation to the outside. They may also have this problem when walking down residential corridors. Windows provide

Semi-Private Zone

orientation, natural lighting, visual relief
from corridors, and ventilation. Skylights
should also be considered for indirect
lighting at the ends of corridors.

● RESIDENTIAL FLOOR LOUNGE AREAS SHOULD
BE PROVIDED. THESE AREAS SHOULD BE EQUALLY
ACCESSIBLE FROM ALL CORRIDORS ON A FLOOR,
BUT VISUALLY SEPARATE FROM ELEVATOR LOBBY
AND APARTMENT UNITS.

On apartment floors where many residents
live, lounge areas can facilitate meeting
others who share the same semi-private zone.
These lounges can also serve as alternative
socializing areas for those who wish to be
with others, yet who do not want to
entertain in their apartment unit or go to
the social spaces on the ground floor.
These lounges are more private than spaces
in the semi-public zone and can be used for
small gatherings such as card groups or
birthday parties. In addition, some
residents occasionally seek a change of
environment from their unit and find these
lounges a different, yet convenient place to
go. Visual connections between elevators
and lounges should be minimized to protect
the privacy of both lounge users and those
passing by. A lounge location should avoid
adjacencies to apartment units to protect
the privacy of residents in thier "home".

Laundry Room Guideline 7

The laundry room can be a source of frustration for elderly residents if it is improperly located and insufficiently equipped. The typical pattern of an elderly resident is to wash a load of clothes once a week. This activity appears to be an important part of the weekly routine.

This guideline is appropriate in buildings with a single laundry facility. A small laundry room on every residential floor is another option that might be considered.

●   LAUNDRY ROOM AS A FUNCTIONAL SPACE

The laundry room is primarily a functional space. It is not treated as a social occasion space by older people. It should have room for an adequate number of machines, chairs for waiting, and a table(s) for folding clothes. Because this area is noisy and often poorly ventilated, residents do not remain in it for extended periods. Those doing their laundry will, however, engage one another in casual conversation while waiting and use provided seating.

●   LAUNDRY ROOM AS PART OF THE SEMI-PUBLIC ZONE AT GROUND LEVEL.

Since substantial periods of time are involved with waiting for wash, location in proximity to social spaces is desirable. Many residents prefer to wait near the laundry to make sure their clothes are not handled

by others but do not want to wait in an unpleasant area. Some will pass the time in social spaces if they are located nearby. Isolated locations in the basement or on one residential floor do not provide this alternative. In addition, a single laundry per building which is located on a residential floor disrupts the more private nature of this zone by generating increased traffic and noise.

●   LAUNDRY ROOM LOCATION NEAR ELEVATOR

For convenience the laundry room should be close to the elevator. With age, carrying bundles of laundry becomes more difficult and thus distance from the unit becomes a crucial factor in location.

●   MINIMAL CONTACT BETWEEN THE LAUNDRY ROOM AND THE PUBLIC ZONE.

Views, noise, and odors associated with laundry room activity should not be apparent to residents and visitors using the entry and public zone. In addition, some residents doing their laundry view it as a personal activity during which they prefer visual privacy.

●   RECOMMENDED RATIOS OF WASHERS/DRYERS

The ratio of equipment to tenants depends heavily on total density and building circulation plan. Residents do not like to wait for machines and often return to their apartments.

5

PRIVATE SPACE:
A CASE STUDY

INTRODUCTION

Case ONE explored methods for evaluating the design of shared or semi-public spaces within moderate to high density housing for older people. The focus in that case was on defining the physical qualities of the particular spaces in terms of expected and observed behaviors. The evaluation (a quasi-experiment) could be cast in terms of independent and dependent variables. In this case, the designs provided the independent variables, while social interactions were the dependent variables.

In Case TWO a different paradigm is formulated. It is much more naturalistic. The questions asked deal with private spaces. How do older people in standardized apartment units organize their private object world? Given identical spaces, are there evident patterns of organization? In what ways do these patterns represent variations in individual represent-ation of self? In what ways do the observed uses of identical apart-ment units exhibit generationally similar characteristics? The goal of Case TWO is to find interpret-ations of residential life-styles which designers (architects) can use.

THE ISSUES

For the older person, the living unit is a container for daily activities and a storehouse of experiences and memories. An apartment unit which is insensitively designed affects the life of occupants by constraining the activities which they wish to conduct and by making it impossible either to retain valued furnishings or to create a setting for such objects consistent with a prior lifestyle.

These issues do not always seem very important to the designer, since adaptation appears to be expected and acceptable. From a psychological and physical standpoint, however, the intimate environment of late life can have a profound effect on health and morale.

It is possible to test every proposed apartment unit design against norms and activity patterns of the user, and thus, to produce more habitable residences.

This case study describes and attempts to interpret the dwelling unit experiences of a sample of elderly people who are living in purpose-built and subsidized housing in the United States.

Recommendations for the design of apartment units for older people often originate from presumptions about the space needs and activity patterns of the elderly. The most widely used guidelines are the Federal Minimum Property Standards (MPS), which were originally developed to guarantee the public interest at least at an acceptable minimum level of design and construction in residential environments. Over the years, however, construction costs, budgeting constraints, and like economies have resulted in the adoption of these minimum guidelines as maximum space allowances. Because the recommendations are described in terms of minimum square footage and furnishability requirements, with little more than the charge that the building design be "suited to the social, economic, and recreational needs of resident families and individuals", there is substantial room for error in translation to built form. A review of many unit plans from Public projects in various parts of the country indicates that the MPS are often inappropriately interpreted with reference to the actual activity and lifestyle needs of the elderly resident. This lack of understanding has resulted in design errors that range from merely aggravating to extremely debilitating.

PURPOSE.

It is the intention of this case study to explore systematically the *habitability* issues of apartment unit living for older persons. The actual responses of residents to living in federally funded units has not been studied before in-depth and in relation to the physical features of these built environments. By providing more *performance*-related information based on activity needs to supplement existing design specifications in HUD MPS, designers should be able to better understand the advantages and disadvantages of certain kinds of apartment unit plans in terms of furniture options, internal circulation, privacy, and activity potentials.

ABOUT THE OLDER APARTMENT TENANTS.

It may come as some surprise that the majority of elderly residing in subsidized apartments previously lived in their own homes of one or two floors. Even when their prior residence was an apartment it was typically considerably more spacious and within a lower density building than those currently provided under public programs. It is estimated that the average prior residence area was 1500 square feet. The average 1 bedroom elderly unit area is 550 square feet.

Residents in our national studies have indicated how difficult the decisions were about what to leave behind and what to bring into their new homes. One third of the elderly respondents had to leave behind some furniture for lack of space in their new unit. Pieces which might have been retained but for the shrinking space tended to be dining sets, bedroom dressers, and double beds. Occasionally items that are over-sized for the dimensions and layout of the new settings are brought anyway and used in rather different ways than formerly dictated by their function. It would appear that there is a conflict between the planned unit and resident needs in terms of providing an environment which would be as much of a home as possible where previously established lifestyle patterns are supported and continued.

In general, the ways in which older people use the apartment units to which they have moved are governed by:

1. the transfer of their varied lifestyles into the new setting;

2. the level of personal and social activity they engage in;

3. the physical characteristics of the unit itself.

The most important point that this material should convey is that older people need variations in the spaces in which they live. This is critical for two reasons:

1. Older people themselves vary greatly in their lifestyles and environmental needs;

2. Because of the increasing amount of time spent within the home, variations within that place need to be provided for stimulation of the individual.

For many elderly, we found that the provision of a range of shared social spaces within the apartment building was not a substitute for the confinements of the unit at all. While shared spaces can, for perhaps 25-30 percent of residents, provide supplemental activity opportunities, the majority of residents have not had a pattern of such interaction with neighbors and non-family. For a large segment, either their activities continue to be focused outside the apartment building, in their apartment with past friends and family, or as rather solitary, insulated behaviors inside their own home.

THE METHODOLOGICAL APPROACH.
Habitability is defined as the ability of a dwelling unit to support the daily activity needs of a resident. For this information to be of any value in the design process, activities must be described in terms of their spatial implications:

What are the typical furniture pieces that are used in support of each activity?

How are these pieces arranged with respect to one another?

How are these pieces positioned with respect to space defining elements such as walls, doors, windows, etc.?

By using this approach to describe how activities are conducted in space, *performance* criteria can then be established for each activity setting.

A variety of different studies, at both the national and local level, provided the data base for the analysis of *habitability* issues. Average furniture pieces and their patterned arrangements were calculated from a detailed survey of 55 apartment units in Cambridge, Massachusetts. Residents in these units were interviewed about their daily activities (some kept diaries) and the adequacy or inability of their space to meet their activity needs and furnishability require- ments. This data was verified and other issues elaborated by an earlier national survey of 53 public housing sites. This survey, which was undertaken in collabor- ation with M. Powell Lawton of the Philadelphia Geriatric Center, established that the findings in our local study were not geograph- ically specific but were character- istic of elderly residents in public housing anywhere in the country. Other studies of the activity patterns of older persons also served as another reliability check.

The case material is organized so that the reader, following several personal tenant scenarios, moves through: activity descriptions which form the basis of the analyses, furnishing characteristics and critiques of unit plans, which applies the findings to a range of actual apartment types located across the United States. Through- out the presentation, information is presented in a variety of ways in order to assist the user in both the design and review processes. A Guidelines section summarizes the case. Data collection methods

and raw data not presented in the text can be found in the Appendices or by communicating with the author.

SCENARIOS

It is often difficult for social planners and designers to comprehend the range of lifestyles that exists across a population of older people who may become residents in elderly housing. The scenarios that follow represent some of the variability between tenants. The daily living patterns of these people are particlly represented in the furnishings within their apartment units. The convergence or non-convergence of these units with the personal histories and lifestyles of the residents is reflected in what they said about and did within their apartment.

Different environmental histories lead directly to different spatial needs. These differences should be reflected in variations in unit sizes within a single project. To provide only one type and size of unit (all efficiencies or all one bedroom units), even if this design approach appears more economical, may be counterproductive in the long run. A project consisting of a single unit type, particularly if it is small, will--

- very likely lead to rejection of the project by those elderly who could contribute to the overall well-being of the setting (e.g. those whose entertaining or activity levels might be of benefit to neighbors),

not allow persons whose health needs require more space to become or to remain residents,

- increasingly select those whose past lifestyles have been most constrained, economically and socially, and

- tend to create psychological discrepancies between past and present identities which could be reflected in the health and well-being of residents, or create unnecessary tensions for couples sharing a unit.

For these reasons it is our studied opinion that policy and practice in the design of housing for the elderly should assure a reasonable mix of unit sizes and types (see Table 1). This recommendation is made particularly with an eye to population trends in terms of continuing marketability of such settings. Our studies indicate that the efficienty unit is an inappropriate residential model for most single elderly. Future trends suggest that more two person groups, whether married, relatives or friends, will be seeking housing accommodations in these settings.

Table 1.

SUGGESTED UNIT MIX FOR AN ELDERLY HOUSING DEVELOPMENT*

UNIT TYPE	RECOMMENDED MIX	RESIDENT PROFILE
Efficiency	10%	Single residents, mostly men, who have little furniture and few possessions as a result of living with others or in a rooming house or hospital.
One bedroom, small	30-35%	Single residents, particularly women, whose lifestyle preferences include the privacy needs of a separate bedroom; single residents who need a larger unit to accommodate their furniture.
One bedroom, large	40-45%	Married couples who are independent and healthy.
Two bedroom	15-20%	Elderly couples, one of whom is disabled enough to require a separate sleeping room; disabled persons or couples with a caretaking relative or non-relative; two elderly adults (sisters, mother and son, friends, etc.) who wish to share a single unit for mutual support; residents with frequent overnight guests.

* These percentages are proposed for subsidized developments. In market rate developments, a significantly higher proportion of two-bedroom units is strongly recommended, as well as a small percent of three or two and den/dining space.

Two residents in the 1976 Cambridge study kept a daily diary, over the period of one week, of their activities within the apartment unit. The average number of hours spent in various spaces is presented below for comparison. On the following pages, more detailed scenarios illustrate the sequence of activities and the use of different spaces during a typical day.

Mr. Watson

Mr. Watson and his wife live in a one bedroom unit. He is an active participant in the activities within his building and devotes several hours a day to card playing in the community room. His wife spends much more time in the unit where she handles all the cooking and cleaning chores.

Mrs. Alexander

Mrs. Alexander, a widow, lives in an efficiency unit. She is an early riser who runs her errands during the morning and relaxes after lunch. At her doctor's recommendation, she rests in her living room, sitting up, instead of lying down on the bed. She visits her daughter several times a week and usually has Sunday dinner with her family.

ACTIVITY SETTING	AVERAGE HOURS PER DAY		AVERAGE HOURS PER DAY	
Bathroom	1.0	shower, shave, oxygen therapy	1.3	bathe, rinse clothes
Sleeping area	8.4	1:30 a.m.–10:00 a.m.	7.5	10:30 p.m.–6:00 a.m.
Living area	7.7	watch TV, read, entertain	7.7	watch TV, rest, read, sew
Eating area:				
Breakfast	.5		.6	
Lunch	–		.5	
Dinner	.9		.8	
Kitchen	–	wife prepares all food	1.3	cook and clean up
Outside Unit	5.5	socialize in building	4.3	shop, socialize in building or at relatives

10am — He awakes and goes to the bathroom to shave and shower.

10·15am — He returns to the bedroom to dress but finds little room for this activity amidst all the furniture and his apparatus for oxygen therapy.

10·30am — Next is breakfast. If Mr. Watson wants to watch TV at the same time, he will set up a TV tray near his favorite chair, the recliner.

11am — He continues to watch TV and read in his recliner until the noon news is over.

12noon — He then leaves the apartment for an afternoon of card playing and socializing in the community room.

5·30pm — He returns to the apartment in the late afternoon for oxygen therapy. The oxygen tanks are brought from the bedroom into the bathroom (which is not large enough to store the equipment), where he takes his therapy in the small, windowless room.

6pm — He and his wife eat dinner at the dining table and spend the evening watching TV and reading, he in his recliner and his wife on the couch.

7·30pm — When they entertain, it is difficult to have more than four guests (they bring in the fourth chair from the bedroom). A high chair for grandchildren is kept in the kitchen.

1·30am — And off to bed.

6am	After she wakes up, Mrs. Alexander goes to the closet for her dressing robe. She must close the door to the bathroom first, in order to open the closet doors.
6·15am	After washing up, she starts coffee in the kitchen and goes down to the lobby to get the morning newspaper.
6·30am	She would like her breakfast and coffee in the kitchen, but because there is no room, she must eat in the living room.
7am	After breakfast the apartment is tidied up, and with some difficulty the bed is made (it is tucked in a corner).
9·15am	Mrs. Alexander then gets dressed to go shopping. She uses the stool in the entry to sit on while she puts on her boots.
11am	After a morning of shopping, she returns to the apartment and sets her groceries on the table. From there she puts them away in the kitchen and starts making lunch.
12noon	Mrs. Alexander eats lunch at her dining table. Afternoons are spent resting on the sofa, sewing, reading and watching TV.
1·30pm	
5pm	Dinner is prepared and then eaten at the dining table. After cleaning up the kitchen, she watches more TV and sews until bedtime. Sometimes she will go out at night, to the community room or to a Beano game at the local church.
6pm	
10·30pm	Mrs. Alexander goes to bed.

Mrs. Alexander

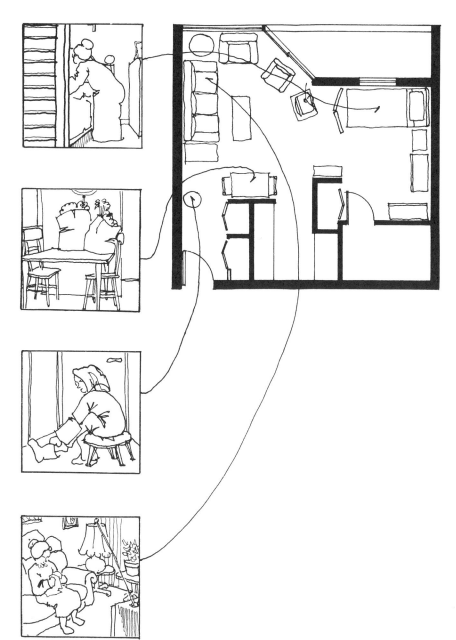

Mr. Anderson

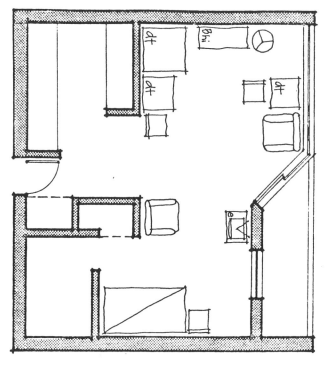

Mr. Danny Anderson is an active 89 year old who enjoys the independence associated with having his own apartment. Before moving into this apartment, he lived in a rooming house for men where he had his own bedroom but shared a bathroom and congregate dining facilities. His desire to cook for himself and to be closer to the neighborhood where he grew up led Mr. Anderson to his present efficiency unit. Although he had no furniture of his own when he first moved in over two years ago, friends and acquaintances have since contributed pieces to his sparsely furnished but comfortable home. One of his favorite pastimes involves the making of paper beads and necklaces for "special ladies". Tables, chairs, and gadgets clamped on kitchen counters are all part of his assembly process. He likes the size of his apartment and the sleeping alcove but doesn't think he needs all the closet and storage space. On a typical day Mr. Anderson will leave the apartment early in the morning to go to the neighborhood newstand where he still has many friends. He returns home after lunch for a nap before commencing his evening activities of dinner, bead-making, and TV-watching.

Mrs. McDonald

Mrs. Marie McDonald moved into her new apartment over three years ago because the building she had lived in for a number of years had no elevator which, for reasons of health, had become a necessity for her. Mrs. McDonald loved her old apartment and was sorry to give away "a lot of things" to which she had become attached. Many of these items were large antiques that she felt would not fit in her small efficiency. She was, however, able to keep one of her china cabinets which is her favorite piece of furniture. She often sits at her table outside the kitchen so she can see both the television and the cabinet where many of her possessions are elegantly displayed. She does not rearrange her furniture; her son placed it in its present location and she feels that there is no room for repositioning. Most important to Mrs. McDonald is the opportunity to serve dinner to her family when they visit--they look forward to her cooking. She must, however, invite them in groups of four in order to serve them comfortably. Ideally, she would very much like to have a dining room so that she might once again entertain them in a large group. One other thing that distresses her is the thought of becoming ill and not being able to retire to the privacy of a bedroom while, perhaps, visitors gather in the living room. She reports that the specter of being in plain view under these conditions makes her "bashful".

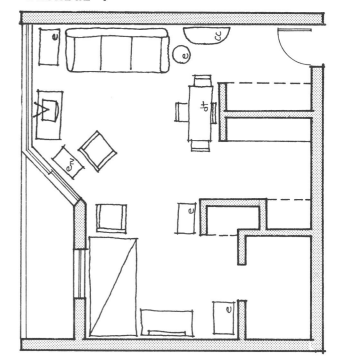

Mrs. Benson

It has been over two years since Mrs. Martha Benson moved from a four room unit to her present efficiency. Not only had her former apartment become too costly, it also lacked the convenience of elevator and shower.   She feels her present unit is not large enough for her needs. Mrs. Benson has had to give away many favorite pieces of furniture and she especially misses her china cabinet. She was also forced to give away her double bed which she replaced with a twin bed. As it is now, she says she has "too much stuff around" and describes her antiques as "too big" for the apartment. Mrs. Benson is active with her needlework and has positioned her couch and rocking chair so that she can sew while watching TV, using the adjacent table and the couch behind her as work surfaces. She points out a need for more storage space in the kitchen, kitchen cabinets which are more easily accessible, and eye-level ovens. She feels that built-in furniture--desks and bookcases-- would have given her the floor space necessary to include items which she had been forced to abandon. When entertaining, Mrs. Benson opens her dropleaf table in front of her window and uses occasional tables; otherwise she does not attempt to rearrange her furniture. The biggest inconvenience Martha Benson encountered upon moving into her apartment was the need to purchase expensive new draperies to accommodate the pulley arrangement above the windows.

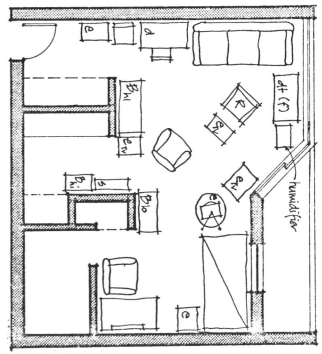

The Samson Sisters

Elizabeth and Ida Samson are sisters who have always lived together. For 38 years they lived in a six room apartment in a triple decker. They moved into their present one bedroom apartment when they found the "old house" too big to keep up and too expensive after Elizabeth's retirement. They feel this apartment is much too small for them, however. When they moved in they had to give away three bedroom bureaus and beds, one dining set, two china cabinets, and a buffet. They had to buy a smaller dining set to fit their tighter spaces. The Samson sisters would prefer a larger, eat-in kitchen so they could entertain more, a larger bedroom because they can barely move around in it now, and more privacy in the living room (they would like a door so they could close the room off when guests spend the night). They use their balcony frequently in nice weather to read and watch others but only in the evenings after the hot western sun has set.

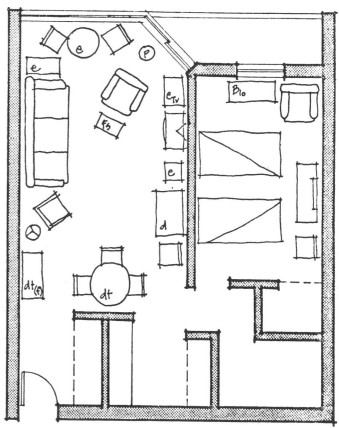

Mr. and Mrs. King

When Adam King retired, he and his wife decided to move from a three family dwelling to their present apartment. Their children were grown and there seemed to be little point in remaining in a neighborhood that was child-oriented. They regard their new unit as a desirable alternative and while they gave away considerable furniture, they acquired replacements with which they are very pleased. In celebration of the move, their daughter gave them a living room set which includes a large couch, two easy chairs, two side tables, and a coffee table. In addition to all this "large furniture" in the living room, there is ample space for a circular dining table and chairs. This dining set is used for daily meals as well as the family dinners which take place three times a month. The Kings would like a separate dining room, however. They also think their bedroom is too small. They pruchased twin beds when they moved in and find it difficult to move about in this room. They definitely feel the need for more closet space. They also view their apartment as "too small for a party" and feel that such an occasion would have to take place in the downstairs social spaces.

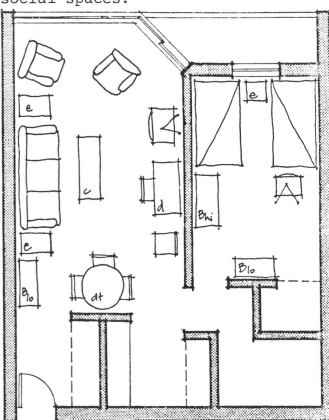

ACTIVITY DESCRIPTIONS

Many studies of the elderly have attempted to enumerate and describe the typical activities which engage this age group in the course of their days. Unfortunately this information has been difficult to translate for design purposes. The older people who participated in the M.I.T. study described, as well as showed us, the ways in which their planned housing was meeting (or in conflict with) their daily activity needs.

Six activities have been selected for detailed analysis. These activities are engaged in by almost all elderly residents and require space, in terms of both floor and wall area, for the activity itself and the furniture associated with it. The elaborated activity descriptions are based on findings from the 1974 M.I.T. National Survey and verified by a literature review of other studies.

Findings on additional activities involving personal care (bathroom), food preparation (kitchen) and storage (closets and cupboards) are reviewed in a later section of this case study. Typically not associated with "habitable" rooms which residents furnish, these activities require greater attention to hardware and equipment items and depend on *human factors* information.

Entering
Leisure Activities
Eating
Visiting
Sleeping and Dressing
Going Outdoors

Entering

Symbolically the entrance to a dwelling unit marks the transition from the outside world to the private domain of the "home". In this transition area the resident might greet friends, chat with neighbors and identify visitors before allowing them to enter the unit.

Most American homes are entered both formally and informally, depending on the intent, status and familiarity of the visitor. The formal entrance, which many residents use for display purposes, provides an introduction to the more personal territory inside the unit. This often takes the form of wall displays or objects and photographs arrayed on a small table or stand. The back entrance serves for informal visiting and the receiving of servicemen in addition to the more functional activities of bringing in groceries and taking out garbage. This entrance typically accesses directly into the hub of activity, the kitchen.

In many low rise housing solutions for the elderly the duality of entering can usually be respected in the traditional manner: the front entrance satisfying the need for formality and display, and the back one, the need for more mundane functions and convenience. However, in urban high rise apartment situations where only one entrance to a dwelling unit is typical, this access must satisfy both front and back door needs, delicately balancing both symbolic and functional components.

It is important to note that residents of an apartment unit with a single entrance view it as being a formal rather than informal access point. They often feel embarrassed and uneasy when visitors can visually invade personal territory immediately upon entering. Some of these embarrassing views include the kitchen sink where dirty dishes might collect, the bathroom, and the sleeping and dressing areas. Many residents feel that visitors should be able to get directly to the public living area where entertaining occurs, without traveling through any other rooms.

In terms of the more functional "back door" aspects of entering an apartment unit, many older persons would like convenient access to the kitchen. When returning home from shopping trips some would rather not track through other areas of the apartment on the way to the kitchen to set their heavy bundles down. The entrance also is where most residents and visitors prefer to take off (and put on) their outer wear before moving into other areas. Some elderly persons will need to sit down during this activity, particularly when it involves the putting on or removal of boots and shoes.

CAMBRIDGE, MASSACHUSETTS:
Although this entrance
hallway is quite narrow,
residents frequently
place small tables here
for display purposes.

M.I.T. NATIONAL STUDY
Selected Comments on <u>Entering</u>

BROOKLYN, NEW YORK: "There is no foyer here; you walk right into the living room."

AUGUSTA, GEORGIA: "I don't like the kitchen at the front door; you see the dishes as you walk in."

SAVANNAH, GEORGIA: "You have to go through the living room to get to the kitchen and rest of the apartment; I put down a plastic cover to keep the floor clean."

LORAIN, OHIO: "This place should have two entrances."

DAYTON, OHIO: "I would like a back door; I feel trapped with only one door."

AUGUSTA GEORGIA: "You don't have but one way out of here."

SAN FRANCISCO, CALIFORNIA: "This is a fire trap with the only exit from the apartment through the kitchen; if I had a kitchen fire I couldn't get out."

Leisure Activities

CAMBRIDGE, MASSACHUSETTS: The favorite piece of furniture for most residents is a large recliner which is typically placed near a window to permit views outdoors and natural light for reading or working on hobbies.

Leisure activity has been defined as "any pursuit which is voluntary, devoid of obligation, unnecessary for subsistence, and engaged in for its intrinsic enjoyment". With retirement and the responsibility of child-rearing behind them, older persons find themselves with more and more time to devote to these activities. Research indicates that the elderly spend more of their waking hours engaged in leisure activities than in maintenance tasks (food preparation and eating, housework, personal care, shopping, etc.). As a general rule, the elderly tend to participate in the same leisure activities that they enjoyed in their previous years (provided, of course, that their present circumstances allow them to do so), the only difference being in the amount of time allocated to each activity. Studies have shown that the elderly whose activity level has increased since retiring and who are able to devote a good deal of time to their favorite activity are the most satisfied with life.

Leisure activities within the apartment unit are typically sedentary (not involving much motion or effort) and involve only the resident(s). (Visiting, which is a social leisure activity, is discussed separately.) Those leisure activities most frequently engaged in within the unit were reported to be:

Watching television
Reading
Hobbies
Watching out the window
Telephoning
Letter writing
Tending plants

Television watching. The elderly spend more of their leisure time watching television than on any other single activity. It is an entertaining pastime which requires a minimal amount of mental and physical effort and can be engaged in alone or in groups. The television is a source of information and entertainment and appears to provide a resource for coping with sadness, loneliness, and tensions.

In 1958, persons 65 years and over were reported to average three hours per weekday in television viewing. Current national trends suggest that even greater amounts of time are devoted to this activity. A review of two weekly diaries kept in 1976 by a single elderly woman and the husband of an elderly couple indicated that an average of 5 to 6 hours per weekday were spent watching TV (range: 3 to 8 1/2 hours per day). These figures may even be higher if weekend viewing had been considered.

This activity, however, is frequently engaged in simultaneously with other activities such as sewing, reading, letter writing, and household maintenance. And although

BRINKLEY, ARKANSAS: Most residents locate their TV sets away from the windows to avoid glare problems.

the television may be turned on, it does not necessarily gain the full attention of those around it. For many older adults, particularly those who are living alone, it might provide background noise for an otherwise quiet and "empty" apartment.

Physiological changes inherent to the aging process render most elderly persons increasingly sensitive to problems of glare. They consequently will take great pains to locate the television set away from window areas to ensure comfortable daytime viewing. Apparently TV viewing with the set placed against a window is least desirable.

Reading. Many older persons also like to read during their leisure hours. One national study showed that approximately 60 percent of persons over 65 read an average of one hour per day. This activity typically takes place in a quiet, well-lit area of the living room or bedroom, or in nice weather, on the balcony or patio. Some housing projects have a communal library on site where residents can borrow books and magazines. It was observed during this study that residents, rather than stay in a library area, often returned to their units so that they could sit in a comfortable, familiar chair.

Hobbies. The types of hobbies which the elderly pursue in their dwellings are as varied as their individual personalities, ranging from such exotic interests as making wood carvings and collecting dolls to the more common pastimes of stamp collecting or knitting and sewing. Most hobbies almost invariabley have been carried on for many years prior to retirement but now attain a new importance due to increased time for leisure.

One survey indicated that although a relatively small percentage of the elderly engaged in certain hobbies (15 per cent in handiwork and one per cent in crafts and collections), those who did allocated an average of two hours per weekday to such activities.

About 10 percent of retired men pursued the hobbies of woodworking and photography, in addition to collecting coins and stamps.

A 1973 survey of Chicago area elderly widows indicated that 40 per cent of the respondents spent time sewing, knitting and crocheting. So for at least some older persons hobbies are an important pastime.

M.I.T. NATIONAL STUDY
Selected Comments on Windows

PARKIN, ARKANSAS: "Windows too high to see out of while sitting; too high to look out easily."
OMAHA, NEBRASKA: "Could have placed windows one cinder block lower so I can sit in a chair and see out."
OMAHA, NEBRASKA: "Windows too high to see out of unless you stand right up there."

Most hobbies (for example, sewing, knitting and stamp collecting) require very good lighting conditions and an adequate work surface. Many hobbies, especially that of collecting, can require disproportionate amounts of storage and display space. Some, such as photography and woodworking, may need specialized equipment for which room might be found in a single family house, but which normally cannot be accommodated in an apartment unit. In compensation, some space in apartment buildings is now allocated to the more specialized hobbies in the form of craft and hobby rooms.

Watching out the window. Watching out the window is a frequently overlooked "activity" often suggesting isolation. It is, however, a legitimate way for many older persons to pass the time, and is not, as is often thought, engaged in only by the financially or socially disadvantaged, infirm or poorly motivated. In the 1974 M.I.T. National Study, one-half of the sampled elderly responded positively to the question: "Do you spend much time sitting by a window to watch people or the view outside?" Many healthy and active older persons well appreciate having the time, opportunity, and peace of mind to sit in a comfortable chair and contemplate the activity in the world outside. However, watching out the window can be seriously hampered by poor window placement in the wall (where bottom sill is higher than 2'6" from floor).

Telephoning. The telephone has become an indespensible convenience in our society, and is heavily relied upon by older persons. Lopata's 1973 study of Chicago area widows indicated that 83 percent of the respondents made at least one phone call per day. The telephone is an essential device for the less mobile, ill, or disabled elderly person, often providing the only form of communication between the living unit and the outside world for extended periods of time.

By and large the elderly engage in telephoning for social purposes, enabling family and friends to "visit" for hours on end without physically being in each others' presence, and for functional purposes such as ordering taxis, and setting up meetings and appointments. But also for most older persons, especially those living alone, the presence of a telephone provides the feeling of security that help may be reached should an emergency situation arise.

There is great variability among the elderly as to the most desirable location for the telephone outlet. Many prefer the living room, as they spend most of the day in this room. Others, such as those who are frequently bedridden or are concerned that they might need to use the phone should an emergency occur at night, would like it in the bedroom near the bed. Some of the elderly in the M.I.T. National Study suggested that telephone jacks be provided in various locations in the dwelling, allowing the phone to be moved as needs require.

The telephone area is often furnished with a chair or other form of seating and a table for writing and storing telephone books.

M.I.T. NATIONAL STUDY
Selected comments on the Telephone

TOCCOA, GEORGIA: "We should have jacks for telephone extensions."
POPLAR BLUFF, MISSOURI: "Need telephone extension in kitchen; now in bedroom only."
SAVANNAH, GEORGIA: "Phone in bedroom and should be here in living room."
AUGUSTA, GEORGIA: "Telephone outlet in wrong place; it should be in bedroom; now on opposite side of living room from bedroom."
CHARLOTTE, NORTH CAROLINA: "Would like phone to reach bed so if I need help I can call."

CAMBRIDGE, MASSACHUSETTS: Residents tend to create a telephone area with a small desk, chair, lamp and wall decoration. It is also used for letter writing.

Letter Writing. For those elderly persons with children, close relations, and friends living far away, letter writing is an essential form of maintaining contact. In one study 53 percent of the elderly reported writing to their children often, an average of 1 1/2 hours per week being devoted to this activity.
A study of Chicago area widows reported that 49 percent of the respondents write at least one letter per week. So although large amounts of time are not typically devoted to letter writing, it is a regular and sentimentally valuable task.

A flat surface of writing height is usually necessary for this activity, although some older persons require only a comfortable chair and do their writing on their laps. Adequate lighting is essential. Due to lack of space in their apartment units some of the elderly may give up writing desks, in which case the dining room table might double as the writing surface.

Tending plants. Gardening is a leisure activity which the active elderly especially enjoy. One study found that close to 20 per cent of the interviewed elderly spent a median number of two hours per day gardening. As this study disregarded older persons in areas with less than 2,500 inhabitants, these figures are probably low.

In urban areas, however, lack of ground space tends to limit this activity. Sometimes ground space near a high rise building is parcelled out to elderly gardeners, a where this has been done, the gard plots appear to be quite popular. Other elderly would prefer to tend plants in their unit or on immediately adjacent patios/porches/balconies. Window sills wide enou for flower pots as well as window boxes were mentioned as desirable. Storage of gardening and plant ten ding materials and equipment is of concern to residents as these item can often consume much space.

M.I.T. NATIONAL STUDY
Selected Comments on Tending Plant

DAYTON, OHIO: 'Husband likes area where he does active gardening.
TOCCOA, GEORGIA: "We don't have a place for rakes and hoes--some put under bed or on porch."
OMAHA, NEBRASKA: "Wants window sil on which to place flowers."
NEBRASKA CITY, NEBRASKA: "Wants flower boxes at window."

Eating

Among the elderly, the activity of eating my take a variety of forms. Some meals will be quick and simple; others will be more substantial, especially if served to one or two others like a spouse or drop-in friend; and still other meals are more elaborate and formal and might involve larger gatherings of friends and relatives. On the average, older persons living alone or with a spouse share one meal a week and holidays with their children and many times these gatherings occur in the older person's home as part of the role of parent and grandparent.

These different types of meals are eaten in various parts of the living unit. For example, light meals and snacks are typically eaten in the kitchen where they are prepared, as the main factor in this form of eating is convenience. One tenant in an elderly housing project in

CAMBRIDGE, MASSACHUSETTS: This resident frequently eats her meals sitting on a high stool at the kitchen counter. The dining table is used only for guests.

Charlotte, North Carolina, where the kitchens do not allow room for even a small table, commented that she eats standing up. Larger meals that require more preparation and eating time than the quick snacks are also often eaten at a table in the kitchen. In the M.I.T. National Study two-thirds of the elderly respondents indicated that they ate in their kitchens. Of the third who never did, approximately 85 per cent said that their kitchen was too small for a table so they could not eat there although they would have preferred to. Only seven respondents gave other reasons for not eating in the kitchen, which included: it was too dark, too hot, had no view, or was too near the cooking area.

Not only did the majority of elderly respondents in this study like to eat in the kitchen, but a substantial proportion (63 per cent) also liked to use their kitchen for informal entertaining. This is a pattern that many developed in their previous residential environments which often had large eat-in kitchens that doubled as a social setting for the family as well as friends. In a recent study in Oklahoma, approximately half of the elderly respondents indicated a preference for the eating area to be part of the kitchen. Only 20 per cent expressed a desire for a separate dining room.

The preference for eating in the kitchen may relate to several issues: (1) for many elderly residents this represents a continuation of a pattern acquired in former family living environments where the eating area was part of the kitchen; (2) a dining table that is perceived as being more a part of the formal living room rather than informal kitchen may be considered "too good" for everyday eating purposes and will be reserved only for use with guests; and (3) as an important issue in everday eating is convenience, many residents may prefer a minimal walking distance for the carrying of food and dishes between the meal preparation area and the dining table. In other words, many older persons may not consider it worthwhile to set a table that is remote from the kitchen for an informal meal.

Formal entertaining of large groups is not a frequent occurrence. It is, however, an important activity for many older persons, particularly when it involves their children and grandchildren. This type of dining has traditionally taken place in a formal dining room or area off of the living room.

The large formal dining room set was the primary furnishing missed by older public housing residents, when asked what they would have wished to bring with them. Many had to replace reluctantly these larger pieces with smaller "kitchenette" sets but some kept their china cabinets. Although adaptation to smaller space appears to be easy. Our research has noted a strong attempt by older people to retain the symbols of past formal and family dining areas

Occasionally some elderly persons will want to eat a snack or even a full meal while watching TV. In some cases TV trays are set up in the living room in front of the TV set or dishes are placed on end tables.

Where once meals were typically social events, when families shared their daily experiences, eating is now more often an individual function for the single older person. Because of the health-related implications, careful attention must be paid to encouraging good eating habits. Research has shown that elderly persons who live alone often neglect nutrient quality and care of preparation in favor of easily

CAMBRIDGE, MASSACHUSETTS: Dining furniture often includes a table, several chairs and a china cabinet.

available "convenience" foods. As a result, environmental supports are needed to stimulate the proper consumption of food. Alternative areas for eating within the unit that provide for different levels of accessibility, convenience, and formality can help motivate the older resident to develop healthy eating patterns. Views from the dining area are also an important stimulus for good eating habits. There may be nothing more unstimulating than eating in a cramped space with one's nose to the wall, and nothing more unappetizing than sitting next to the bathroom.

Natural light and a view to the outdoors make eating a pleasurable experience for young and old alike, but may have an especially beneficial effect on the older person who now often eats alone.

M.I.T. NATIONAL STUDY
Selected Comments on Eating

EAST HARTFORD, CONNECTICUT: "I like that we can put a table in the kitchen."

YONKERS, NEW YORK: "They should make the kitchen bigger; it would be nice to eat in it."

CHARLOTTE, NORTH CAROLINA: "There is not enough room in the kitchen; I would have to eat standing up."

DAYTON, OHIO: "I would like a little alcove (in the kitchen) big enough for a table so I wouldn't have to eat in the living room."

DAYTON, OHIO: "I would like a larger kitchen where there is a place to sit."

CHARLOTTE, NORTH CAROLINA: "There is no room in the kitchen; guests have to stand."

OMAHA, NEBRASKA: "The kitchen and living room are together so I put up a screen to separate the table from the kitchen."

CLEVELAND, OHIO: "Kitchen is too small; I am not able to have people for dinner."

BRONX, NEW YORK: "I don't like the kitchen next to the bathroom.

NEW HAVEN, CONNECTICUT: A high counter has been provided at the window. Residents can eat at this height or they can slide a small table underneath which can be pulled out to eat on.

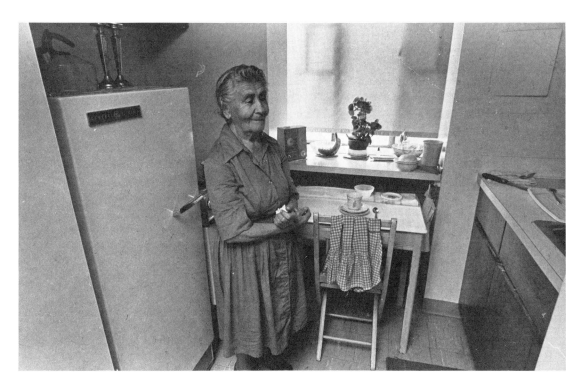

Visiting

The activity of visiting includes all forms of social contact that occur within a dwelling unit, from sitting with a friend, chatting over coffee, to having the family over for Sunday dinner. Visiting can be planned or informal when friends, neighbors, or relatives drop-in. It frequently involves the sharing of food. It may include having someone stay overnight, so that although most visiting takes place in the living and dining areas, it can involve other areas of the home as well.

Visiting is an important activity for older persons as it helps keep them in touch with the world outside the living unit. (This is especially true for the less mobile elderly person.) In the 1974 M.I.T. National Study, 63 percent of the respondents were visited in their apartments by friends at least once a week (53 percent themselves visited in friends' apartments weekly). An earlier national survey indicated that two-thirds of the persons over 65 visited daily (for an average of about two hours) with others either inside or outside their home.

The majority of visiting takes place on an informal basis where friends and neighbors might drop in to chat or have coffee. Entertaining, which implies more formal contact, occurs less frequently, but as an occasion is more time-consuming and usually includes the preparation of a meal or snacks. It is an important activity, even if not a frequent one, because it often involves maintaining previous patterns and role obligations (eg. the once-a-month family gathering for dinner at grandmother's house) Lack of space for entertaining was frequently mentioned as a problem by residents at both the national and local sites. Adequate floor area was viewed as necessary for seating groups of 6+ people around a dining table or in the living room for conversation purposes. In addition, several residents thought their kitchens were prohibitively small for the preparation of food for a large gathering.

Conversation is an integral part of the activity of visiting whether it be at the dining table or in the living room. Studies have found that in general, two people conversing prefer to sit across from one another or at a slight angle rather than side by side, the maximum nose to nose distance being 5 and 1/2 feet. These studies took place in a large lounge and it is believed that conversation distance in a smaller space such a a living room may be greater. However, many older persons may require closer distances due to hearing problems. For the elderly, conversation furniture typically includes a sofa with two end tables, a coffee table, and one or more arm chairs arranged in a closed loop. Should more seating be required, dining chairs or floor cushions are often used.

Elderly residents occasionally have overnight guests. One study reported that 46 percent of people over 65 have had their children stay overnight at least once a year. In addition, one-third of this age group had company other than children spend the night one or more times a year. To accommodate these guests, many of the elderly would like a separate bedroom.

When others visit, the issue of visual invasion of private spaces must be addressed. As with most people, the elderly tend to feel self-conscious when little can be hidden from their guests. This uneasiness is often translated into a reluctance to invite others into the apartment and, as a result, social interaction is further limited. Areas within the unit that residents most frequently mentioned as needing visual privacy include the sleeping area, the bathroom, and the kitchen sink.

In a few multi-unit housing projects an extra one bedroom unit has been set aside for tenant guests. Incidental evidence suggests that these are not well used, that residents either crowd guests in or forego the pleasure of such intimate occasions.

M.I.T. NATIONAL STUDY
Selected Comments on Visiting

MARKED TREE, ARKANSAS: "I need another small room for a bed for company."

WEST HELENA, ARKANSAS: "I would like another bedroom for relatives staying overnight."

HARTWELL, GEORGIA: "I would prefer a two bedroom apartment. My daughter came to visit with her husband and two children and they could not stay here."

TOCCOA, GEORGIA: "There should be another small bedroom for guests."

HARTWELL, GEORGIA: "When people have children who come and visit they need more room."

CHARLOTTE, NORTH CAROLINA: "The kitchen is too small if you want to cook for more than two people."

CLEVELAND, OHIO: "The kitchen is too small; I am not able to have people for dinner."

Sleeping and Dressing

Sleep, one of the basic needs of the human body, has a direct effect on the health and general well-being of elderly persons. The total amount of sleep required varies greatly from one individual to another, and may depend on life attitudes and general health as well as actual physical needs. On the average, an elderly person spends about 9 hours per night sleeping. Many older persons need to rest during the daytime as well, so that an average of 1.4 hours daily is devoted to taking naps.

Although most sleeping takes place in the bedroom, many elderly persons may use other areas of their home as well. Some like to nap on the living room couch during the day (perhaps to avoid rumpling the made-up bed); others might doze off while sitting in front of the TV in an easy chair. Such elderly persons, having obtained a large part of their required sleep "informally" during the day, may sleep very little at night.

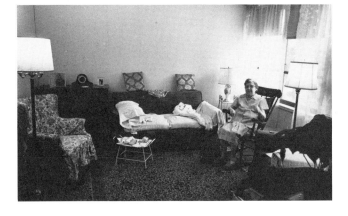

CAMBRIDGE, MASSACHUSETTS: *During the day this resident naps on her living room sofa.*

The elderly often spend time in bed for reasons other than sleeping. Many enjoy reading or watching TV in bed, and in times of illness it is the natural retreat. Due to ill health some older persons spend large amounts of time in bed and therefore are especially sensitive to the bedroom environment. Noise, drafts, view, and privacy are just some of the factors that play a par in determining the levels of comfor and enjoyment available in the sleeping area of a dwelling.

Privacy is one of the most acute issues associated with the activity of sleeping, for both psychological and functional reason Because of the inherent vulnerabili of the sleeping person and the sexu connotations of the bed, views of the bed, along with the furniture associated with it, are in most cases considered taboo to the stranger and casual visitor. The bedroom traditionally houses the occupant's most personal items such as momentos and photographs, person clothing, and bedside medicines which the resident may wish to keep from the visitors' scrutiny. It is the place where many private activities such as dressing, un-dressing and lovemaking occur and where many married couples tradi-tionally retreat to discuss private matters.

Many of the residents in the M.I.T. National Study commented on the inadequacy of their sleeping areas.

Those in efficiency units, particularly the single women, wanted a separate bedroom for privacy or at least a sleeping area large enough to accommodate a double bed as well as other bedroom furniture (dressers, tables, chairs, etc.) Limited floor space at some of the national sites forced several residents to sleep on hide-a-beds which they made up every evening. Some expressed extreme embarrassment.

when visitors had full view of their bed and many regarded overnight guests as an impossibility. And although most of the elderly preferred convenient access between bedroom and bathroom, some mentioned being uncomfortable when guests had to pass through the sleeping area to reach the bathroom. These reactions can have strong repercussions on the social life of the older person.

CAMBRIDGE, MASSACHUSETTS: This sleeping alcove is not large enough to accommodate all of this resident's bedroom furniture. As a result, some bureaus are placed in the living room.

In a recent survey of Oklahoma elderly residing in public housing it was found that the greater the separation of the sleeping area from the rest of the apartment the greater percentage of satisfied respondents. Again this reinforces the need for privacy in the sleeping area.

Several of the elderly residents in the M.I.T. National Study also expressed a desire for a second bedroom. Their comments, as well as other studies (Tucker), have indicated that this additional bedroom is used to: (1) accommodate overnight guests; (2) provide separate bedrooms, for reasons of privacy and/or health, for two residents sharing a unit; and (3) offer space for hobbies and/or the storage of furniture and other belongings.

Bedroom furniture among the elderly, like all the rest of their belongings is a reflection of a lifestyle developed over many years. Some recently widowed women (for both financial and sentimental reasons) will cling to their double bed, and many elderly couples, due to either health or habit, have twin beds. In the M.I.T. National Study, the two pieces of furniture that the interviewed elderly would have kept from their previous residence that they now have no room for are beds (particularly double beds) and dressing bureaus. It is psychologically difficult for such persons to have to adjust to new arrangements due to lack of space for their old furniture. This may reduce the marketability of buildings.

The activity of dressing typically takes place in the bedroom or sleeping area in close proximity to the clothes closet. Photographs of bedroom areas in some of the national sites indicate that the bureaus are often located near the closet to form a convenient dressing area. Adequate floor space in this area is an issue for the movement necessary to putting on or removing clothes as well as accessing clothing in the drawers or behind closet door

BRINKLEY, ARKANSAS: Inadequate wall space in bedroom, vanity against a window and easy chair in front of closet door.

FURNISHING PATTERNS

The preceding activity descriptions illustrate that there are similarities in what older persons do in their private environment. Are there also *patterns* that emerge concerning the furnishings they use in the support of these activities? To test for issues of furnishability, 55 similar apartment units were evaluated for their capabilities to support the activity and furnishing needs of residents with varied lifestyles and environmental histories. By controlling for similarities in design, the issues of furnishability emerge as *patterns* of resident definition of their activity settings within a given fixed space.

THE SAMPLE

Apartment units. The 55 units in the sample are located in three buildings in Cambridge, Massachusetts which were designed by one architectural firm, Benjamin Thompson & Associates, constructed and occupied simultaneously in 1974. Although these buildings differ in terms of massing, the same working drawings and specifications for the individual apartment units were used for all three. As a result, all units are identical, with the exception of location of unit entrance and the presence or absence of a separate bedroom.

Apartment unit types were sampled in relative proportion to their representation in the three buildings studied. The four variations in unit types are: Unit A, efficiency with center entrance (22 cases); Unit B, efficiency with side entrance (17 cases); Unit C, one bedroom with center entrance (9 cases); and Unit D, one bedroom with side entrance (7 cases). The approximate gross square footage is 380 (430 including the balcony) for the efficiency units and 520 (570 including the balcony) for the one bedroom units. Because of the difference in square footage, bedroom definition, and number of occupants (the efficiency is for single residents only while the one bedroom unit is typically occupied by two residents), these two unit sizes (A/B and C/D) will be analyzed separately.

Resident sample. Seven (18 per cent) of the residents occupying the 39 sampled efficiencies were single men (they comprise approximately 15 per cent of the total resident population at these sites). The breakdown of residents in the 16 sampled one bedroom units included two widows (two units), two sisters (one unit), two mother/daughter living arrangements (two units), and eleven married couples. At the time they were interviewed, all had lived in their units for more than six months and 80 per cent had been in their units for at least two years. Almost half had previously lived in duplexes or triplexes before their move and another third came from other public housing projects. The majority of the residents have lived in Cambridge for a substantial part of their adult lives.

DATA COLLECTION

Prior to any contact with residents, permission to undertake this study was requested from the Cambridge Housing Authority as well as the managers and tenant council presidents at the sites. Each council president subsequently informed their tenant organization of our study and presence in the building. All residents in the sampled units were then sent a letter which further described the type of information needed and a date and time for a visit to the individual unit was proposed. The residents were also informed that participants in the study would receive five dollars for their time and information. Approximately 90 per cent of the residents approached in this manner were cooperative.

A variety of data collection methods was employed to elicit information from sampled residents on activities, furnishings, and other lifestyle variables. (Examples of these data collection instruments can be found in the Appendix.)

Interviews. Residents in 31 of the 55 units were interviewed about the perceived adequacy of their unit for both furnishings and activities. They were specifically asked about the furniture that was both given away and acquired as a result of the move into the present unit, the frequency of rearranging furniture, entertainment patterns, and layout preferences for various spaces. As this questionnaire followed a longer, more extensive one on activities outside of the unit (which also included a brief description of the previous living environment), it was kept as short as possible.

Furniture maps. After the interview, the furniture pieces in each unit were drawn in their appropriate locations on a scaled (1/4"=1') unit plan. Standardized definitions (based on both functional and dimensional differences) and graphic codes of typically observed furniture pieces were developed after several pilot mappings. Furniture templates at the same scale as the unit plans were then used by the interviewers in mapping to increase accuracy and efficiency. Dimensions of major furniture pieces that consistently varied in shape and size (i.e. dining tables) were noted. An additional 24 furniture maps were constructed from photographs taken in those units where the residents were not interviewed.

Photographic documentation. Each of the units was systematically photographed with a wide angle lens (28 or 35mm) from the same series of approximately ten vantage points. This series provided a complete documentation of all furnished areas in each unit (bathrooms were excluded) as well as a systematic record of how any one area in the same unit type was furnished by a sample of residents. Each unit was photographed with both black and white print film and color slides: the prints are used for detailed analysis, verification of the furniture maps, and as illustration for written reports while the color slides are used for group presentations and team analysis.

Field notes. Much of the information that residents volunteered during the course of an interview, although very informative, was not specifically asked for on the questionnaire format. As a means of recording this additional data, interviewers were asked to keep field notes on each unit visit. Information recorded by this method included such personal characteristics as general health and physical handicaps or limitations, family ties, and a more detailed description of previous living situations.

Interviewer debriefing sessions. Upon completion of all field visits, the interviewers reviewed each sampled resident/unit for other members of the research team. The series of slides taken in each unit was shown and accompanied by a summary of findings from the interview and field notes. Members of the research team then responded to each visual/verbal description with questions and comments which lead to further clarification and elaboration. These sessions, which were taped and subsequently transcribed, proved to be a major vehicle for developing hypotheses on lifestyle patterns and a basis for validating observations.

The following figure summarizes the characteristics of the units and persons sampled in the pilot explorations of Private Space, Habitability of Elderly Housing.

Description of Pilot Sample and Unit Types, Private Space, MIT Design Evaluation Project, 1978.

	UNIT TYPE	SAMPLE SIZE	DESCRIPTION OF OCCUPANTS
	A Efficiency, center entrance	22	19 single females 3 single males
	B Efficiency, side entrance	17	13 single females 4 single males
	C One bedroom, center entrance	9	2 single females (widows) 6 married couples 1 mother and daughter
	D One bedroom, side entrance	7	5 married couples 1 mother and daughter 1 two sisters

AVERAGE FURNISHINGS

For each of the four apartment unit types a tally of the various furniture pieces observed in the sampled apartments was taken. Based on both the mean and the mode, average furnishings were then calculated. On an average, there are 19 furniture pieces in the efficiency unit and 23 pieces in the one bedroom unit. These calculated averages are substantially higher than those recommended in HUD Minimum Property Standards (MPS). The MPS require enough space to accommodate 13 pieces of furniture in the efficiency unit and 14 pieces in the one bedroom unit (double occupancy). Only two of the 55 apartment units studied had as few furnishings as those specified in the national standards.

HUD standards do not adequately reflect the number of tables and easy chairs in a typical living room arrangement. And, in general, the MPS places little emphasis on dining furniture. Most residents seek to retain their former dining set (table, 30 x 40 inches, with possibility of extension using leaves; four matching chairs; and occasionally, a china cabinet) while HUD recommendations assume that residents have a small kitchenette set (table 30 x 30; two chairs). This discrepancy possibly accounts for the general inadequacy of dining areas in existing HUD units.

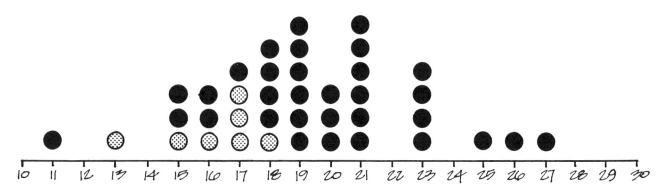

Distribution of furniture pieces in 39 efficiencies

The following graphic compares the furniture pieces specified in the HUD MPS with those calculated from observations of occupied units.

Efficiency Unit (single occupancy)

One Bedroom Unit (double occupancy)

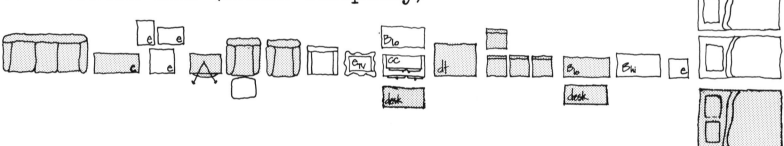

The table on the following pages lists the average furnishings that have been calculated from the 39 efficiencies and 16 one bedroom units. It includes a graphic code for each piece (1/8"=1')* and a description of the frequency of occurrence in efficiencies and one bedroom units. In several instances three or four similar items (in terms of use or size) were clustered together as options for an average furniture piece.

The difference in the amount of furnishings between the efficiency and one bedroom units might be attributed to the difference in square footage as well as the number of occupants.

INVENTORY OF FURNITURE PIECES

Efficiency unit: center entrance

FURNITURE PIECES:	Apt. A.1	Apt. A.2	Apt. A.3	Apt. A.4	Apt. A.5	Apt. A.6	Apt. A.7	Apt. A.8	Apt. A.9	Apt. A.10	Apt. A.11	Apt. A.12	Apt. A.13	Apt. A.14	Apt. A.15	Apt. A.16	Apt. A.17	Apt. A.18	Apt. A.19	Apt. A.20	Apt. A.21	Apt. A.22	TOTAL
RESIDENT(S) SEX	F	F	F	F	F	F	F	F	F	F	F	F	F	F	F	F	F	F	F	M	M	M	
Love seat							1	1		1						1	1				1		6
Sofa/couch	1		1	1	1	1			1		1	1		1			1	1	1	1	1		14
Easy chair		2	1	2	2		2	1	4	2	2	1		2		1	1	1	1	1	1		28
Foot stool		1	1	1	1		1		1	2	1	1	1				1				1		13
Arm chair	4	3	1			2			1	1			1	2	1	1		1	1	2		1	23
Side chair	3	2	3	5	5	4	3	7	2	4	2	2	4	3	3	3	2	5	3	4	2	3	74
Dining table	1	1	1	1	1	1	1	1	2	1	1		1	1	2	1	1	1	1	1	2	3	26
Coffee table									1	1	1		1				1	1	1				11
End table	6	5	2	5	2	2	2	4	4	7	5	5	6	2	4	5	3	5	4	2	3	1	84
China cabinet													1			1		2					4
Shelving						1		2	4	2	1						1	2		1			14
Desk			1											1									2
Vanity	1	1		1			1			1	1	1	1				1		1				10
Lo bureau		2	3	1		2			1		1	2			2		1	1			1		18
Hi bureau			1					1	1	1	1	2		1	1	1		2	1	1			14
Single bed	1	1	1		1	1	1	1	1		1	1	1	1		1		1	1	1		1	19
Double bed																		1			1		2
TV	1	1	1	1	1	1	1	3	1	1	1	1	1	1	1	2	1	1	1	3	1		27
TV tray							1		3				1										5
TV tray stand				1					1														2
Floor lamp	1						1	1		1	1		1		2		1		1	1		1	12
Room divider																		1		1			2
Step stool			1	1				1															3
Plant stand	2	1			3											1					1		8
TOTAL PIECES	21	19	19	23	15	18	15	25	26	27	20	21	11	20	18	18	21	17	15	18	13		421

Efficiency unit: side entrance

RESIDENT(S) SEX	Apt. B.1	Apt. B.2	Apt. B.3	Apt. B.4	Apt. B.5	Apt. B.6	Apt. B.7	Apt. B.8	Apt. B.9	Apt. B.10	Apt. B.11	Apt. B.12	Apt. B.13	Apt. B.14	Apt. B.15	Apt. B.16	Apt. B.17	TOTAL
	F	F	F	F	F	F	F	F	F	F	F	F	F	F	M	M	M	
FURNITURE PIECES:																		
Love seat		1				1												2
Sofa/couch	1		1	1	1		1		1	1	1	1			1	1		13
Easy chair	1	2	1		1	2	2		2	1	3	1	3		1	1	1	23
Foot stool		2	2	1				1	1			2	2				1	12
Arm chair	1	1	1	2	1		1	2		1			3	1	1			15
Side chair	2	2	4	2	3	5	2	4	2	3	4	3	3	1	5	1	3	49
Dining table	1	1	1	1	1	1	1	1	1	1	1	1	1	1	1	2	1	18
Coffee table		1	1	1		1					1	1		1	1	1		10
End table	5	6	4	3	5	5	3	4	6	6	2	4	7	4	3	3	4	74
China cabinet		1				1		1				1						4
Shelving	1		1	2		1			1			2	2	1	2	1		15
Desk							1				1							2
Vanity	1	1	1		1	1	1		1	1	1				1			11
Lo bureau			1	1		1		1	1	1	1		1		1			9
Hi bureau		1				2					1	1		2	1			8
Single bed	1	1	1	1	1	1	1	1	1	1	1	1	1	1	1	1	1	17
Double bed																		0
TV	1	1	1		1	1	1	1	2	1	1		1	1	2	1	1	19
TV tray		1		1	1	3	1											
TV tray stand										1							1	2
Floor lamp			1	1							1			1	1		1	6
Room divider		1											1					2
Step stool	1		1		1													3
Plant stand						2		1										3
TOTAL PIECES	16	24	23	19	19	22	24	18	19	20	16	19	23	16	18	17	17	**324**

One bedroom unit: living area furniture

RESIDENT(S) SEX	Apt. C.1	Apt. C.2	Apt. C.3	Apt. C.4	Apt. C.5	Apt. C.6	Apt. C.7	Apt. C.8	Apt. C.9	Apt. D.1	Apt. D.2	Apt. D.3	Apt. D.4	Apt. D.5	Apt. D.6	Apt. D.7	TOTAL
	F	F/M	F	F/M	F/M	F/M	F/M	F/M	F/M	M	F	F	F/M	F/M	F/M	F/M	
FURNITURE PIECES:																	
Love seat	1				1												2
Sofa/couch	1	1	1	1	1		2	1	1	1	1	1	1	1	1	1	16
Easy chair	1	1	2	2	2	2	2	3	2	1	1	2	1	1	3	2	28
Foot stool	1	1		1	2		2	1		2	1			1		1	14
Arm chair		1			1		1	1	2		1		1	1	1	1	11
Side chair	1	3	4	2			5	3	6	4	5	4	3	4	3		47
Dining table		2	1	1	1			1	1	2	1	1	1	1	1	1	15
Coffee table	1	1	1		1		1				1	1			1	1	9
End table	2	2	2	5	4		4	3	4	3	4	2	1	2	5	2	45
China cabinet		1	1	1	1		1				1				1	1	8
Shelving				1		1					1		1				4
Desk									1		1						2
Vanity																	0
Lo bureau	1	1	1	3	1	2		1			1					1	12
Hi bureau				1							1						2
Single bed																	0
Double bed																	0
TV	1	1	1	1	1	1	2	1	1	1	1	1	1	1	1	1	17
TV tray	3		2	1	2			1								1	10
TV tray stand				1	1												2
Floor lamp		1		1	1	1			1	2		1	1			2	11
Room divider																	0
Step stool		1									1						2
Plant stand										1				1	1	1	4
TOTAL PIECES	13	6	15	23	17	11	6	17	13	24	21	15	13	13	18	9	261

One bedroom unit: bedroom furniture

	Apt. C.1	Apt. C.2	Apt. C.3	Apt. C.4	Apt. C.5	Apt. C.6	Apt. C.7	Apt. C.8	Apt. C.9	Apt. D.1	Apt. D.2	Apt. D.3	Apt. D.4	Apt. D.5	Apt. D.6	Apt. D.7	TOTAL
RESIDENT(S) SEX	F	F/M	F	F/M	M	F/M	F/M	F/M	F/M	F/M	F	F	F/M	F/M	F/M	F/M	
FURNITURE PIECES:																	
Love seat																	
Sofa/couch																	
Easy chair	1									1	1						3
Foot stool																	
Arm chair				1	1								1				3
Side chair	1	3			1	1				1	1						8
Dining table																	
Coffee table																	
End table				1	1	1	2				1	1	2				10
China cabinet																	
Shelving													1				1
Desk											1						1
Vanity	1		1								1						3
Lo bureau	1	3		2	1	1					1	2					12
Hi bureau	1	1		1	1	1							2				7
Single bed	1		2	2	2	2					2	2					13
Double bed		1									1		1				3
TV		1		1								1					3
TV tray	1																1
TV tray stand																	
Floor lamp	1																1
Room divider																	
Step stool				1													1
Plant stand																	
TOTAL PIECES	8	10	5	9	6	7				6	6	6	7				70

FURNITURE DIMENSIONS

A standardized dimension has been calculated for the following pieces of furniture. These dimensions are based on several sources:

- HUD Minimum Property Standards (HUD),1973 edition

- Central Mortgage and Housing Corporation (CMHC), Canada, in The Use and Design of Space in the Home, 1974. Furniture sizes resulted from a study of moderately priced furniture on the Canadian market.

- Michigan State Housing Development Authority (MSHDA), in Housing for the Elderly Development Process, 1974. Appears to be based on HUD Minimum Property Standards.

- Graphic Standards (GS) 1938, 1945 and 1970. Gives dimensions for a wide variety of furniture types. Only the dimensions for those pieces that were similar in style to observed elderly furnishings were referenced.

- Time-Saver Standards for Building Types (TSS), 1973. "Furniture sizes may vary slightly; those indicated are the averages commonly met with in upper middle-class homes, and are little affected by changes in style or similar matters of individual preference."

- Sears 1976. As many of the furnishings in the elderly households are similar to those found in a Sears catalogue it was used as a reference for dimensions. Again, care was taken to include only dimensions of furniture that was similar in style to observed furnishings in elderly residents' units.

- Design Evaluation Project (DEP), 1977. Actual dimensions for some furniture pieces were collected as part of the Apartment Unit study at the Cambridge sites.

The recommended dimensions for a piece of furniture frequently varied from one source to the next. In an effort to accommodate the greatest number of cases as well as reflect the central tendency, final dimensions are slightly greater than the mean average. Therefore, the majority of elderly residents will have furniture no larger than this study's recommendations.

FURNITURE	RECOMMENDED DIMENSIONS	SOURCES
SOFA	36x82 *There is great variation in size amongst the sources as well as in the DEP observed apartment furnishings. A larger than average dimension is recommended: if this larger sofa can be accommodated in an apartment then so can the smaller sized sofas.*	36x82 HUD 34x80 CMHC 36x82 MSHDA 34x80 GS 1945 30x72 GS 1970 36x84 TSS 35x71 Sears 32x76 DEP (range 66-84)
LOVESEAT	32x55 *Again, the larger rather than average size is recommended to accommodate the majority of cases.*	30x54 GS 1938 32x55 GS 1970 30x54 TSS 32x49 Sears
EASY CHAIR	34x36 *Many of these chairs are large recliners which average 34x36 (Sears).*	30x36 HUD 32x34 CMHC 30x36 MSHDA 33x33 GS 1970 30x36 TSS 34x36 Sears
FOOT STOOL	18x22 *The smaller foot stool is more prevalent; large ottomans were rarely observed at the Cambridge sites.*	21x24 GS 1970 (hi) 18 dia. Sears (lo) 18x22 Sears (ave.)

Note: All dimensions are in inches.

FURNITURE	RECOMMENDED DIMENSIONS	SOURCES
ARM CHAIR	24x29 *The most prevalent arm chair was a rocking chair.*	28x30 CMHC 23x23 GS 1970 (ave.) 20x25 GS 1970 (image) 27x30 TSS 24x29 Sears (rocker)
SIDE CHAIR	18x18	18x18 HUD 18x20 CMHC 18x18 MSHDA 18x18 TSS 18x18 Sears
DINING TABLE	30x40 *This dimension reflects the average horizontal surface area of tables observed at the Cambridge sites whether they were folded or unfolded.*	30x30 HUD 36x48 CMHC (5-6 persons) 36x36 MSHDA 30x36 Sears (ave.) 30x40 DEP (ave.)
COFFEE TABLE	18x48	18x48 CMHC 18x30 MSHDA 24x36 TSS 20x42 Sears (ave.) 18x48 DEP (modal ave.)

FURNITURE	RECOMMENDED DIMENSIONS	SOURCES
END TABLES		
• by sofa	18x30	18x30 HUD
		18x26 CMHC
		18x30 MSHDA
		15x24 TSS
		21x26 Sears
		18x30 DEP (modal ave.)
• by bed (nightstand)	18x18	16x20 CMHC
		18x18 MSHDA
		17x18 TSS
		18x18 Sears
• other areas	24x24	20x20 TSS
		24x24 DEP (ave.)
	This is an approximate dimension for the many other tables of various sizes, shapes, and heights found in apartments.	
CHINA CABINET	18x42	18x48 CMHC (buffet)
		18x42 MSHDA
	The china cabinet is typically a hutch (taller than 32") and not a buffet (32" or shorter).	15x54 GS 1970 (buffet)
		15x38 TSS (ave.)
		16x36 Sears (buffet)
		16x48 Sears (hutch)
		18x42 DEP (hutch)
SHELVING	14x30	10x30 Sears
		12x30 Sears
		11x36 Sears
		9x21 Sears
		14x30 DEP (ave.)

FURNITURE	RECOMMENDED DIMENSIONS	SOURCES
DESK	20x42	20x42 HUD
		18x36 CMHC (work surface)
		20x42 MSHDA
		24x48 TSS
		17x40 Sears (ave.)
TV	20x32	16x32 HUD
		16x32 MSHDA
	Typical TV at Cambridge sites is a large portable sitting on a moveable TV stand or end table.	20x24 Sears (TV stand)
VANITY	18x48	18x48 DEP
LO BUREAU	20x42	20x42 TSS
		20x42 DEP
HI BUREAU	18x42	18x42 HUD (dresser)
		18x52 MSHDA (dresser)
		20x36 TSS
		18x48 Sears
		18x42 DEP
SINGLE BED	39x82	39x82 HUD
		39x78 CMHC
	82" length accommodates long mattress (80") plus headboard/frame.	39x78 MSHDA
		39x82 TSS

FURNITURE	RECOMMENDED DIMENSIONS	SOURCES
DOUBLE BED	54x82 *82" length accommodates long mattress (80") plus headboard/frame.*	54x82 HUD 54x78 CMHC 57x78 MSHDA 54x82 TSS
TV TRAY	15x22	15x22 DEP
STEP STOOL	11x15	11x15 Sears (ave.)
FLOOR LAMP	16 dia.	16 dia. Sears (ave.)
PLANT STAND	*Sizes vary too much to establish an average dimension. Range: 5" dia. to 24"x42".*	

AVERAGE FURNISHINGS

FURNITURE	EFFICIENCY UNITS		ONE BEDROOM UNITS	
sofa/couch 36x82	1	One sofa was present in 70 per cent (27/39) of the efficiency units. An additional 8 loveseats (2 seaters) were observed in other units. Only one resident had both a couch and a loveseat. In addition to being used for occasional napping, several of the sofas folded out into a bed for overnight guests.	1	94 per cent (15/16) of the one bedroom units were furnished with at least one sofa. One unit had both a sofa and a loveseat and another had two sofas. Residents used the fold-out sofas for themselves as well as for over-night visitors: when one member of a couple was sick, the other would sometimes sleep on the sofa in the living room; and, in one instance where a mother and daughter shared a unit, the daughter always slept on a fold-out sofa in the living room.
easy chair 34x36 *large upholstered chair including club chair, wing chair, and recliner*	1	In the 39 units, a total of 51 easy chairs were observed. While six units did not have this type of chair, there were others that had three or four of these chairs. Easy chairs were most frequently mentioned as the favorite piece of furniture in the unit. For the most part, they were strategically located to have a view of both the TV and the outdoors.	2	In the one bedroom units, 28 easy chairs were found in the living area and another three were in the bedroom, for an average of almost two chairs per unit (31/16).
foot stool fs 18x22	1	At least one foot stool could be found in 50 per cent (20/39) of the units (a total of 25 were observed). The foot stool was most frequently associated with an easy chair in all units.	1	14 foot stools were observed in 11 of the 16 units. They were all found in areas other than the bedroom.

FURNITURE	EFFICIENCY UNITS	ONE BEDROOM UNITS
arm chair ▢ *24x29* *unupholstered chair with arms (at the Cambridge sites this was typically a rocking chair)*	1 67 per cent (26/39) of the units had at least one arm chair. A total of 38 such chairs were observed with some residents (3) having as many as three or four.	1 11 arm chairs were found in the living rooms of 16 units and another three were located in 10 observed bedrooms. No one bedroom unit had more than two arm chairs.
side chair ▢ *18x18* *chair without arms (typically part of a dining set)*	3 Two-thirds (26/39) of the units had at least three side chairs with several units (6) having 5-7 side chairs. In the 39 units, a total of 123 chairs were observed. Although primarily used for sitting on, these chairs were occasionally used as end tables near sofas and as display surfaces in entrances.	3 47 side chairs were observed in 16 living rooms and an additional 8 chairs were found in 10 bed-rooms. 1* In addition to the average of two easy chairs, one arm chair, and three side chairs found in the living room, 9 of the 10 bedrooms observed had at least one of these chairs. This chair was typically a side chair, however.
dining table ▢ dt *30x40* *table 28" to 30" high which is used for eating; includes both formal dining tables and small kitchenette sets.*	1 Only one of the 39 units did not have a dining table. Four units had two tables and one unit had three tables. Not all of these tables were used for dining on a daily basis however. Several were folded against the wall and used only when others visited. At least three were used solely as hobby tables.	1 75 per cent (12/16) of the units had at least one dining table (two had two tables). Those without dining tables ate at TV trays or end tables while sitting in favorite chairs in the living room.

* in bedroom

FURNITURE	EFFICIENCY UNITS	ONE BEDROOM UNITS
coffee table `c` 18x48 *low tables 16" high typically placed in front of the sofa*	1 — 21 of the 39 units (54 per cent) were furnished with a coffee table. No unit had more than one such table (used for display and setting things on).	1 — More than 50 per cent (9/16) of the units had a coffee table, all of which were centered directly in front of the sofa/couch.
end table `e` `e` `e` 18x30 *20" (+2") high table found in various parts of the unit and used to set objects on as well as for display*	4 — 158 end tables of various sizes were counted in the 39 units. At least one table was associated with the sofa and another with an easy chair or arm chair. In many instances, an end table was used for display surface near the entrance. Typically there was also one table (nightstand) located near the head of the bed.	3 — 45 end tables were observed in the 16 living rooms. End tables adjacent to the sofa typically had a lamp on them as well as display objects and family photographs. Tables were also located near the windows to set plants on. 1* — In 8 of 10 observed bedrooms, a total of 10 end tables (night-stands) were located at the head of the bed(s).
TV 20x32 *typically a large portable set sitting on a movable TV stand or on an end table*	1 — Every unit had at least one TV. Three residents had two TVs and two residents had three TVs.	1 — 17 TV sets were found in 16 living rooms and another three were present in 10 observed bedrooms.

FURNITURE	EFFICIENCY UNITS	ONE BEDROOM UNITS
china cabinet, shelving, or desk	1 64 per cent (25/39) of the efficiency units had at least one of these large storage/display pieces of furniture.	1 75 per cent (12/16) of the one bedroom units had at least one of these storage/display pieces. Any one of these three pieces should be accommodated in a living room.
china cabinet *cc* 18x42 *a large, often glass front unit for the display and storage of dishes, glassware, and related items*	China cabinets were observed in approximately one-fifth (7/39) of the units. Although it was a piece that did not show up frequently, for a few residents it was very important. Approximately one-fourth of the interviewed residents (7/31) gave away a china cabinet when they moved into their unit and many would have kept it if there had been room for it.	50 per cent (8/16) of the units were furnished with a china cabinet. With two persons (especially a married couple) sharing a unit, dining appeared to retain more importance and formality on a daily basis than in an efficiency where the incidence of snacking and quick meals increased.
shelving *s* 14x30 *open shelves including bookcases and large plant shelves/stands*	Some form of shelving was found in almost half (19/39) of the units. More than one shelving unit was found in nine units.	Of five shelving units found in these units, four were in the living room while one was found in the bedroom. Typical objects on shelves included plants, family photos, and knick-knacks.
desk *d* 20x42	10 per cent (4/39) of the units had a desk.	Three desks were observed: two in the living room and one in the bedroom.

FURNITURE	EFFICIENCY UNITS	ONE BEDROOM UNITS
vanity, lo bureau, or hi bureau	**2** A total of 70 bureaus (vanity, lo, and hi) were present in these 39 units. Almost half (19/39) of the units had at least two of these pieces. They were typically located near the sleeping area and used for clothes storage.	**2*** 80 per cent (8/10) of the bedrooms were furnished with at least two bureaus. A total of 22 pieces were observed in 10 bedrooms: 12 lo bureaus, seven hi bureaus, and three vanities. An average bedroom space should accommodate a lo and hi bureau.
vanity ▭ *18x48* *low bureau with a large mirror which limits its placement against windows*	A total of 21 vanities were observed in the sleeping areas of these 39 units. Women were more likely to have this piece of furniture than men (20/30 females with vanities vs. 1/7 men with this same piece of furniture).	Only three vanities were observed in these units and they were all in the bedroom.
lo bureau ▭ B₁₀ *20x42* *storage unit (32" or shorter) with drawers/doors; includes cedar chests*	27 lo bureaus were observed in 21 of the 39 units. They were equally distributed between the living and sleeping areas.	**1** Of the 24 lo bureaus present in 11 of the 16 units, half were located in the living room and half in the bedroom. Several residents had as many as four or five of these bureaus.
hi bureau ▭ Bₕᵢ *18x42* *storage unit taller than 32" with drawers/doors*	22 hi bureaus were present in 47 per cent (18/39) of the units. Although some of these bureaus were observed in the living area, they were more frequently (16/22) located in the sleeping area.	Seven hi bureaus were found in 10 bedrooms and another two were found in 16 living rooms.

FURNITURE	EFFICIENCY UNITS		ONE BEDROOM UNITS	
beds 39x82 54x82	1	92 per cent (36/39) of the units had a single/twin bed. The majority (15/24) of interviewed residents in these units, however, gave away double beds when they moved in and purchased single beds for the small sleeping alcoves. They indicated a desire for a larger sleeping area that would accommodate a double bed.	2*	Six sets of twin beds were found in 10 bedrooms. Another three bedrooms were furnished with double beds and one widow had a single bed. Two people (married couples, mothers and daughters, sisters, etc.) living in a one bedroom apartment were more likely to have two twin beds than a single double bed.
floor lamp, TV tray, step stool, or plant stand	1	In addition to the above major pieces of furniture, there were other, sometimes smaller pieces found around the unit including 18 floor lamps and 12 TV trays. Six of the residents had step stools, typically in the kitchen, which they used for reaching high shelves. And although plants could be found on almost all surfaces in the units, eleven large plant stands were also observed. Any one of these pieces could be found in an average apartment	1	At least one floor lamp was observed in 9 of the 16 living rooms (an additional one was found in a bedroom). Three step stools, four TV trays, and four plant stands were also observed. Although any one of these items could be found in a one bedroom unit, the most likely item is the floor lamp.
			17 6*	general living area in bedroom
TOTAL	19		23	

AVERAGE FURNISHINGS

Efficiency Unit

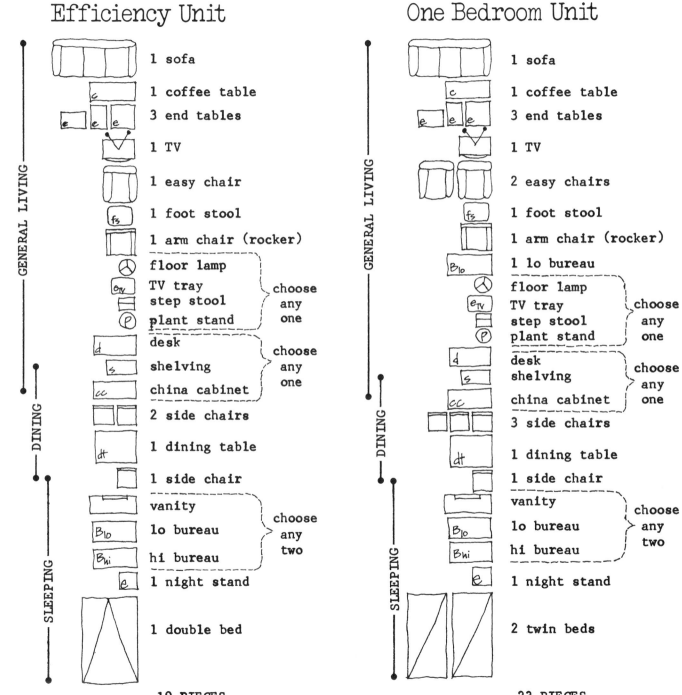

GENERAL LIVING

1 sofa
1 coffee table
3 end tables
1 TV
1 easy chair
1 foot stool
1 arm chair (rocker)

floor lamp
TV tray
step stool
plant stand
} choose any one

DINING

desk
shelving
china cabinet
} choose any one

2 side chairs
1 dining table
1 side chair

SLEEPING

vanity
lo bureau
hi bureau
} choose any two

1 night stand
1 double bed

19 PIECES

One Bedroom Unit

GENERAL LIVING

1 sofa
1 coffee table
3 end tables
1 TV
2 easy chairs
1 foot stool
1 arm chair (rocker)
1 lo bureau

floor lamp
TV tray
step stool
plant stand
} choose any one

DINING

desk
shelving
china cabinet
} choose any one

3 side chairs
1 dining table
1 side chair

SLEEPING

vanity
lo bureau
hi bureau
} choose any two

1 night stand
2 twin beds

23 PIECES

Scale: 1/8" = 1'

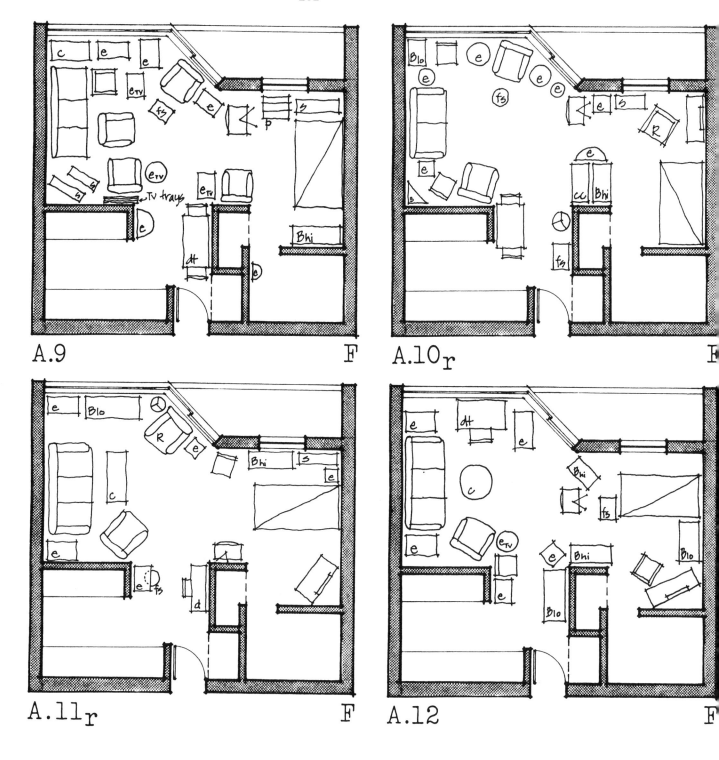

A.9   F

A.10r   F

A.11r   F

A.12   F

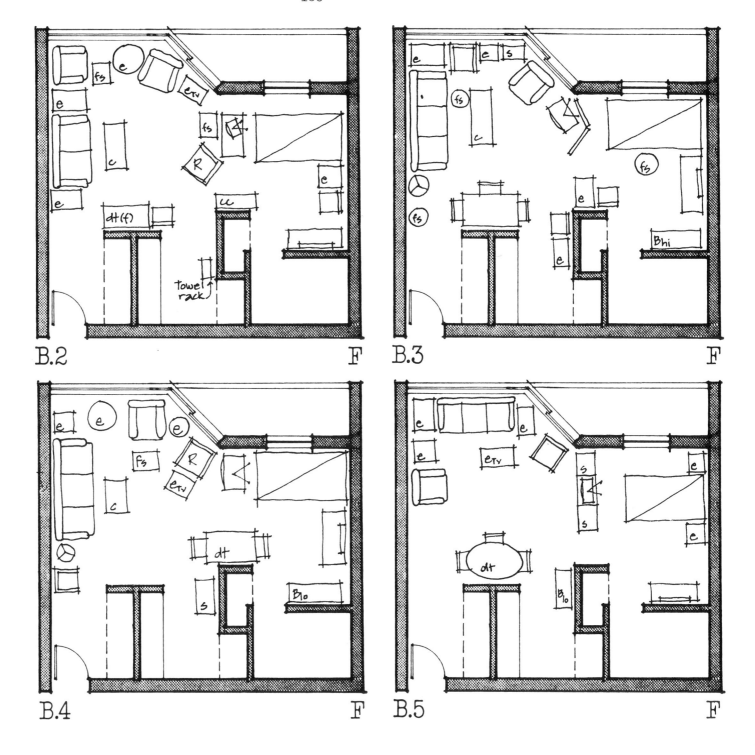

B.2   F

B.3   F

B.4   F

B.5   F

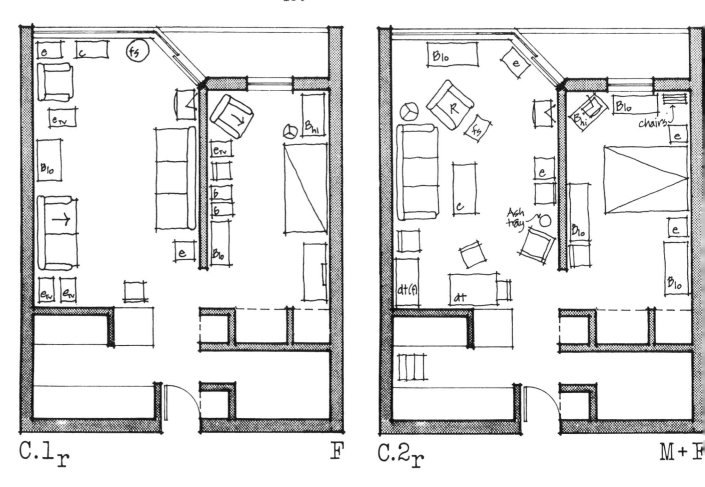

C.1r   F   C.2r   M + F

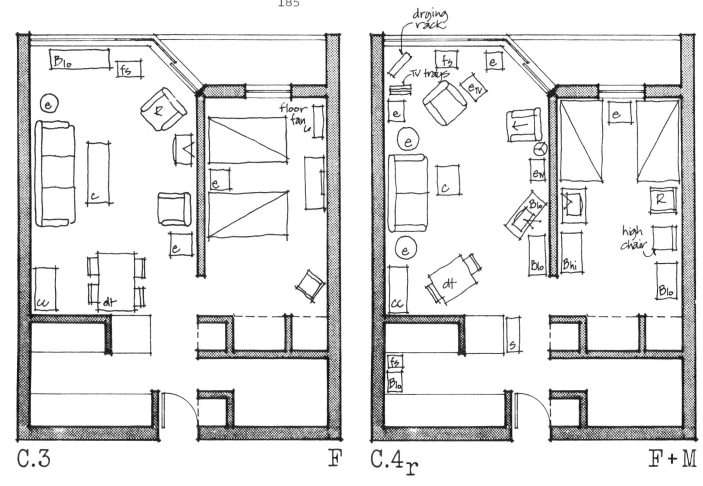

C.3   F

C.4_r   F + M

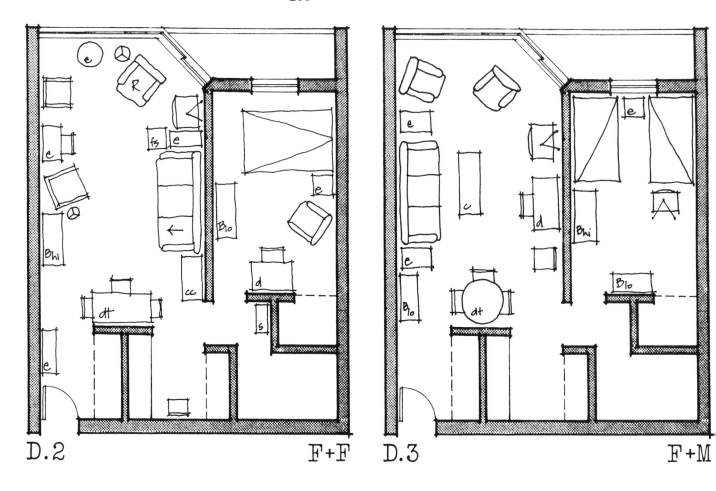

D.2   F+F   D.3   F+M

PATTERNS OF USE

As a result of the detailed analysis of furnishings and activities within the studied units, patterns of use of the standard units, by this age group, began to emerge. Consistencies in furniture type, placement of furniture pieces in relationship to other pieces and to design features, such as windows and walls, began to surface.

General adequacy of the units. In response to an opening question on the size of the apartment unit, 72 percent (21/29) of the interviewed residents stated that it suited their needs "just fine." The remaining 28 percent thought the unit was too small. (There was no difference in responses to this question between residents in the one bedroom units and those occupying the efficiencies.) Further exploration of this general level of satisfaction, however, indicated that residents had made many accommodations to their new, typically smaller apartments. For example, more than 200 pieces of furniture were given away by residents in 31 of the sampled units when they moved in. Although many of these residents wanted to get rid of their old and worn furniture and replace it with pieces more

appropriate for a "new home," several mentioned they would have liked to have kept some of these items if there had been more space in the unit. Over 100 new pieces of furniture were acquired but these were typically smaller versions of larger pieces that would not all fit in the new apartment. Two-thirds of the interviewed residents (21/31) said that they never re-arranged their furniture because "nothing else can be done in such a small space."

Such information about the inability of the apartment to accommodate desired furnishings as well as other indicators of changes in activity patterns, particularly in entertaining, suggest conflicts between resident lifestyles and several design features of the apartment units. These conflicts and patterns in the definition of activity settings are presented in the following section. Due to the differences in square footage and number of occupants, the 39 efficiencies and 16 one bedroom units are analyzed separately.

Efficiency Units

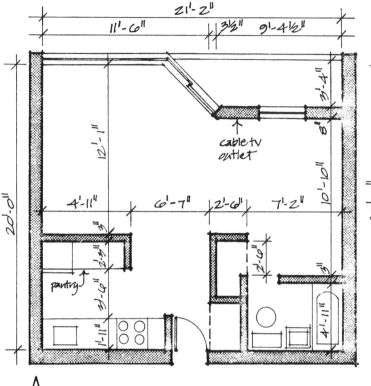

A

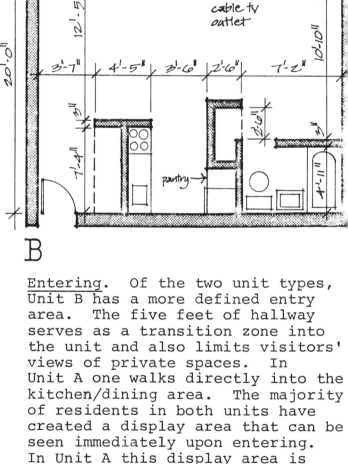

B

Unit B: Displays in unit entry

Of the 39 sampled efficiency units, 22 have center entrances (Unit A) and 17 have side entrances (Unit B). There was no difference between these two efficiency types in terms of the amount of furnishings observed in each (both averaged 19 pieces). However, because of the difference in entrance location which creates different circulation patterns, the placement of these furnishings did vary between unit type. The capabilities of Units A and B to accommodate various activities are discussed in the following sections.

Entering. Of the two unit types, Unit B has a more defined entry area. The five feet of hallway serves as a transition zone into the unit and also limits visitors' views of private spaces. In Unit A one walks directly into the kitchen/dining area. The majority of residents in both units have created a display area that can be seen immediately upon entering. In Unit A this display area is typically along the short wall at the kitchen edge, while residents in Unit B have placed tables and shelves covered with photographs, knick-knacks and other memorabilia in the already narrow entrance hallway. Several chairs were also observed in this hallway which are used by residents for setting packages on when returning from shopping trips. When interviewed about the entrance location, 15 per cent (2/13) of the residents in Unit A complained about seeing the kitchen upon entering while none of the residents in Unit B minded going through the living room to get to the kitchen when coming home with groceries.

Leisure activities. The majority of daily activities like TV watching, hobbies, reading and watching outdoor activities take place in the living area. The typical furniture layout in both units includes placement of the sofa along the long wall surrounded by end and coffee tables, an easy chair against the window, and a TV opposite the sofa at a distance of 10 to 12 feet. The consistent placement of the sofa against the longest wall may be related to several factors:

(1) the long wall allows for a more formal arrangement of end tables on both sides of the sofa (table lamps are typically placed on these end tables)

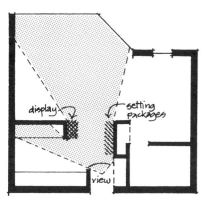

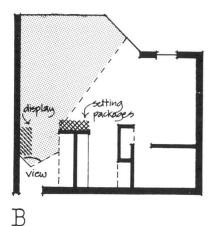

Views from unit entrances

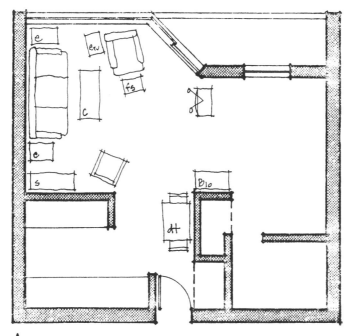

A Typical living area arrangement

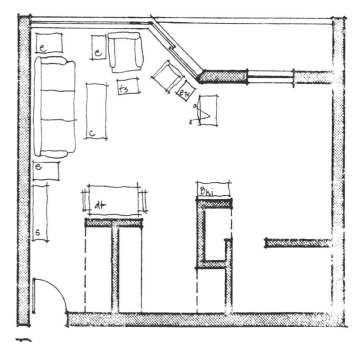

B Typical living area arrangement

(2) this sitting location permits views of both the outdoors and other parts of the unit, including the entrance

(3) sofa placement against the window is discouraged by cold drafts from the windows, location of the baseboard electric heating unit along the exterior wall (residents mentioned not wanting to place large furniture pieces in front of this heating source), and lack of a view to the outdoors for visual release.

Unit A: Resident's furnishing of living area

The television set is typically located near the exterior wall between the sliding balcony doors and the window in the sleeping area. (Although this is the location of the cable TV outlet, it does not necessarily prohibit the placement of the television set in other areas of the unit.) From this location, the TV is directly in front of the sofa (75 percent of the television sets are found in the central 60° angle of vision with respect to the sofa). As most of these sets are portable and rest on a TV stand or an end table, they can be easily turned around and viewed from the bed. Glare was a frequently mentioned problem which kept many residents from placing their set against the windows.

When questioned about "favorite" pieces of furniture, most residents responded with the easy chair. Here they spent long hours watching television, reading, or talking with friends. Their criteria for the location of this "favorite" piece were (1) within viewing distance of the TV; and next to the window for (2) visual release and (3) natural lighting for daytime reading or sewing. Footstools are typically found in front of or near the easy chair.

Due to circulation patterns, Unit A can accommodate a more *enclosed* arrangement of living area furniture than Unit B. In Unit A the furniture is arranged against three walls while only two walls are available in Unit B. Although the same amount of furniture is found in both settings, the arrangement in Unit A provides more seating options with views as well as a more comfortable area for group conversation.

Although these housing sites have a communal library area with a collection of reading materials, residents who borrow these books and magazines usually return to their unit so that they can sit in a comfortable, familiar chair with adequate lighting and read without distractions.

Several of the residents have hobbies that they pursue in their apartments. Many of the women engage in such handicrafts as sewing, knitting, and crocheting. One elderly man makes paper bead necklaces and another sews and stuffs toy animals. In all cases, pieces of furniture in the living area are specially arranged for each hobby. Almost all hobbies require a layout space such as a centrally located table, tables lined up against a wall, or chairs and sofas arranged in such a way as to create a work surface. These residents also mentioned a concern for adequate lighting and many locate their work area and equipment near the windows to take advantage of the natural light.

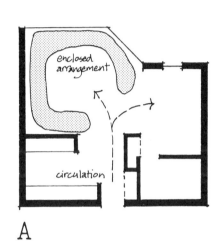

A

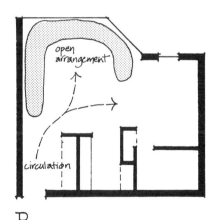

B

Arrangement of living area furniture

The telephone outlet in these efficiencies is centrally located on the closet wall between the living and sleeping areas. This is a convenient location for all areas in the apartment, including the sleeping area. Several residents furnished this wall with a desk or telephone stand and a chair to create a comfortable setting for both telephone conversation and letter writing.

Several, if not many, plants were observed in most of the efficiencies. These plants are most typically "displayed" in the living area near the windows on a series of odd-shaped tables of varying heights.

Eating. Although the efficiencies are large enough to accommodate a small eating area, the size and design of the perceived dining space has limited the continuation of a former dining style. Half (11/24) of the interviewed residents in these units gave away a dining table and chairs when they moved in. Of these residents who gave away a dining table, half kept a smaller, older one suggesting that their former lifestyles included two types of dining, one formal and one informal. The other half exchanged their old dining furniture for a new, smaller "kitchenette" set indicating perhaps that the dining space was perceived as too small to accommodate previously owned furniture. A survey of table dimensions shows that dining tables brought to the new apartment from former situations measured, on an average, 36 inches by 46 inches while newly purchased dinette sets averaged 27 inches by 40 inches.

For many of the residents, particularly the women, an important part of the dining set is the china cabinet which is used for storage as well as display. Three of the women specifically mentioned that they would like to have kept this piece of furniture if there had been space for it in the apartment. Seven other women did bring this large piece of furniture with them and found space for it either against a wall (typically near the dining table) or created another "wall" with it between the living and sleeping areas.

Although there is some variation in the location of the dining table in the efficiencies, most are located near the kitchens. In Unit A, 70 percent (16/23) of the tables are placed in the small area adjacent to the kitchen: 9 tables are against the longest wall while 7 are located next to the short wall. The next most popular location is against the windows. Two tables are located in the middle of the living area: one is a round dining set while the other is a banquette, both of which are difficult to place against a wall. In Unit B, more than 80 percent (14/17) of the tables are located against the wall immediately outside the kitchen. An additional two tables are placed against the windows.

There is greater variation in the location of the dining area in Unit A than in Unit B. Although this could imply that there are more options available to residents in Unit A for dining areas, it appears that it is the inadequacy of the eating area near the kitchen rather than the appropriateness of other areas in the unit for dining that might account for the variability. For example, the larger tables in Unit A are typically found in the living area, suggesting that they cannot easily be accommodated next to the kitchen. In Unit B, both large and small tables are found along the wall closest to

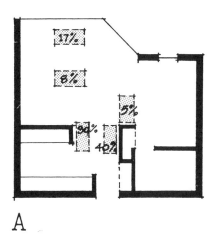

A

B

Percentage location of dining table

Unit B

the kitchen. Secondly, there is a greater tendency in Unit A to locate tables close to the windows suggesting a desire to be near natural light. In Unit B where the typical dining area is four feet closer to the windows than in Unit A, this is not as evident. In addition, more chairs are found around the typical dining table location in Unit B than in Unit A indicating the greater inability of Unit A to accommodate a complete dining set.

When interviewed about their preference for eating arrangements, 68 percent (15/22) of the residents in both units said they liked their present arrangement while 23 percent (5/22) expressed a desire for an eat-in kitchen and 9 percent (2/22) would prefer a separate dining room. These figures should be used cautiously, however, as research has shown that there is a tendency for people to

prefer their present, real environment over other options they are not familiar with. In the MIT National Study, two-thirds of 196 elderly respondents indicated that they ate in their kitchens. Of the third who never did, the majority indicated a desire for an eat-in kitchen but found their present kitchen too small for such an arrangement. There was some evidence in photographs of the Cambridge kitchen areas that residents ate some of their meals at the kitchen counter while sitting on a step stool or high chair.

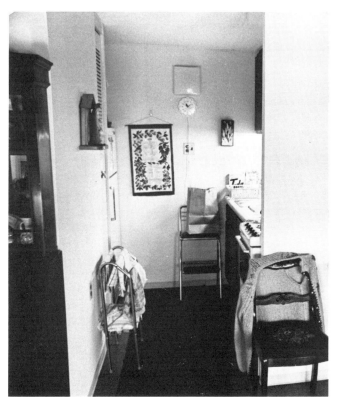

Unit B

In the 1974 National Study, 63 per cent of the interviewed residents indicated that they were visited by at least one on-site friend during the previous week. During this same time period, 53 per cent said they visited at least one friend in the project.

Visiting. Of the 24 interviewed residents who live in efficiencies, only one said she does not have any visitors in her apartment. The frequency of visitors varies:

FREQUENCY	NUMBER OF RESIDENTS	PERCENTAGE
Every day	3	13
Several times a week	2	8
Once a week	5	21
Several times a month	2	8
Infrequently	11	46
Never	1	4
TOTAL	24	100

Anywhere from one to ten visitors are entertained on an occasion with the average being four to five guests. These visitors are typically relatives.

Many of the residents mentioned having difficulties in accommodating groups of this size in their small unit, particularly if it involves serving a meal. Their response to this problem varies: a few have decided not to have people over for dinner at all; one women who cannot entertain her large family at one gathering has elected to have them over in smaller groups; and another solves her shortage of space problem by having her family sit on a quilt on the floor around a large ottoman that is adapted to a "buffet table." Approximately one third of the residents have extra furniture they set up for entertaining which includes TV trays, folding tables and chairs, and leaves of dining tables. Dining tables are typically pulled away from the wall and chairs are up around it. This presents some difficulty in Unit A where the

Foldaway bed stored in bathroom.

standard dining area is limited in floor space.

Several of the residents also mentioned having overnight guests in their unit, the most frequent being grandchildren. With inadequate floor space and storage area for a foldaway bed, many resort to the use of sleeping bags. In several instances where this is not a satisfactory arrangement, the grandchildren no longer spend the night with their grandparent.

Sleeping and dressing. With the exception of one woman who sleeps on a fold-out couch in the living area, all residents sleep at night on a bed (typically a twin) in the sleeping alcove. Some occasionally nap during the day on the sofa or in an easy chair. A total of 20 beds were given away by the 24 residents in the efficiencies, of which approximately 75 percent were double beds. Many wanted to keep their larger beds but did not think the sleeping alcove could accommodate this size. A total of 12 new beds were purchased (11 twins and one double). These figures suggest many of the residents had more than one bed in their former living situation.

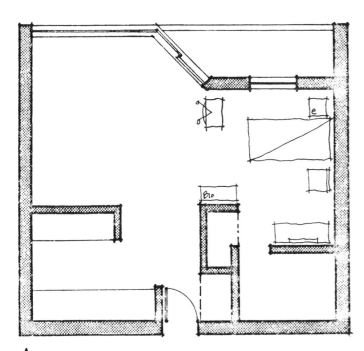

A *Typical sleeping area arrangement*

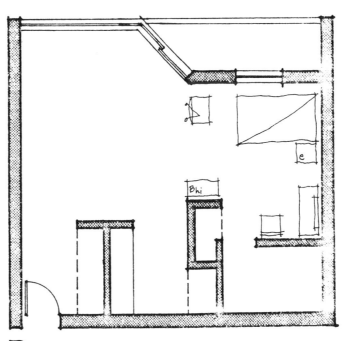

B *Typical sleeping area arrangement*

Data from the MIT National Study also indicated that one of the pieces of furniture most frequently discarded at the time of the move was the double bed because it was too large for the apartment unit. It appears that most single older people have a double bed which they would like to keep with them.

In both units the beds are typically located perpendicular to the long wall and near the window. The majority are placed

Unit B: Screen blocks view of bed

in such a way that they can be accessed from three sides. A nightstand is usually present at the head of the bed for lamps, clocks, and medications.

Many of the female residents dislike the *openness* of the sleeping alcove to the living area. They would prefer the privacy of a separate bedroom. In an attempt to gain more *visual privacy*, several residents have placed large pieces of furniture which act as barriers between the living area and sleeping alcove. These pieces of furniture include tall bureaus, bookcases, china cabinets, and wooden screens. One resident is even considering constructing a wall of concrete blocks.

There is a greater tendency for residents in Unit B to construct high visual barriers (taller than 40") than in Unit A. In Unit A,

Unit B: Resident uses china cabinet to provide privacy in the sleeping area

only 18 percent (4/22) of the residents have tall pieces of furniture separating the sleeping alcove from the living area while 35 percent (6/17) of the residents in Unit B have tall visual barriers. This might be attributed to the differences in entrance location: In entering Unit A, one's visual attention is directed to the living area and not the sleeping alcove. In addition, the circulation path into the unit further separates these two areas. In Unit B, however, there is less definition between the living area and sleeping alcove. When one turns the corner from the entrance hallway, both of these areas are in full view and one's attention is actually directed toward the sleeping alcove. As a result, there is some tendency to read the alcove as an extension of the living area rather than as a separate space. This implicit breach of privacy could account for twice the frequency of high barriers in Unit B.

Bedroom bureaus are typically placed near the closet and bathroom to create a small dressing area. A chair is also included in this area which residents use to sit on or to set clothing on while dressing. Substantial floor area is available in front of the dresser to gain access to the drawers.

A total of 14 bureaus were given away by the 24 interviewed residents. Nine of these bureaus would have been kept if there had been space in the unit. Those residents who have two bureaus keep one in the living area because the sleeping alcove cannot easily accommodate two.

Going outdoors. The majority of the interviewed residents in efficiency units said that they use

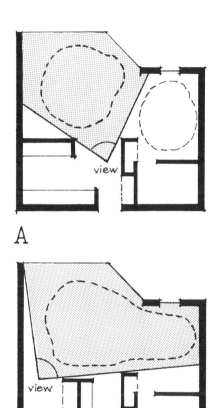

A

B

Direction of visual attention in units

their balcony to sit and enjoy the view, read, sew, talk, etc.

Reported Balcony Use	Number of Residents	Percentage
Often	38	56
Sometimes	14	21
Rarely	7	10
Never	9	13
TOTAL	68	100%

Those who said they rarely or never use their balconies cited several reasons: residents in wheelchairs cannot get over the 2 inch threshold or turn around in the small area (balcony width is 3 feet); some residents cannot tolerate the hot summer sun (their balconies typically have south and west orientation and only a shallow overhang); other residents have no desire to use this area for anything but storage.

Residents were also asked if they would prefer other unit amenities (i.e. larger rooms or a separate bedroom) to their balcony. Almost half (33/69) said they would trade their balcony for another space, the majority (29/33) wanting a separate bedroom. Two would prefer a larger kitchen; one would like a larger living area; and one resident would trade the balcony for a window in the kitchen.

Summary. These two efficiency types, Unit A and Unit B, are both furnished, on an average, with 19 pieces of furniture. This is substantially more furniture than the 13 pieces recommended by HUD Minimum Property Standards. In addition, much furniture was given away by residents when they moved into these units because it could not all be accommodated in the smaller living space.

In terms of activity settings, these efficiencies appear to provide adequate area and definition for daily activities like reading, watching TV, and plant tending. However, for such activities like sleeping, eating and entertaining, the units provide less satisfactory settings. Many of the residents, particularly the women, find the sleeping alcove lacking in visual privacy and would prefer a separate bedroom instead. The relatively small area for dining forced many of the residents to give up their larger dining sets and china cabinets in exchange for kitchenette sets. Entertaining groups of visitors numbering over three or four also presents problems for many of the residents due to lack of floor area. Overnight guests are difficult to accommodate.

A brief summary of the activity settings in Unit A and Unit B follows.

Unit A Summary

The circulation path and lines of vision created by the center entrance in Unit A serve to define two separate areas: the general living area and the sleeping alcove. Because the living area is defined by three walls, an enclosed and formal seating arrangement is possible which creates an appropriate setting for watching TV, looking outdoors, or entertaining visitors. The eating area, however, is quite small and very little floor area is available for serving groups of four or more around a dining table. Residents appear to treat the sleeping alcove as distinct from the living area. Although there is a general preference for a separate bedroom, particularly for the single female, very few high barriers have been erected to insure visual privacy to this area in Unit A.

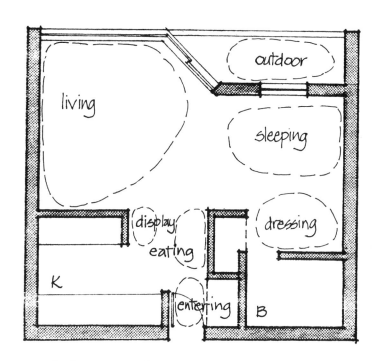

Activity settings

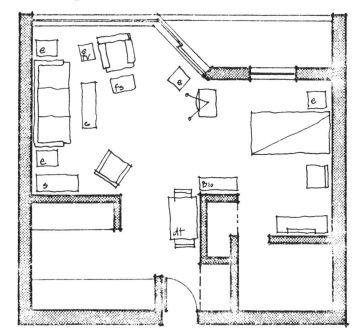

Typical furniture arrangement

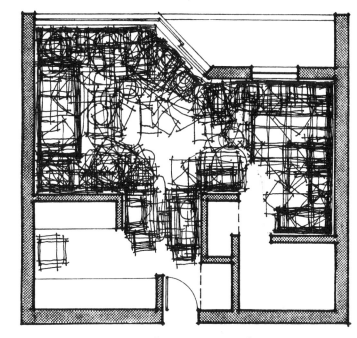

Aggregate furniture mappings of 22 units

Unit B
Summary

Although the entry area in Unit B is small and quite narrow, residents use it to display personal items. At the edge of this hallway, the main living area as well as the sleeping alcove are completely visible. Several of the residents have created high barriers with bureaus, china cabinets, and screens to visually separate the sleeping area from the rest of the unit. The living area is defined by only two walls creating a more open furniture arrangement. This appears to be less functional for conversing with several visitors. All residents use the same location for their dining area. This area (and wall) is large enough to accommodate larger sized tables and floor area is available to pull the table out away from the wall for entertaining large groups.

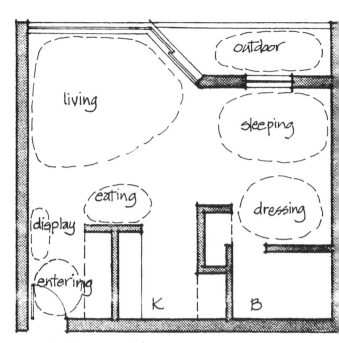

Activity settings

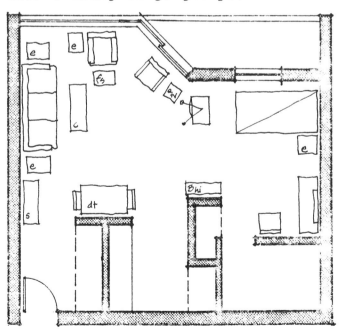

Typical furniture arrangement

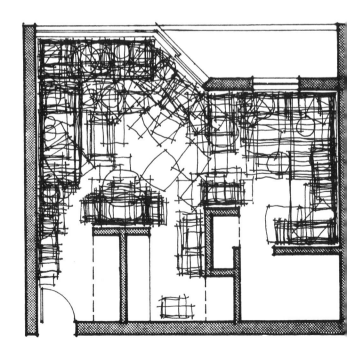

Aggregate furniture mappings of 19 units

One Bedroom Units

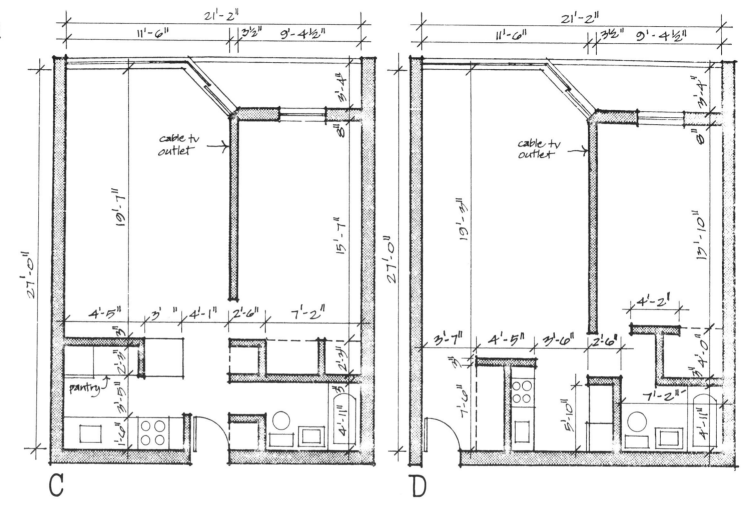

C

D

Of the 16 sampled one bedroom units, 9 have center entrances (Unit C) and 7 have side entrances (Unit D). In both unit types, an average of 23 furniture pieces was observed. Although the square footage is identical for these units, the difference in entrance location and circulation paths has led to variations in the location and definition of activity settings.

Entering. In Unit C there is no area inside the front door for a small display table or chair. In only one of these nine units is there a small shelf next to the open kitchen counter. Residents do, however, use this counter as a

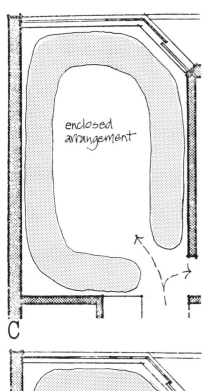

enclosed
arrangement

C

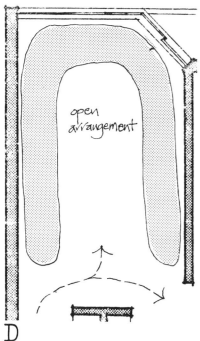

open
arrangement

D

*Arrangement of living
room furniture*

display area as it is immediately seen upon entering. In Unit D several residents have put small shelves and tables in the entrance hallway for the display of photographs and other personal objects.

Leisure activities. The living room is the setting for the majority of the daily activities. The furniture layout in these two unit types has many similarities: the sofa is located

against the longest wall with end tables on both sides and a coffee table in front; one easy chair is in the corner by the window and another is directly across from the sofa; there is an end table near the windows which is typically covered with various plants; the television set is also placed across from the sofa in the central 60° angle of vision (the cable connection is located along this interior wall). From this standard sofa location (there is only one

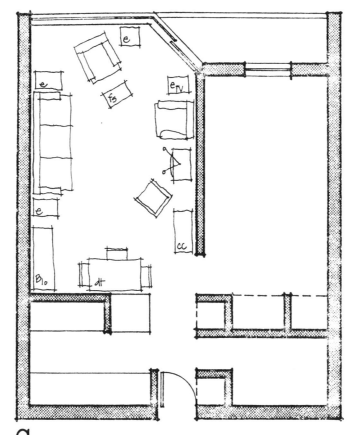

C *Typical furniture layout in living room*

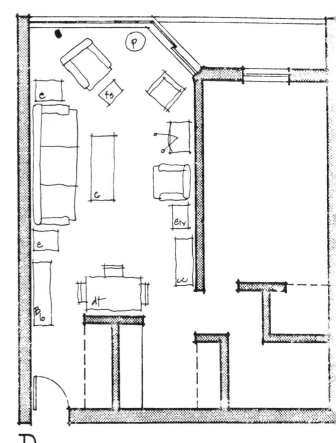

D *Typical furniture layout in living roo*

deviation from this location in each unit type), there are views of (1) the outdoors through the sliding glass doors to the balcony; (2) the TV set; and (3) the focal point of circulation between all rooms including the entrance. The one piece of furniture that does vary in placement between unit types is the arm chair. In Unit C it is typically located at the end of the room nearest the kitchen creating almost complete closure of the living room furniture. In

Unit C, center entrance

Unit D, however, this chair is placed along the wall opposite the sofa and a horseshoe configuration is formed by the furniture. The end toward the kitchen is open as this area is used for circulation.

As is the case in the efficiencies, the most frequently mentioned "favorite" piece of furniture is the easy chair. It is found in essentially the same location between the sofa and the windows. This chair is used most frequently by the husband for watching TV, reading, talking, and relaxing. From this position residents can view the outdoors, the TV, or the rest of the unit.

In these units TV watching also occurs in the bedrooms. There is an additional TV set in four of eleven observed bedrooms. These sets are typically found at the foot of the beds.

Unit D, side entrance

Many of the hobbies require good natural lighting conditions

living room, the wife might be busy in the kitchen or both might be watching TV in different rooms One of the occupants sometimes leaves the unit to spend time in other parts of the building or to run errands off site. Whether this is a function of a small living space for two people (several did mention this fact) or whether it is the continuation of a previously established pattern should be further investigated.

Eating. More than half of the interviewed residents gave away a dining set when they moved into their one bedroom apartments. The majority replace their older sets with new smaller ones while some had two sets and kept only one. This suggests, as in the efficiencies, that residents are adapting their dining needs to a much smaller setting. In general, however, the tables that are in the one bedroom apartments are larger than those in the efficiencies and are furnished with more chair around them.

One area in each of the unit type is consistently perceived as the dining space. This area is against the wall immediately outside of the kitchen. Those table that are not placed directly against the wall are typically round and have a full complement of chairs (4) around them. All o

Plants, which are most frequently the hobby of the wife, are found throughout the unit but the majority are located near the windows in the living room on plant stands and end tables.

It was discovered in the course of interviewing residents in the one bedroom units that during an average day the two occupants do not spend much time in the unit or in the same room together. When the husband is watching TV in the

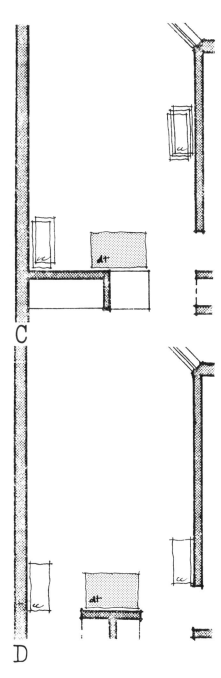

*China cabinet locations
relative to dining table*

the residents in Unit D have dining tables but one-third of the residents in Unit C have no table. These residents say they eat on TV trays in the living room. This percentage having no dining table plus the typical off-center location of the existing tables in Unit C suggests that some of the residents do not view the outer kitchen wall as a continuous surface from wall to outside counter edge. They rather see it as two surfaces--a half wall and a full wall--and do not center the table between the two. The dining table is more typically found at the end near the counter. Several residents suggested either removing this counter or taking out the cupboards underneath so chairs could be slid under it to use as an eating surface.

Half of the residents in the one bedroom units have china cabinets. This is a much more frequent occurrence in these units than in the efficiencies which might indicate that married couples place greater importance on formal dining patterns and the retention of a previous lifestyle than do single residents. In addition, there is more space in these units to accommodate such a large piece of furniture. These cabinets are placed close to the dining table and, although functional, are also major display pieces in the living room.

Kitchen wall/counter phenomenon.

When asked about preferences for eating arrangements, three residents said they like their present arrangement, two would like an eat-in kitchen, and another would prefer a separate dining room.

Visiting. On an average, residents who share a one bedroom unit entertain less frequently than the single residents in efficiencies. Those interviewed said they have visitors no more often than once a week and the majority entertain several times a month or infrequently. Anywhere from one to eight persons are entertained on these occasions. Additional furniture is typically brought out of storage for these visitors and includes card tables, folding chairs, and TV tables.

Residents find overnight guests difficult to accommodate in one bedroom units. The guests typically sleep in the living room on a couch, fold-out sofa, or on day-beds (residents complain about inadequate storage space for these large items). Two sisters sharing one apartment expressed a desire for doors or some other means of closing off the living room so their overnight guests could have more privacy.

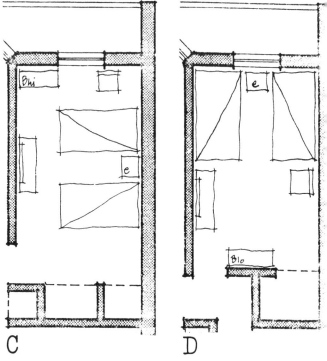

Typical bedroom arrangement

Unit D

<u>Sleeping and dressing.</u> In eleven furnished bedrooms, there are six sets of twin beds, four double beds, and a single twin bed (this belongs to a recent widow). With the exception of this single twin bed, all other beds are placed with the head against a wall. There appears to be no preferred location of these beds as they are equally distributed against the left, right, and window walls at the far end of the room. This suggests that the bedroom size and layout can accommodate several alternative arrangements for these

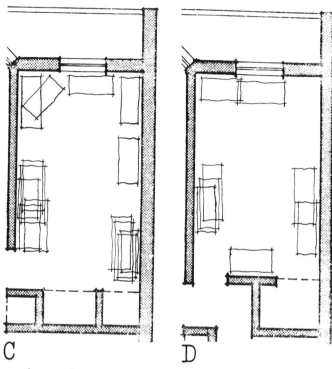

Bedroom bureau and vanity mapping

sickness of one spouse, difference in sleeping habits between two occupants, and privacy for non-married occupants such as sisters, mother and daughter or mother and son. In one unit shared by a mother and daughter, the mother sleeps and dresses in the bedroom while the daughter sleeps on a fold-out couch in the living room where her dresser is also located.

An average of two bureaus is found in each bedroom. These are typically placed against walls near the closet. Also included as part of this *dressing area* is a chair for sitting on or setting clothes on. In almost all cases, a substantial amount of circulation space has been left in front of the bureaus so they can be easily accessed. In two instances the bureau is located against the

large furniture pieces. Eight of the eleven bed arrangements are accessible from three sides for ease in making the bed as well as in getting in and out of it without disturbing the other occupant. A nightstand is typically placed between the twin beds or adjacent to the head of the double bed. In no instance is a bed located directly under the window.

Several residents expressed a desire for a second bedroom. Situations that might call for separate bedrooms include the

Little space is left between beds and bureau

sitting & watching	
reading	
sewing & knitting	
listening to radio	
talking	
eating & drinking	
gardening	
sleeping	
watching tv	
writing	
sunning	
drying laundry, storage	

Relative distribution of reported balcony activities.

wall at the foot of the beds. As the room is only 10 feet wide, very little space is left between the beds and the bureau which can only be accessed while standing between the two beds.

Going outdoors. As is the case in the efficiency units, approximately four-fifths of the residents in one bedroom units said they use their balconies. The major activities engaged in in this outdoor space are sitting and watching, and reading.

Only one-fifth of these residents (6/29) said they would trade their balcony for another amenity in unit design. Of those six who would trade, three want a larger kitchen, two a second bedroom, and one would prefer a larger bedroom. And then there is one wife who emphatically stated: "I would trade my living room space for a larger balcony but it should be wider so I can use it as a yard for plants. I love that balcony —I sleep out there at night. I even asked to live on the top (12th) floor so we would be away from the noisy traffic." Systematic studies of actual balcony use have not been conducted.

Summary. On an average, 23 pieces of furniture are found in both the center and side entrance unit types. Six of these pieces are found in the bedroom. Several of the residents in the 16 sampled units mentioned a need for a second bedroom: relatives (mother and daughter, two sisters) living together want separate bedrooms; some married couples need a second bedroom if one person is sick; and others would like an area for overnight guests. The dining area in these units is larger and more formal in its arrangement than that found in the efficiencies. The dining tables are larger, more chairs are found at the tables, and there is a greater tendency for a china cabinet to be present. Brief summaries of the activity settings in Unit C and Unit D follow.

Unit C Summary

In this center entrance one bedroom unit, the kitchen counter is used as a display area as it is visible from both the entry and the living room. The dining table, when there is one, is located against this counter wall. Several of the residents in this unit type do not have a dining table; they eat at TV trays in the living area instead. There are 3 1/2 walls available for furnishing in the living room which permits a more enclosed arrangement for entertaining. The closet door locations in the bedroom limit the available wall area at that end of the room. As a result, one bureau is typically placed at the foot of the beds (difficult to access) and the other bureau is found near the window.

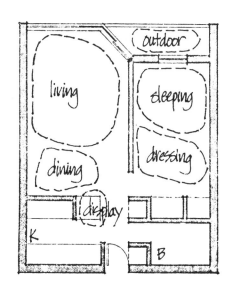

Activity settings

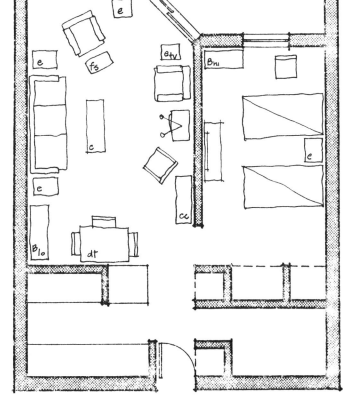

Typical furniture arrangement

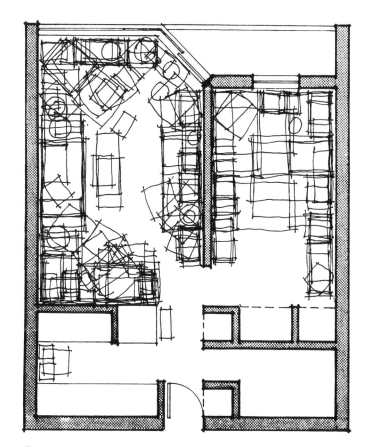

Aggregate furniture mappings of 9 units

Unit D Summary

The side entrance in Unit D creates a small hallway which is used for display. The furniture in the living room is arranged in a U-shaped configuration and is open at one end where the major circulation path is. All of the dining tables in this unit are located against the closet/kitchen wall and china cabinets are placed against the walls to either side. As there is more wall space available near the closet in this unit type, there is a greater tendency to put the two bureaus at this end of the room to create a dressing area.

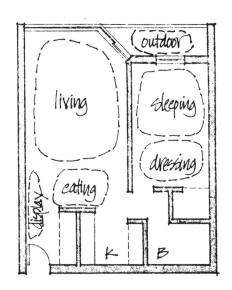

Activity settings

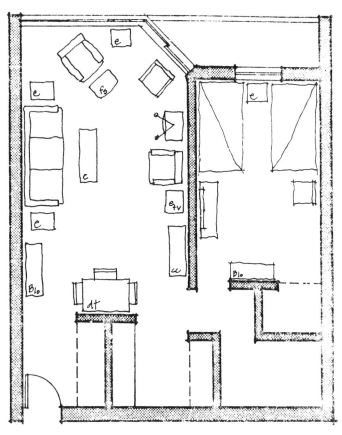

Typical furniture arrangement

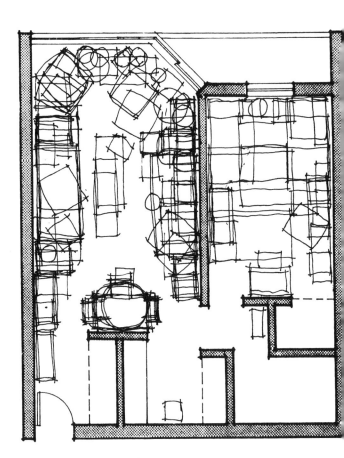

Aggregate furniture mappings of 7 units

Summary of Unit Studies

The study of the 55 Cambridge units illustrates that there are basic similarities in the activities and furnishings of residents in subsidized housing for the elderly. The use patterns are not unique to a particular geographic area but are characteristic of other regions, as evidenced in the photographs and comments from a national sample of older residents. Although the amount of time devoted to a particular activity and the time of day it occurs may vary from one resident to the next, all residents engage in the same basic activities of eating, sleeping, dressing, visiting, watching TV, reading, etc.

For most older persons, the move into these subsidized units, which are typically smaller in size than previous residences, requires some lifestyle alterations. Typical of changes precipitated by a smaller living space include the following:

- Many furniture pieces are discarded, some reluctantly if they have functional importance or sentimental value.

- Entertaining, particularly when it involves meal preparation or overnight guests, is a problem because of inadequate floor area and storage space.

- On an average day two occupants do not spend much time together in the same space. They are either in different rooms engaging in different activities or one leaves the unit to go elsewhere.

- There is no rearranging of major furniture pieces after the move as residents seldom perceive other alternatives in their restricted living space.

Within the single occupancy units, there are differences in furnishability patterns of men and women. In general, the elderly women have more furniture, are more attached to it, and are more critical of their private environment than are the single men. The single women also have a more expressed need for visual privacy in the sleeping area and find the efficiency unit an unacceptable living arrangement while the men often prefer its convenience and simplicity.

There are also patterns in the type, amount, and placement of furniture pieces that support the various activities within the home. Most importantly, *furniture is not "floated" in space* (as many architectural floor plans would indicate) *but is typically backed up against a wall*. In other words, residents rely more on walls as defining edges of an activity setting than on furniture placement. Other major furniture patterns follow:

Typical Furniture Arrangements

Living Area

- a sofa, flanked by two end tables and a coffee table, is placed against a wall preferably perpendicular to a window wall for views

- TV against opposite wall becomes a focal point (the majority of all TVs are placed in the central 60° angle of vision relative to the sofa)

- the "favorite" easy chair is at the window end of the sofa with views of the TV, outdoors, rest of unit, and natural light

- furniture pieces are arranged in a closed, cul-de-sac setting for visiting in groups

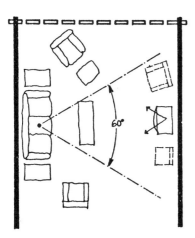

Dining Area

- for everyday use, table (30"x40") with two chairs is placed against a wall in or near the kitchen

- for entertaining, table is pulled away from wall, expanded with leaves, and chairs placed around it

- other chairs to dining set, when not in use, are dispersed throughout the unit

- china cabinet is nearby, against a wall, and typically in a visually prominent area

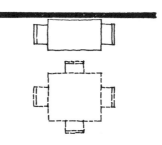

Sleeping Area

- typical furnishings include double beds for single residents and twin beds for married couples; hide-a-bed is not a viable alternative for everyday use

- a nightstand is located at the head of the double bed or between twin beds, which are always parallel to one another

- heads of beds are placed against a wall and not under a window to avoid drafts and permit views out of unit while in bed

- beds are placed so they are accessible from two sides and one end for bed-making and possible nurse care

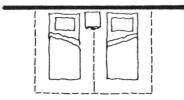

- two bureaus and a chair are often clustered together near the clothes closet to create a "dressing area"

- clearance space is needed in front of bureaus for pulling out drawers

- many of the bureaus are tall and cannot be placed under windows

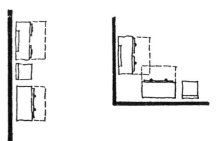

Visual Access

Within the apartment unit there are both public and private areas that should be respected not only in terms of physical access but also in terms of visibility. Views of the more private areas from the public areas should be avoided in order for the resident to maintain a sense of propriety and dignity in the home.

Doors should be located in such a way that the toilet is not visible from any part of the unit. Views into the sleeping area in an efficiency should be minimized by providing alcoves. Views into a bedroom from the entry area should be particularly avoided. Visual protection of the kitchen sink from the entry, eating and living areas should also be available. With consideration to careful door location, various levels of visual privacy can be provided without having to close doors.

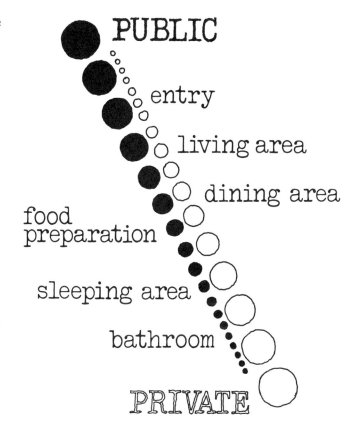

PUBLIC
entry
living area
dining area
food preparation
sleeping area
bathroom
PRIVATE

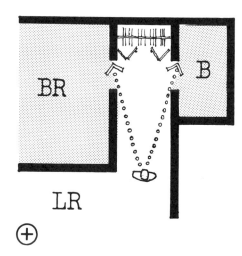

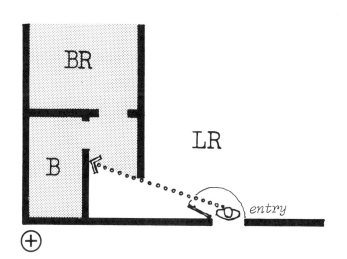

Room Proportions

The ratio of the length of a room to its width has an affect on how the particular pieces of furniture found in an activity setting are arranged in relation to each other.

The living and dining areas are focused and centralized activity settings. As a result, each is more easily accommodated in a squarish as opposed to rectangular area. In the study of living areas, the longer spaces tend to have a parallel arrangement of furniture (this is particularly true if one end of the space is a window wall) while the square areas tend to have more closed or circular furniture groupings.

Living and dining activities, which are somewhat compatible in terms of privacy levels, can be accommodated in the same room if each activity setting can define an area unto itself. This is more easily accomplished in a rectangular-shaped room than in a squarish room.

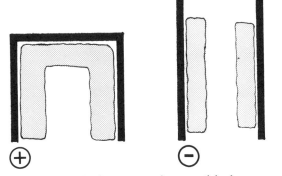

Single activity setting: living area

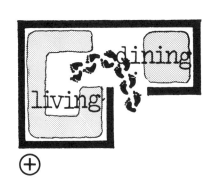

Two activity settings: living and dining

Room Dimensions

Living area. The dimensions of a room are strong determinants of its furnishability. For example, in the living area one wall should be at least 14 feet long to accommodate the standard arrangement of a sofa, two end tables, and one corner easy chair. The more walls that are at least this length, the greater the flexibility in furniture arrangement. The minimum width of the room should be 11 1/2 feet, based on furniture dimensions and access area. This approximates the recommended conversation distance of 10 feet measured from center points of sitting furniture. An additional 2 feet in width, for a total of 13.5 feet, is suggested as a miximum dimension for maintaining comfortable conversation and TV viewing distances.

Dining area. A wall in or near the kitchen should be at least 8 feet long for the table, chairs, and access ares, with another wall nearby to accommodate the 42 inch long china cabinet. Enough floor area should be available for seating 6 to 8 persons around a table.

Sleeping area. In the single occupancy sleeping area, one wall should be at least 9 feet long. For double occupancy, one wall should be a minimun of 11.5 feet in length to accommodate the standard furniture pieces and necessary access areas. Access to a closet area at either end of the room will require additional space. Minimum room widths are 10 feet if no bureaus are to be placed at the foot of the beds and 11.5+ feet if they are.

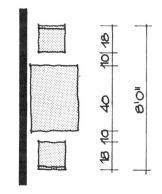

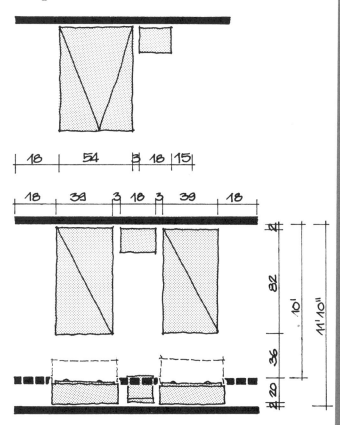

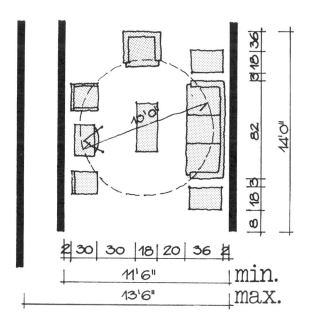

Walls
Corners
Niches

Walls. The preferred arrangement for all furniture, particularly the larger pieces, is against a wall. As a general rule, taking into consideration room dimensions and circulation routes, the more wall area available in a unit, the more furniture it will be able to accommodate.

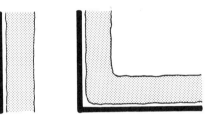    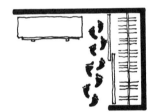

Corners. Corners are also important furnishable areas as they are out of the way of circulation. Right-angled corners are particularly furnishable as most furniture is rectilinear and easily is nestled along the two intersecting walls. Tables are frequently located in the 90° corners.

More furnishable   *Less furnishable*

Niches. Niches in walls (regardless of their depth or protrusion) read as breaks in a continuous surface. Furniture is typically placed on either side of the break and large pieces (sofas, dining tables, china cabinets, etc.) will not usually be placed in front of it.

Circulation and Doors

Circulation routes are defined by the placement of doors and the layout of activity areas. Those paths which lead directly through a single functional area such as the living room disrupt the setting by dividing it into two separate areas.

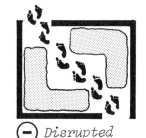 
Ⓞ *Disrupted*   ⊕ *Not disrupted*

Circulation routes can also be used to help define different activity settings located in one large room.

Furniture will typically be placed against all walls, even if it appears to be in the path of the most direct access route between activity settings.

   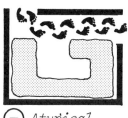
⊕ *Typical*   Ⓞ *Atypical*   ⊕ *Typical*   Ⓞ *Atypical*

The way a door is hinged also affects issues of furnishability as well as safety. Doors should ideally open against a dead wall area which is perpendicular to the closed door position.

 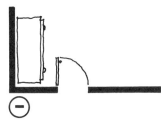 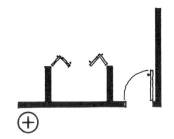
Ⓞ   Ⓞ   ⊕

Window Placement

Window placement in plan and elevation is a strong determinant of furniture location. Major sitting furniture and beds are typically placed perpendicular to windows to take advantage of the view and natural light. Placement of TVs under or against a window is avoided for reasons of glare.

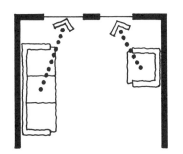
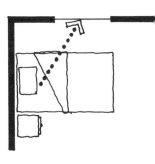

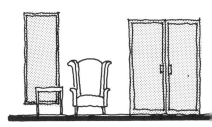

Furniture of all types and heights can typically be placed under a clerestory window.

Low furniture such as tables or cabinets is placed under the standard window where the sill height is anywhere from 30 to 40 inches. Sitting furniture, however, is not typically placed with its back to this window height because of possible drafts on the back of the neck and minimal viewing opportunities.

Very little furniture is placed directly in front of a low window that terminates near the floor, as it block views out of the unit One exception might b a plant stand.

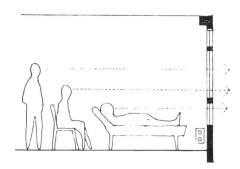

CRITIQUE OF NATIONAL UNIT PLANS

Given the activity needs and furniture patterns typical of older residents, what are the specific characteristics of the surrounding built space that make it more suitable and supportive of a particular activity? Some of the characteristics about spaces, including their shape, dimensions, and boundaries, have been identified in the Cambridge studies. However, such analysis is limited by the specific design characteristics of the studied units. To extend this information base on both the supportive and constraining features of a dwelling space, we tested a variety of unit types for their ability to accommodate typical daily activities and associated furniture pieces. Most of these units were visited in the 1974 national M.I.T. study and actual comments from interviewed residents living in a particular unit have been included in the critiques. Those design features which were found to have the greatest impact on habitability of an apartment unit are summarized at the end of this chapter.

Walls·Corners·Niches
Room Proportions
Room Dimensions
Circulation and Doors
Window Placement
Visual Access

Irvington, New Jersey
efficiency 350 sq. ft.

— jogged corners could make
it difficult to arrange
some types of furniture

— sleeping alcove has
minimal wall area
thus limiting the
amount of, and
placement options for,
bedroom furniture

— unit layout prohibits
the cul-de-sac clustering
of living area furniture

— the area in front of the
closet doors is unfurnishable
and can only be used for
circulation

— there is no visual separation
between living, sleeping and
dining areas, and the unit is
not large enough to use
furniture as barriers

— there is no space near
the dining table for a
china cabinet

+ entry area can
accommodate a chair
as well as several
small tables/shelves
for the display of
personal objects

Charlotte, North Carolina
efficiency 400 sq. ft.

*"...need a different arrangement.
I want a place for a bedroom.
There is thrown-away space."*

— minimal wall area
is available for
the placement or
rearrangement of
living area
furniture

— no physical or visual
separation exists
between living,
sleeping, and dining
areas

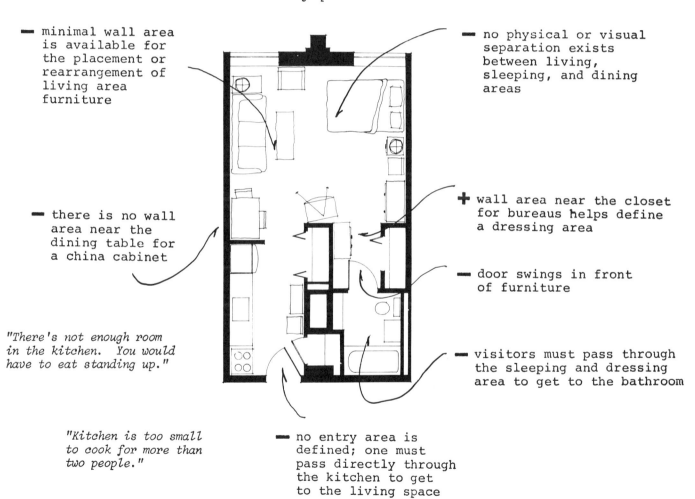

— there is no wall
area near the
dining table for
a china cabinet

+ wall area near the closet
for bureaus helps define
a dressing area

— door swings in front
of furniture

*"There's not enough room
in the kitchen. You would
have to eat standing up."*

— visitors must pass through
the sleeping and dressing
area to get to the bathroom

*"Kitchen is too small
to cook for more than
two people."*

— no entry area is
defined; one must
pass directly through
the kitchen to get
to the living space

Gloucester, Massachusetts
efficiency (renovation) 755 sq. ft.

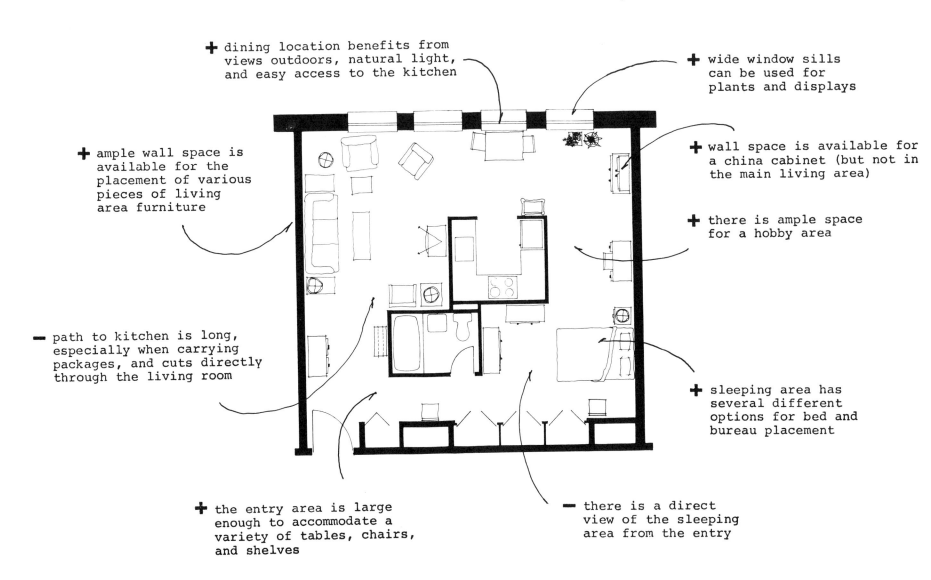

+ dining location benefits from views outdoors, natural light, and easy access to the kitchen

+ wide window sills can be used for plants and displays

+ ample wall space is available for the placement of various pieces of living area furniture

+ wall space is available for a china cabinet (but not in the main living area)

+ there is ample space for a hobby area

– path to kitchen is long, especially when carrying packages, and cuts directly through the living room

+ sleeping area has several different options for bed and bureau placement

+ the entry area is large enough to accommodate a variety of tables, chairs, and shelves

– there is a direct view of the sleeping area from the entry

Cleveland, Ohio
one bedroom 500 sq. ft.

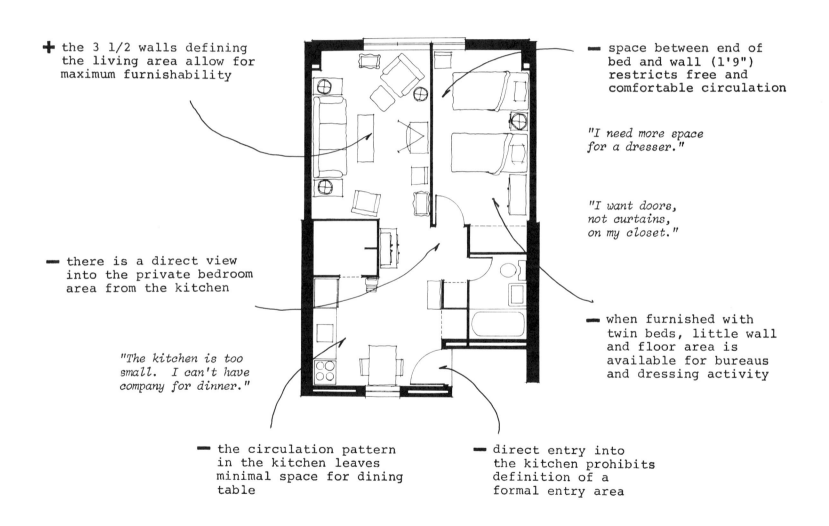

+ the 3 1/2 walls defining the living area allow for maximum furnishability

— space between end of bed and wall (1'9") restricts free and comfortable circulation

"I need more space for a dresser."

"I want doors, not curtains, on my closet."

— there is a direct view into the private bedroom area from the kitchen

— when furnished with twin beds, little wall and floor area is available for bureaus and dressing activity

"The kitchen is too small. I can't have company for dinner."

— the circulation pattern in the kitchen leaves minimal space for dining table

— direct entry into the kitchen prohibits definition of a formal entry area

Brooklyn, New York
one bedroom 530 sq. ft.

− structural elements
could make placement
of furniture awkward

＋ furniture can be arranged
in a cul-de-sac pattern
against the walls

＋ dining alcove is easily
accessible from the kitchen
and can serve as both an
informal and formal dining
setting

− placement of the china
cabinet in the dining
alcove is not possible
due to the minimal wall
area

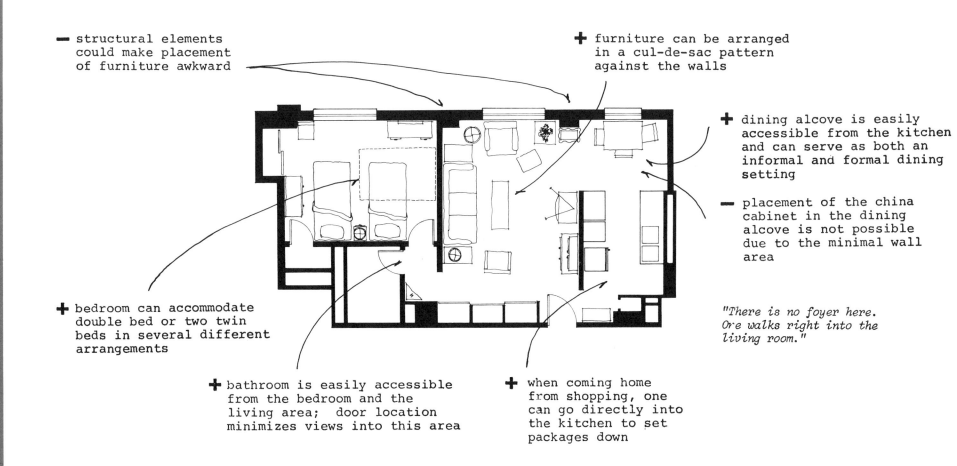

*"There is no foyer here.
One walks right into the
living room."*

＋ bedroom can accommodate
double bed or two twin
beds in several different
arrangements

＋ bathroom is easily accessible
from the bedroom and the
living area; door location
minimizes views into this area

＋ when coming home
from shopping, one
can go directly into
the kitchen to set
packages down

Irvington, New Jersey
one bedroom 560 sq. ft.

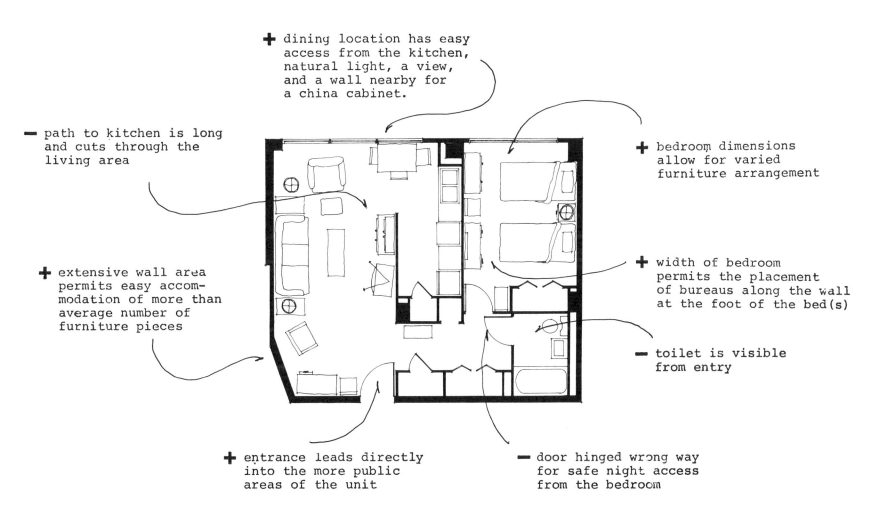

+ dining location has easy
access from the kitchen,
natural light, a view,
and a wall nearby for
a china cabinet.

− path to kitchen is long
and cuts through the
living area

+ bedroom dimensions
allow for varied
furniture arrangement

+ extensive wall area
permits easy accom-
modation of more than
average number of
furniture pieces

+ width of bedroom
permits the placement
of bureaus along the wall
at the foot of the bed(s)

− toilet is visible
from entry

+ entrance leads directly
into the more public
areas of the unit

− door hinged wrong way
for safe night access
from the bedroom

Ames, Iowa
one bedroom 516 sq. ft.

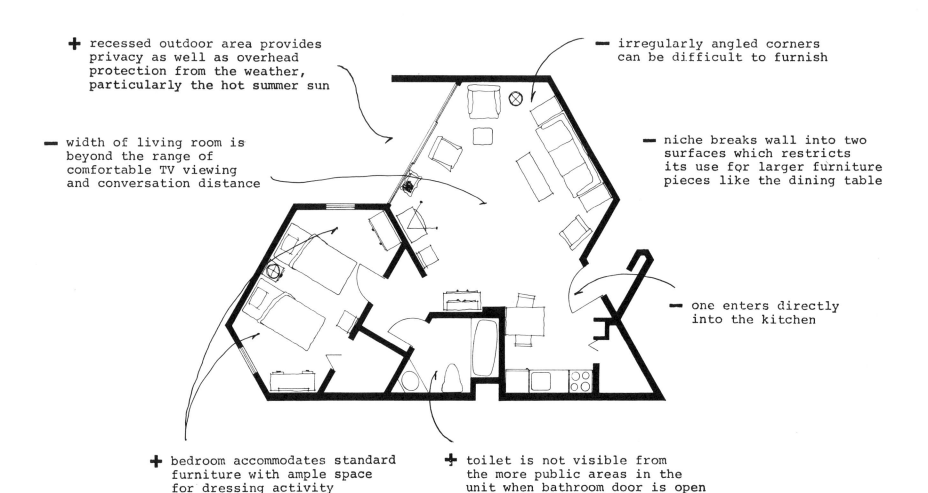

+ recessed outdoor area provides privacy as well as overhead protection from the weather, particularly the hot summer sun

− irregularly angled corners can be difficult to furnish

− width of living room is beyond the range of comfortable TV viewing and conversation distance

− niche breaks wall into two surfaces which restricts its use for larger furniture pieces like the dining table

− one enters directly into the kitchen

+ bedroom accommodates standard furniture with ample space for dressing activity

+ toilet is not visible from the more public areas in the unit when bathroom door is open

Boston, Massachusetts
two bedroom 695 sq. ft.

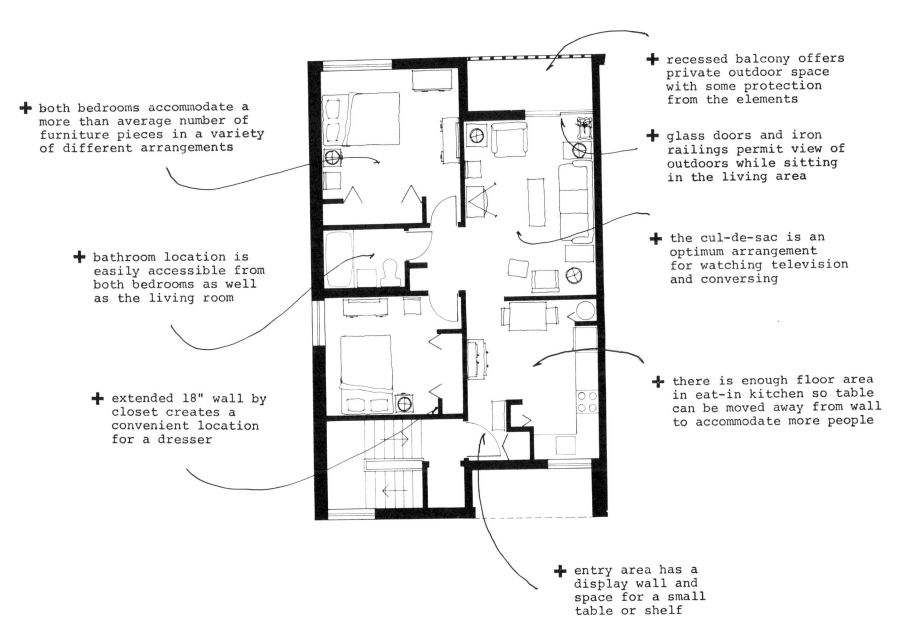

+ recessed balcony offers private outdoor space with some protection from the elements

+ glass doors and iron railings permit view of outdoors while sitting in the living area

+ the cul-de-sac is an optimum arrangement for watching television and conversing

+ there is enough floor area in eat-in kitchen so table can be moved away from wall to accommodate more people

+ both bedrooms accommodate a more than average number of furniture pieces in a variety of different arrangements

+ bathroom location is easily accessible from both bedrooms as well as the living room

+ extended 18" wall by closet creates a convenient location for a dresser

+ entry area has a display wall and space for a small table or shelf

GUIDELINES

The intention of the following guidelines is to elaborate on the *habitability* needs of older residents in purpose-built housing and not to dictate new standards of apartment unit design. This information supplements rather than supplants existing national guidelines in the form of HUD Minimum Property Standards. Our studies suggest that the design of more habitable living spaces does not necessarily require additional square footage but instead more careful attention to spatial definition in terms of walls, corners, windows, circulation paths, etc. With one exception, the recommendations, which are based on the systematic study of resident activities and furnishings, can be incorporated within the existing square footage constraints

specified by the MPS. The present findings indicate a need for more square footage in the bedroom. This discrepancy in bedroom size is due in part to the difference i' bedroom furnishings recommended by the HUD MPS as compared to those observed in the M.I.T. study.

For each of the following guidelin there is a summary of the *activity description* as well as the *furniture* pieces typically used in support o the activity. Specific items that should be attended to in the desig of the particular setting are listed as *design considerations*. Sever examples of small scale design solutions are offered as possible *design alternatives*. These options are not exhaustive or mutually exclusive.

SQUARE FOOTAGE COMPARISON BETWEEN HUD MPS AND MIT STUDY: One bedroom, double occupancy

AREA	HUD Minimum Property Standards		MIT Study	
	Square Footage	Least Dimension	Square Footage	Dimensions
Living	160	11'0"	160	one wall at least 14'0" minimum width 11'6" maximum width 13'6"
Dining	100	8'4"	100	one wall at least 8'0" another wall at least 3'6"
Bedroom	120 with one wall at least 10'0"	9'4"	160*	one wall at least 11'6" minimum width with dresser 11'6 placed at foot of bed

* Calculated on a room 11'6" x 14"0" (11'6" for twin beds plus approximately 2'6" for closet acc

Entering

Design Considerations:

○ In front entry areas, floor and wall space should be available for the display of personal objects on shelves or a small table.

○ Inside the front door there should be a coat closet and an adjacent area for a side chair for putting on and taking off outer wear.

○ Avoid direct views from the entry of the more private areas in the unit like the bedroom, bathroom and kitchen sink.

○ The path from entry area to kitchen should be minimized for the convenience and safety of residents returning home with heavy bundles.

○ The entry area should lead directly to the main living space without passing through more private areas.

Activity Description

In entering a home, there are both functional and symbolic consider-ations. In the entry area, visitors are identified and greeted, neighboring occurs, and outer wear is removed or put on. It also serves as the transition zone between the outside world and the private domain of the home. Here, where the formal "presentation of the self" occurs, symbols and displays provide an introduction to the more personal territory inside. Residents prefer that only the more public areas of the home be viewed from this transition area. Most older persons who previously have resided in single family or duplex dwellings, are accustomed to having two entrances: the informal back door where servicemen enter and household goods are carried in and out, and the formal front door where visitors are greeted and personal objects are on display. When building densities permit only a single entrance, all of these functions must be accommodated in one area.

Furniture

Most residents have a small table or set of shelves for displaying objects or setting packages on when returning to their apart-ments. A chair may also be used in the entry way for sitting down while putting on and taking off outer wear. This is typically placed near the coat closet where these items are stored.

Design Alternatives for ENTERING

① A separate vestibule area uses a half wall for definition and to place furniture against.

② A built-in shelf near the entry can be used for setting packages on or for display.

③ By tiling the floor in the entry and kitchen, these trafficked areas can be easily maintained.

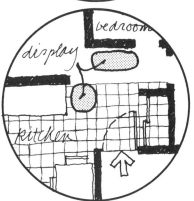

Leisure Activities

Activity Description

With retirement and childrearing behind them, older persons devote much of their time to leisure activities within the home. More time is spent watching television than on any other activity, many watching TV an average of 5 to 6 hours per weekday. Most older persons also enjoy reading and will settle down in a comfortable chair preferably near a light source. Some engage in hobbies such as sewing, knitting, stamp collecting, woodworking, plant-tending, etc. which require good lighting conditions, a work surface and possibly storage and display space. Most elderly residents also spend time looking out their windows at outdoor activities and views. Some time each day is spent keeping in touch with family and friends in the form of telephoning and letter-writing. The telephone has become a particularly important instrument and its preferred location varies from one resident to the next: many would like it in the living room or kitchen as most of the waking hours are spent in these areas while others prefer the bedroom location in the event of illness or night time emergencies.

Furniture

All elderly residents have at least one TV which in modern times has replaced the fireplace as the focal point in the living room. It typically is placed against a wall directly across from the sofa. The sofa is always placed against a wall. Residents avoid putting it under a window where there is a potential problem with drafts on the back of the neck. Residents sit here to watch TV or in their "favorite" easy chair which is usually placed at the end of the sofa and near a window to take advantage of natural light and outdoor views. This is also the favored setting for other leisure activities like reading, sewing, and watching outdoors. End and coffee tables accompany these primary seating areas to hold table lamps and materials associated with various other activities. Depending on the specific interests of the residents, there might also be a sewing machine, work surface, or storage and display piece for a particular hobby. Some residents might define a "communications area" with a desk and chair for telephoning and letter-writing.

Design Considerations:

◯ Provide at least one unbroken wall in the living area, preferably perpendicular to the window wall, long enough to accommodate one sofa and two end tables.

◯ Locate TV antenna outlets on interior walls (away from windows and potential glare problems) in positions that maximize options for TV location in the living and sleeping areas.

◯ Space should be available near a window for the "favorite" easy chair to take advantage of natural light, views to the outdoors, and a potential view of the TV set.

◯ Provide an area in the apartment that can be used as a hobby corner or niche for such activities as sewing, painting, bead-making, etc.

◯ Design at least some windows in the living area that permit a view to the outdoors from a seated position (in the easy chair or sofa) and that have sills deep enough for flower pots and window boxes.

◯ Locate telephone jack(s) so that residents have a choice of places/rooms to put a telephone and its related furniture.

Design Alternatives for LEISURE ACTIVITIES

① A built-in shelf area visible from the living area can be used for the display and storage of hobby collections.

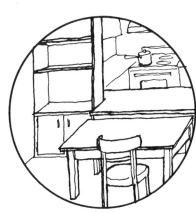

② Wide window sills provide ideal areas for plants as well as the display of other personal objects.

③ A niche in any habitable area of the unit, particularly one near a window, can be a setting for such activities as reading, sewing, watching outdoors, etc.

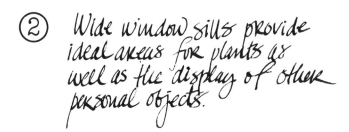

Eating

Activity Description

The activity of eating can take a variety of different forms. Most meals are informal and frequently involve nothing more than a quick snack. As a matter of convenience, elderly residents prefer to eat these meals in the kitchen where they are prepared. Many of the residents are also accustomed to informal socializing around the kitchen table and would like a kitchen large enough to accommodate this activity. Although formal entertaining with the serving of a meal is a less frequent occurrence, it plays an important role in maintaining relations with family and friends. For these occasions a more formal dining area which can accommodate larger gatherings is often desired.

Furniture

To support this activity, most residents have a dining table and four side chairs as well as a china cabinet. The table is typically placed against a wall with two of the chairs while the other chairs are located in other areas in the apartment. For formal meals with visitors, this table is pulled away from the wall and chairs are placed around it. For many older residents, particularly women, the china cabinet is an important piece of furniture as it typically symbolizes a previous role in the family as well as serving for the display and storage of dinnerware.

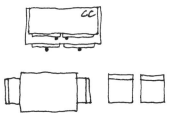

- The walk between the dining and food preparation areas should be short and direct (avoid level changes and turns) to minimize the effort and hazards in carrying food and dishes back and forth.

- Floor area should be available for opening up the dining table and seating 6 to 8 guests around it for a meal.

- Uninterrupted wall area is needed near the dining table for the possible placement of a china cabinet.

- Direct views to avoid from the dining area include the bathroom and kitchen sink where dirty dishes might collect.

- Provide a window near the eating area for natural light and ventilation and views out of the unit.

Design Alternatives for EATING

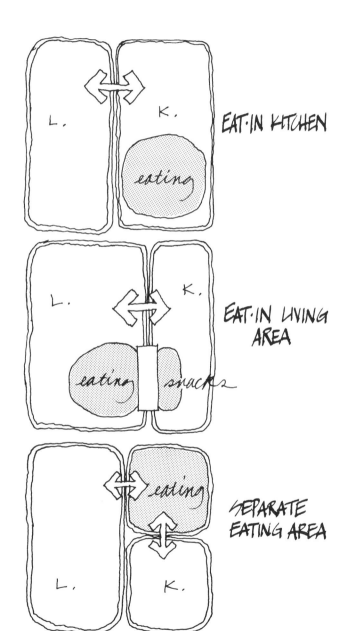

EAT·IN KITCHEN

EAT·IN LIVING AREA

SEPARATE EATING AREA

① Eat-in kitchen has view to living area and windows; can be used for informal socializing

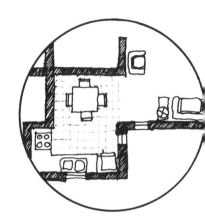

② Pass-thru counter can be used with chairs for informal eating; more formal dining occurs in the living room

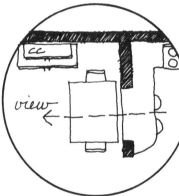

③ L-shaped living room defines a separate multipurpose eating area

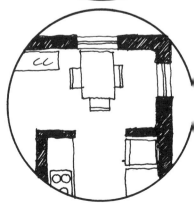

Visiting

Activity Description

Visiting includes various forms of socializing within the apartment unit. It can be informal in nature where friends and neighbors drop in to chat or have coffee. Although formal entertaining is less frequent, it is an important occasion that is time-consuming and usually involves the preparation of a meal. These activities take place in comfortable chairs in the living area or around the dining table. Overnight guests are also a possibility for which many of the older residents would like a separate bedroom to ensure privacy.

Furniture

Conversation furniture typically includes a sofa with two end tables, coffee table, rocker, and one or more easy chairs arranged in a closed loop. Recommended distance between seats for comfortable conversation is 10 feet. If more seating is required, dining chairs or floor cushions are often used. When a snack or meal is served as part of the visit, the dining table is typically pulled away from the wall and chairs are arranged around it. For entertaining large numbers, some residents have folding tables and chairs which they keep stored away in closets when not in use. Some also have folding beds which they set-up for overnight guests.

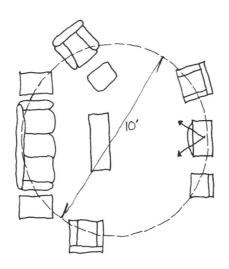

Design Considerations:

○ Provide adequate floor area for seating at least 6 to 8 people around a dining table or in the living room.

○ Define living area in terms of walls and corners so that the conversation furniture can be arranged in a small cul-de-sac without having to "float" furniture pieces.

○ Avoid circulation routes which lead directly through this living room as they can divide and disrupt the setting.

○ Storage areas within the unit should be available for furniture used for visiting activities (e.g. folding tables and chairs, table leaves, TV trays, cots).

○ Minimize visual invasion of private spaces (sleeping area, bathroom, and kitchen sink) from the more public areas of the apartment where visiting typically takes place.

① There is enough floor area
to open up the dining table
and seat 6 to 8 people.

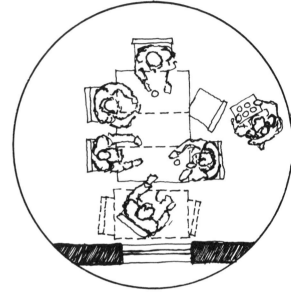

② Furniture can be placed at a
comfortable conversation distance;
the grouping is supplemented
by folding furniture for
large gatherings.

Sleeping & Dressing

Activity Description

For older persons, the activities of sleeping and dressing are considered private in nature. As many of the residents' most personal objects such as photographs, mementos, personal care items, and medicines are kept in the sleeping area, there is a desire for visual privacy. Auditory privacy is preferred by many to minimize disruptions during sleep. This area is also used as a retreat from other occupants or visitors or during times of illness. Activities associated with the sleeping area include dressing and bed-making.

Furniture

For single residents, typical furniture in the sleeping and dressing area includes a double bed, two bureaus, a night stand, and a chair. Double occupants (who are most frequently married couples) are more likely to have twin beds rather than a double bed. Heads of beds are placed against walls, perpendicular to a window to permit a view of the outdoors while lying down. Placement of the head of a bed under a window is avoided because of problems with drafts. For ease in making the bed(s), residents prefer to place it so it is accessible from two sides and one end. A nightstand is located at the head of a bed (between twin beds) upon which is usually found a table lamp, clock, medicines, and other personal items. The two bureaus, along with a chair, are typically clustered near the closet(s) to form a convenient dressing area.

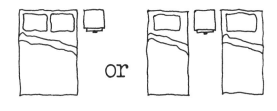

or

Design Considerations:

○ Avoid direct views into the sleeping area from more public areas like the entry and living room.

○ Guests should not have to pass through the sleeping and dressing area to reach the bathroom.

○ Provide a direct and safe route between sleeping area and bathroom (avoid turning corners).

○ Provide enough floor area so beds can be accessed from three sides and do not have to be placed in a corner.

○ Window placement should allow for views of the outdoors while lying in bed.

○ Provide floor and wall area near the clothes closet(s) for placement of the bureaus and chair and definition of a dressing area.

An Overnight Visit to Grandma's House.

Photo: George Gardner

6

TOWARD A FUTURE

THE LIMITS OF PATTERNS OF USE.

Evaluating the match between design and use has its own critical deficiencies. Only those environments and the particular qualities that have been constructed and occupied can enter into the evaluation. Consequently, only the uses observed and reported for these settings and the self selected tenants are recorded.

What about the human potential in relation to different environments? Suppose, based upon behavioral science *performance* statements, a group of designers decided that special variations in design or building might better meet the social and psychological needs of aging persons within a particular community? At the present time it would be exceedingly difficult to gain acceptance of deviant patterns of design and construction. Further, there is no mechanism in the United States by which a series of alternatives in design could be built and tested against behavioral hypotheses. Design, as a creative and innovative endeavor, shrivels under such constraints. The loss is to user populations who might have elected and tried adaptations to a new environment and, in doing so, provided us with richer information on *patterns of use*. The absence of research in energy conservation and habitability is a good case in point.

One apparent potential for exploration, given the current state of the construction industry in the United States, is in *Adaptive Re-Use*. In *adaptive re-use*, buildings, and their historically relevant features, may be differentially deployed to array private and shared space in combinations that might meet the variabilities inherent among any given population of aging people. The question to be asked of the building industry, the regulatory authorities and the program planners is what are the attributes of older buildings which appear to provide greater design flexibility than seems to be able to be produced by the new construction process? The author has seen very poor reconstitutions of old factories and schools into housing for elderly, in which the result only replicated the prototypes of new construction. She has also experienced creative innovation, utilizing existing older structural spans that allowed free manipulation of internal space and re-use of architectural elements in order to create environmental stimulation and variation that must, surely, make a new living environment recognizable and unique.

EXISTING HOUSING IN USE.

A critical base-line study yet to be conducted is that of patterns of use by aging people of the single family home in its variations. If, as is the fact, the majority of elderly do not and may not move to congregate-type settings, what are their relationships to place and space as life constricts?

A RESEARCH-PRACTICE AGENDA.

Let us begin the development of a stable and additive data file for use by researchers and practitioners designing for aging.

In order to secure such a file, each of us, and the agencies that we deal with, will have to maintain *convergible* records. At the present time each party to applied research in housing is accumulating information on program, activities and processes with little relation to the collective need. Often the data is never reviewed evaluatively. This appears certainly to be the case with HUD specification forms and plans for individual projects at regional and local levels.

For researchers conducting *post-occupancy evaluations* as single case studies, the systematic testing of interview items and observation modes needs to be extended and further validated in relation to particular architectural solutions. Each of us now asks similar questions of tenants. How similar are the styles of response? What is lost or gained in design-relevant information across settings? How specific to a setting should activity and attitude questions and observations be? What information about the physical parameters of a particular setting under study should precede any interview and observation program?

INFORMATION RETRIEVAL.

Architects often retain records on a completed project that appear to be legally necessary to file or a potential source of information for future projects. Design researchers are encouraged to collaboratively explore this promising and retrievable pool of data. It may be that the answers to the multi-faceted problem of using behavioral information in design is imbedded in a kind of input-output analysis of project documents. Perhaps this is an appropriate study for the American Institute of Architects to support? Academic researchers might, in addition, encourage designer panels to retain particular types of process information, from program through construction, as a means of improving what are now more incidental retrospective studies of design intention. A firm should be able to retrieve information rapidly on prior decisions made and the rationale or research basis for those decisions. Decisions are not now so ordered.

Early reviewers of this book strongly recommended the inclusion of a discussion about the costs of individual design recommendations. Even were those types of generalizations possible, that is not the issues for user-sensitive design. Particular design-behavior issues only become the focus in user needs research. To cost out each individual solution is irrational accounting. Design solutions at the level of particular spaces, building elements and fixtures are the product of the quality and care taken in pre-planning and architectural programming. The costly element in the design segment of the housing production process is *time*. When a nearly final design is reviewed and found weak in meeting habitability needs for aging, it is probably too late, because it will be too expensive, to make major modifications in unit distribution and spatial relations. In some cases, perhaps many, a critical reorganization of spaces would involve a complete reprogramming effort, involving significantly different decisions about the orientation of the building on the site, the choice and application of a particular industrialized building system and its fitted elements, or a revision of unit size and number, all of which the financing agency had already agreed to.

criteria under which either settings are designed and constructed or behaviors and their environmental meanings are assessed.

Grow old along with me
The best is yet to be.

LEFT UNSAID.

The production of a problem-oriented manuscript leaves writer and reader with their feet firmly planted in mid-air. Much that should and could be said about the populations of aging, the built environment and the methods of relating them both is left unsaid.

Why are we so uncomfortable with indeterminacy? As a psychologist, the author suggests that we still hold many myths about the surety of science and about the appropriateness of certain physical science methods to human behavior. The role of applied mathematics in science is partly at fault. Somehow, the presentation of an equation that specifies a relationship between variables or the provision of a definitive central tendency makes us feel secure. In the matter of designing for patterns of human behavior nothing could be further from the truth than determinant solutions, unless you believe we have reached the end of the trail as a creative species.

The author is arguing for a *trial and error* approach to designing environments for people, but that the approach become systematic and recorded. A further proposition is that the practitioner and researcher, alike, take risks in challenging the established

APPENDIX

APPENDIX

The selection of materials for this appendix was determined by three goals:

To assist architecture and behavior science researchers to replicate and refine methods of data collection in conducting *Post Occupancy Evaluations*;

To encourage design and planning pract-itioners to conduct more systematic pre-programming studies;

To exemplify the quantitative analyses which have been conducted on the data collected.

For the expected audience of this book, the last goal was least important. The author intends to contribute primary data files to a national archive in order that it can be freely massaged by other researchers.

Calendar Summary of Research Process.

1973 Development of plan for Restudy of
Lawton (1971) National Public Housing
Sites.
Preparation of Neighborhood study plan.
Modification and supplementation of
interview schedule.
Development of pilot interview on
apartment adequacy.
Development of site-specific architect-
ural information file.

1974 Exploration and preparation of Environmental Analysis methods.
Conduct national field study.
Data Analyses.
Reorganization and integration of
interview and environmental observation
data.

1975 Methodological Studies A: Computergraphic
explorations -
neighborhood resource use
Interview item, validity review
Identification of information gaps and
formulation of directions
for new hypothesis and study.
Development and conduct of architecture-
specific studies (Shared Space).
Data Analysis

1976 Methodology Studies B: Translation.
Preparation of data for research transfer.
Consultation with architects on in-
formation needs.

1977 Methodology Studies C:
Research translation and transfer to
architects.
Dissemination and test of transfer
document, in use.
Development of apartment study plan.
Conduct Private Space study, Cambridge,
MA.

1978 Methodology Studies D:
Analysis and integration of apartment
unit data.
Explorations of open-end interview and
field note information.
Exploration of photodocumentation of
life-style and furnishing patterns.
Test applications to architectural
theory and methods (SAR).
Computergraphic explorations of unit
furnishability
Preparation and dissemination of
Private Space transfer document.

MIT Design Evaluation Project 1973-1978
Principal Investigator, S. Howell

Summary: Selected Variables, Methods of Collection and Sample Size

DESIGN EVALUATION PROJECT
1973-76

TA VARIABLE	METHODS OF COLLECTION	SAMPLE
mographic and Housing History		
st residential type	structured interview	662 National Subjects
st residence (duration)	"	"
oximate neighborhood	"	"
st living arrangement	"	"
esent living arrangement	"	"
andard personal variables including health, marital status, etc.	"	"
cation of apartment in building/on site	sample sheet	662 units
thin Building Activities	structured interview	662 National Subjects
equency visit others	"	"
cation of visited others	"	"
equency being visited	"	"
cation of visitors	"	"
rticipation in activities	"	"
miliarity with tenant population	"	"
ilding and Site Variables		53 sites
ighborhood land use	detailed mapping	"
e and "character" of neighborhood	photographs	"
ilding/neighborhood scale	photographs	"
ilding density	HUD form	"
te plan	site plans	12 sites
ilding height	HUD form	53 sites
ilding specifications (selected)	HUD form	53 sites
ilding plan	floor plans	12 sites
ilding massing	simulated from photographs and specifications	45 sites

DATA VARIABLE	METHODS OF COLLECTION	SAMPLE
Building and Site Variables		
building entry (orientation)	photographs	45 sites
unit plans	HUD form; floor plans	12 sites
unit furnishing characteristics	photographs; mapping	8 sites; 70+ units
Hardare/fixtures	tenant interview	662 subjects
pieces wish to retain	structured interview	199 subjects; 15 site
perceived window issues	structured interview; unstructured responses	160 subjects; 15 site

perceived storage issues	structured and unstructured
	   responses; photography;
	   annotation
		160 subjects; 15 site

furnishability	tenant interview; mapping;
	   photographs
		200 subjects; 20 site
		  55 units

perceived spatial adequacy	tenant interview	200 subjects; 20 unit 55 units

use of key fixtures
  (if present)
   grab bars
   peep holes
   intercom
	tenant interview	160 subjects; 15 site

heating-ventillation issues	tenant interview	160 subjects; 15 site

Appendix A-1.

NEIGHBORHOOD USE TENANT INTERVIEW

A-3

1-3

4-6

Q. 33 FOR THE FOLLOWING DETERMINATION OF "FUNCTIONAL NEIGHBORHOOD", FIND OUT WHETHER FACILITY LIES WITHIN THE MAPPED AREA. IF IT DOES, DETERMINE ITS LOCATION BY A VERBAL DESCRIPTION (INCLUDE STREET FACILITY IS ON AND CLOSEST CROSS STREET), AND BY MARKING IT DIRECTLY ON THE MAP NOW OR AFTER THE INTERVIEW IS COMPLETED.

Read: Now I'd like to find out the kinds of places you go to for pleasure and for your errands. This will help us plan better housing locations in the future.

Ask: Where do you go to: _____? Is it in your neighborhood?

How accomplished 1=respondent goes 2=respondent manages alternate means (phone, mail, etc.) 3=other does for resp. 4= resp. doesn't use; never does; no one goes for resp.	Location 1=on site 2=Zone 1 3=Zone 2 4=beyond Zone 2, in locality 5=outside locality 9=DK, NA Name of facility Description Location: give cross streets	Did you go there during the past week? 1=yes 2=no 9=DK, NA	About how often do you usually go? 1=daily 2=2-6/wk. 3=weekly 4=2-3/mo. 5=monthly 6=less often 7=never 9=DK, NA	How do you usually get there? 1=walk. What route do you take? 2=own car 3=another's car 4=bus 5=subway 6=taxi 7=train 8=other 9=DK, NA	About how long does it take to get there? (one way) RECORD NUMBER OF MINUTES INCLUDING WAITING TIME 999=DK, NA	Is this the closest _____? (facility) 1=yes 2=no 9=DK, NA For each "No" ask about closer facility	Why don't you use a _____ that (facility) is closer?
	Code			Code Route			
1. Shop for food and groceries? Location 1							1. grocery
Location 2							
2. Shop for clothing?							2. clothing
3. See a doctor?							3. doctor
4. Go walking for exercise or pleasure?							4. walking
5. Cash your checks?							5. cash checks

**Design Evaluation Project
MIT National Survey, 1974.**

Appendix A-1

A-3

Q. 33 (Cont'd)

How accomplished 1=respondent goes 2=respondent manages 　alternate means 　(phone, mail, etc.) 3=other does for resp. 4=resp. doesn't use; 　never does; no one 　goes for resp. 9=DK, NA	Location 1=on site 2=Zone 1 3=Zone 2 4=beyond Zone 2, in locality 5=outside locality 9=DK, NA Code ｜ Name of facility Description Location: give cross streets	Did you go there during the past week? 1=yes 2=no 9=DK, NA	About how often do you usually go? 1=daily 2=2-6/wk. 3=weekly 4=2-3/mo. 5=monthly 6=less often 7=never 9=DK, NA	How do you usually get there? 1=walk 2=own car 3=another's car 4=bus 5=subway 6=taxi 7=train 8=other 9=DK, NA Code ｜ Route	About how long does it take to get there? (one way) RECORD NUMBER OF MINUTES INCLUDING WAITING TIME 999=DK, NA	Is this the closest _____? (facility) 1=yes 2=no 9=DK, NA For each "No" ask about closer facility	Why don't you use a _____ that (facility) is closer?
6. Get your hair done/cut?							6. hair cut
7. A drugstore?							7. drugstore
8. Go to church or synagogue?							8. church
9. Get a meal or snack?							9. meal/snack
10. Get public transportation?							10. public trans.
11. Visit a friend who doesn't live in _____ (name of project) Where does he/she live?							
12. Visit another friend who doesn't live in _____ (name of project) Where does he/she live?							

Design Evaluation Project
MIT National Survey, 1974.

Appendix A-2

Design Evaluation Project - Social Activities

LABEL

EXTENDED LABEL

RELCONTC   **CONTACT WITH RELATIVE 74   HI=HI CONTACT**

History

From the 1974 tenant interview, three questions were selected which measured the frequency with which tenants were in contact with three different relatives. The questions, methods of recoding, and methods of scoring are listed below:

Q.#	DK. & COL.	ITEM	LABEL
			RL1TOUCH
32a2	701:45	About how often are you in contact with relative #1?	
		1 = daily	
		2 = 2-6/weeks	
		3 = weekly	
		4 = twice/month	
		5 = monthly	
		6 = less often	
		9 = NA, DK	
			RL2TOUCH
32b2	701:55	About how often are you in contact with relative #2?	
		1 = daily	
		2 = 2-6/weeks	
		3 = weekly	
		4 = twice/month	
		5 = monthly	
		6 = less often	
		9 = NA, DK	
			RL3TOUCH
32c2	701:65	About how often are you in contact with relative #3?	
		1 = daily	
		2 = 2-6/weeks	
		3 = weekly	
		4 = twice/month	
		5 = monthly	
		6 = less often	
		9 = NA, DK	

Recode all:
1 = 6
2 = 5
3 = 4
4 = 3
5 = 2
6 = 1
9 = 0

Each of the tenant's responses to the questions were summed and recoded as above.

Source: Final Report (Lawton), Design Evaluation: Social Uses of Elderly Housing. 1973-76. Howell & Lawton

LABEL   EXTENDED LABEL

ELCONTC   CONTACT WITH RELATIVE 74   HI= HI CONTACT [continued]

LABEL   EXTENDED LABEL

RELCONTC   CONTACT WITH RELATIVES 74   HI= HI CONTACT
[Range = 00-18]

	N	%
00	35	5.3
1	13	2.0
2	19	2.9
3	23	3.5
4	30	4.5
5	39	5.9
6	75	11.3
7	30	4.5
8	45	6.8
9	35	5.3
10	54	8.2
11	38	5.7
12	63	9.5
13	29	4.4
14	34	5.1
15	24	3.6
16	32	4.8
17	20	3.0
18	24	3.6
	662	100.0

Median = 9.129
Mean = 9.035
S.D. = 4.824
Skewness = -0.024

LABEL | EXTENDED LABEL

FRENSON | SEES FRIENDS ONSITE | HI=MORE CONTACT

History

Four questions from the 1974 tenant interview were selected which described the tenant's contacts with friends living in the same housing site. The questions and scoring methods are listed below:

Q.#	DK. & COL.	ITEM	LABEL
26	701:31	**Is that person [you confide in] a friend, a relative or someone else? Is that person from the project or somewhere else?** 1 = friend in project + 2 = friend outside 3 = relative in project 4 = relative outside 5 = other in project + 6 = other outside project 9 = NA, DK	CONFIDE2
27	701:32-33	How many people here do you consider very good friends? 00 = none or few 01-03 = number listed 04-97 = number listed + 05 = several, many + 98 = majority, all, 1/2, 1/3 99 = NA, DK	NUMBFREN
28	701:34-35	In the past week, which friends here did you visit here in their apartments? 00 = none or few 01-97 = number listed + 05 = several, many + 98 = majority, all, 1/2, 1/3 99 = NA, DK	YOUVISIT
30	701:39-40	In the past week, which friends here [not relatives] visited you in your apartment? 00 = none or few 01 = number listed 02-97 = number listed + 05 = several, many + 98 = majority, all, 1/3, 1/3 99 = NA, DK	VISITYOU

For each of the tenants, the designated "+" responses were summed

Appendix A-2

LABEL

FRENSON

EXTENDED LABEL

SEES FRIENDS ONSITE   HI=MORE CONTACT [continued]

LABEL

FRENSON

EXTENDED LABEL

SEES FRIENDS ON SITE   HI=MORE CONTACT
[Range = 0-4]

	N	**%**
0 =	125	18.9
1 =	162	24.5
2 =	183	27.6
3 =	141	21.3
4 =	51	7.7
	662	100.0

Median = 1.740
Mean = 1.745
S.D. = 1.208
Skewness = 0.117

LABEL | EXTENDED LABEL

ACTIV74 | ACTIVITY PARTICIPATION 74 | HI= ACTIVE

History

Two questions were selected from the 1974 tenant interview which illustrate the amount of the tenant's participation in activities both inside and outside of the building site. Original questions, responses, method of recoding, and scoring follow:

Q.#	DK. & COL.	ITEM	LABEL
66	704:31-32	Which organizations or activities have you participated in within the housing site during the past year? Code total activities mentioned: 00 = none 01-98 = number mentioned 99 = NA, DK *outside*	NUMBACT
67	704:33-4	Which activities or organizations have you participated in within the housing site during the past year? Code total activities mentioned: 00 = none 01-98 = number mentioned 99 = NA, DK Recode both: 99 = 00	ACTOUT

For each tenant, the total number of activities were summed

LABEL | EXTENDED LABEL

ACTIV74 | PARTICIPATION IN ACTIVITIES | HI= ACTIVE
[Range = 00-20]

	N	%	
0	246	37.2	
1	166	25.1	Median = 1.012
2	86	13.0	Mean = 1.630
3	68	10.3	S.D. = 2.103
4	46	6.9	Skewness = 2.345
5	18	2.7	
6	10	1.5	
7	8	1.2	
8	5	0.8	
9	1	0.2	
10	2	0.3	
11	0	0.0	
12	3	0.5	
13	1	0.2	
14	1	0.2	
15	1	0.2	
	662	100.0	

Appendix A-2

LABEL

EXTENDED LABEL

MOBILE71   TENANT MOBILITY 71   LO= HIGH MOBILITY

History

In order to replicate in the 1974 study the 1971 study's index measuring the tenant's degree of mobility outside of the building and the neighborhood, the following questions were selected from the 1974 tenant interview. Variable MOBILE71 is comparable to 1971's MOBILE. The questions original responses, and methods of recoding, and methods of scoring are as listed below:

Q.#	DK. & COL.	ITEM		LABEL
17	701:24	About how often do you go out of this [building] [house] in good weather?		EXITBLDG

1 = 5 days a week or more
2 = 2-4 days a week
3 = once a week
4 = 2-3 days a month
5 = once a month
6 = less than once a month
7 = never
9 = NA, DK

Recode: 9 = Missing

| 18 | 701:26 | About how often do you leave this neighborhood? | | EXITNABR |

1 = 5 days a week of more
2 = 2-4 days a week
3 = Once a week
4 = 2-3 days a month
5 = once a month
6 = less than once a month
7 = never
9 = NA, DK

Recode: 9 = Missing

MOBILE71's score reflects the sum of the tenant's responses to both questions. However, if either question was missing (9), the subject was eliminated from the computations.

LABEL

EXTENDED LABEL

MOBILE71   TENANT MOBILITY 71   LO= HIGH MOBILITY
[Range = 2-14]

	N	%		N	%
2	84	12.8	9	21	3.2
3	109	16.6	10	19	2.9
4	126	19.2	11	6	0.9
5	69	10.5	12	17	2.6
6	71	10.8	13	2	0.3
7	59	9.0	14	8	1.2

Median   = 4.630
Mean   = 5.320
S.D.   = 2.701
Skewness = 0.940

Appendix A-2

SSPD INDICES

A social space x distance variable [SSPD] was created for each relative a tenant visited and for each facility a tenant traveled to. The following computational example used Rl1 variables for illustration.

Step 1 Select the tenat if he has a "1" punch in RL1VISIT [i.e., he goes to visit Relative 1]. If he has any other punch for that variable his score for RL1SSPD is "0."

Step 2 If a "1" punch is found multiply RL1RVSE by RL1WHERE. [RL1RVSE is RL1OFTEN recoded so that a high code reflects the most frequency of visiting]. The resultant variable is called RL1SSPD.

RESULTS

SOCIAL SPACE: DISTANCE X FREQ-REL1

SOCIAL SPACE: DISTANCE X FREQ-REL2

SOCIAL SPACE: DISTANCE X FREQ-REL3

SOCIAL SPACE: DISTANCE X FREQ-FOOD SHOP 1

SOCIAL SPACE: DISTANCE X FREQ-FOOD SHOP 2

RL1SSPD

Range	0-24
Median	4.446
Mean	6.379
S.D.	5.279
Skewness	0.683

RL2SSPD

Range	0-20
Median	3.628
Mean	4.002
S.D.	4.493
Skewness	1.151

RL3SSPD

Range	0-20
Median	0.0
Mean	2.299
S.D.	3.716
Skewness	1.835

FD1SSSPD

Range	0-30
Median	10.216
Mean	10.029
S.D.	6.668
Skewness	- 0.020

FD2SSPD

Range	0-25
Median	0.0
Median	4.934
S.D.	6.516
Skewness	0.998

Appendix A-3

NEIGHBORHOOD MAPPING PROTOCOL

PURPOSE:

Housing varies widely in its access to shopping, transportation, medical care and other resources. One of the many factors as to whether older people avail themselves of needed resources is the distance between their dwelling and the resource. Of course, being near the resource does not guarantee that it will be used. However, if the resource does not exist, or is inconveniently located, the older person is faced with the problem of satisfying his needs. The purpose of the mapping is to be able to describe what is physically accessible, and what is utilized by the tenant.

Since aspects in their neighborhood other than resources may be important to the older person's well-being, the mapping is designed also to provide information on the kinds of spaces, natural and man made structures in the vicinity of the housing, as well as transportation, traffic, and barriers to ambulation.

EXPLANATION:

Your description of the "neighborhood" in map and checklist form will be the basis upon which we can determine how elderly use their "neighborhood" and what problems they have with the area as it now presents itself.

Since a non-resident of a neighborhood cannot presume to know what services exist and are used by residents, nor to understand the "why" of use (e.g., fear, safety, unfamiliarity, cost of services or products), a list of resources and other aspects is being provided for the interviewer to observe and record on a detailed block map, prior to any interviewing.

In turn, interviews with tenants about where they actually do and do not go will verify, supplement and modify the interviewer's observations.

MTP Evaluation P

MATERIALS TO BE PROVIDED:

(1) maps
    (a) 24" mounted site area map
    (b) large folded site area map
    (c) city map
(2) Code sheet
(3) grid recording sheet
(4) 7 colored markers
(5) slope measurement device
(6) gridded mylar
(7) drafting tape
(8) push pins in small envelope
(9) precut and stamped sheets of tracing paper
(10) dots

Site Area Maps, Explanation of Zone #1

Two types of maps will be provided for every interviewer -- the road map of the locality, and the site area maps (of which there will be two different sized copies). The smaller scale road map is a city map of the locality showing the target site. The smaller site area map is mounted on board for ease of field use. The folded map is the final copy the interviewer will return to M.I.T. along with the city map(s). These site area maps have been further subdivided to show Zone #1 and the target site.

Zone #1 is the area in which the resources tenants walk to are located. Of course, we have no way of accurately determining this area prior to talking with the tenants, therefore the interviewer will be responsible for marking the actual Zone #1 after talking with all the tenants. However, to get an idea as to what area needs to be mapped intensively, a square to show a suspected Zone #1 has been drawn around the immediately-adjacent blocks to the target site, some-times in red.

Note: Land use mapping is usually done every five or ten years; therefore the interviewer may find maps for a particular site to be out of date. Whole

Appendix A-3

blocks may have been changed, streets added or eliminated; and often, buildings are shown which are either no longer at a location, or are not being used in the way shown. The interviewer should plan to make hand-drawn map corrections as needed! There will be instances where the staff will not have had enough information on which to make changes, and the interviewer may find this necessary upon the initial scanning of the neighborhood.

Code Sheet

The purpose of the code sheet is two-fold. First, when mapping the environment, it provides information as to how to code and color the essential resources on the map. Second, the code sheet provides the final codes for the grid recording sheet. Hopefully, it is self-explanatory, as to what needs to be recorded, in what color, and how it is to be marked.

Tracing Paper

There should be a precut, prestamped sheet of tracing paper for every tenant you interview. Please remember to fill in the required information on each sheet and draw the registration marks!!

Slope Measurement Device

The slope measurement device is a styrofoam board, plumb and bob instrument designed to measure both the percentage and degree of slope of a given land parcel. It is operated by being held upright with the string and weight dangling toward the ground. Then the upper edge is used as the sighting line which the researcher lines up with his/her eyes. The reading of percentage slope is taken when the researcher is either standing on the crest of the hill, or at the base and sighting toward the other. When sighting uphill toward the crest, sight to your own eye level above the ground, lining eyes with uphill side, and when on the crest sighting down to the base, line eyes up with "downhill" side and sight to a point your percentage of slope measure is most desired. Instructions and practice for use will be included in training.

Grided Mylar

You may have one or two sheets of mylar, depending on the scale of the area site maps for your site(s). The rows and columns are marked and numbered consecutively so that the row numbers run down the left hand side of the sheet and the column numbers run across the top. Each grid number is comprised of the row number and then the column number; e.g. (12,6). Always use the mylar with frosted side up (or the shiny surface underneath) for ease of legibility.

In the case where you have two sheets of mylar, you will need to piece the two together so that the row numbers still run down the left-hand side, column numbers run consecutively across the top, and most importantly, the grids match up as closely as possible. This must be done with transparent tape, so that the map is clearly visible through it.

Please note: this looks like an insurmountable number of grids, but the interviewer will only be concerned with those that fall over those areas of the map which have resources already located.

Grid Recording Sheet

The grid recording sheet has a horizontal row for each grid on the area marked as being used on the site area maps. A vertical column is provided for each category to be recorded and coded (as per the coding sheet), for each of the grids used.

Record the number of each facility from each of the categories found on the grid in the column provided for that category, and the row for that specific grid. (See example.)

GRID #	LAND USE	RESIDENTIAL TYPE	BANK
2,4		B C	3
2,5	2-I	B	0
2,6		B	0
2,7		A	1
3,2	1-I	A B	0
3,3		B C	0
3,4		B C	0
3,5		B	0
3,6		A B E	2
3,7		B C	0
3,8		B	0

All of the categories are directly transferrable from the map with the follow-ing clarifications: all industrial land use should be coded under "land Use" as "I", using a sub-number which makes explicit the number of times industrial fac-ilities are to be found in each grid. For example, I_{12} means that twelve factories/warehouses/other industrial facilities were found in that grid. Vacant lots (S_2) will be included in "Open Land (S_1)", the combined total figure being recorded for each grid under "open".

Other Materials

Colored markers, push pins, and drafting tape are provided in order to do the recording on the maps themselves.

PROCEDURE:

(1) First Day's Visit

The first day's visit to the site should include a scanning of the neighbor-hood in the predetermined Zone I to locate and record the location of all of the resources directly on the mounted map that are delineated below. This first day's scanning of the neighborhood should also permit you to make any map corrections due to major neighborhood changes since the maps were drawn. Corrections made at this stage will save many headaches later on.

Appendix A-3

Tools needed: mounted site area map; red marker.

Print the location and name of the following resources on the map itself in Zone #1 in red according to the designated code. Since this map is your own copy and will not have to be returned, you may find it to your advantage to record as specifically as possible the name of each of the resources, so that when a tenant tells you the "First National Bank around the corner", you can refer to the exact location by having the name of that bank on your map.

Resource	Code
Bank	Bank
Bar	Bar
Beauty Shop	Beauty
Barber Shop	Barber
Church, synagogue	Church
Clothing Store	Clos
Doctor's Office (dentist, podiatrist, chiropractor, psychiatrist, etc.)	Doc
Drugstore	Drug
Grocery Store	Groc
Restaurant, Luncheonette, Drive-In, etc.	Eat
Supermarket	Super

(2) Question #33 of the Tenant Interview

Tools: Both mounted and larger site area maps (Zone II with first visit information marked; city map; overlay sheets; red, blue orange and black pencils.

In the context of the tenant interview, the one question directly pertaining to the neighborhood mapping process is Question #33. While interviewing, it is necessary to have the larger site area map and city map on hand. As specific resources are volunteered, they should be recorded on the interview sheet specifically enough to locate later on the map. No recording on the map itself will be done during the interview; however, locational information needs to be as clear as possible so it can be located on a piece of tracing paper immediately after the interview. Be sure to note the tenant's number & the site number; draw registration marks, etc., as tracing paper is marked.

Use one overlay per tenant. Locate the resources the tenant uses on his/her over lay sheet when possible, recording the code designated below for each re- source in the color designated.

It is also necessary to draw pathways on the overlay, for those resources which the tenant walks to and for the routes which the tenant uses for exercise or pleasure. Be sure the directions for the route are recorded specifically on the Q. #33 interview sheet during the interview.

Mark the pathways in black, following the example below.

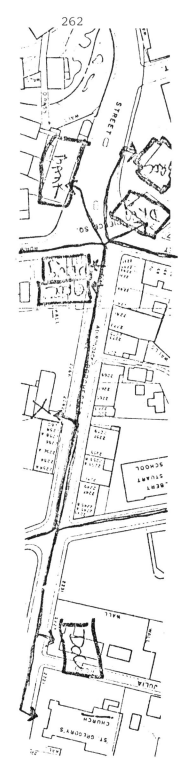

Circle in orange on overlay all resources which the tenant uses (i.e., write resources codes in red and blue; black is for the pathways.)

Black - Routes walked for exercise or pleasure or to resource.

Blue - Residential Resource: freind/Code; Frein; relative/Code: Rel.

Red - See "First Day's Visit" section for Resources and Codes.

After the second site mapping, circle in orange on the neighborhood area maps all those resources which the tenants walk to. (Go back to the individual over- lays and to the interview sheets. Some tenants may use different transportation means to get to the same resource.) A tenant walks, according to the interview, circle resource in orange; if a tenant uses any transportation, circle resource

Appendix A-3

From the interview we will also learn about resources in Zone 1 and outside Zone 1 which tenants get to by means other than walking. These resources should be circled in red on the neighborhood area maps., instead of orange, for walk.

The resources the tenant does not walk to also need to be located, even though the pathways taken there are irrelevant. There is, however, the possibility that these resources may not be close enough to the site to be found on the site area maps. When this is the case, mark the location of the resource on the city or road map with a dot, being sure to number these dotted locations, and attach a sheet to the map explaining what each numbered dot represents. For those resources located beyond the city map, just note that it is outside the city on the interview form.

After completing all the interviews make (1) a composite pathway overlay; (2) an interview resource list.

(1) Compile all the pathways used by tenants on a new overlay to be used only for this purpose. Begin with the first tenant interview and recopy all the pathways which appear on Tenant 1 overlay. For each successive interview, add only new pathways not used in previous interviews to the composite pathway overlay. Even though a pathway is used by all 20 tenants interviewed, it would appear only once on the composite. The boundaries of this composite become the "actual"zone 1 map.

(2) Make a list of all the resources and their locations which the tenants volunteered they used. Take this list into the field on the second site mapping expedition - to fill in resources missed in Zone 1 and to map for the first time those resources outside of Zone #1.

Appendix A-3

(3) Second Site Visit : After all interviews

Tools Needed: Actual zone I map with resources located; interview resource list; red, yellow, blue, green markers; instruction-code sheet.

After completing all the tenant interviews, you are ready for the second site visit. Map all the actual Zone I, recording all of the residential, open - space, industrial and commercial land usage as explained in the instruction sheet. Then map just those used and specify resources outside the predetermined Zone I.

The resources that need to be mapped in Zone #2 are those which the tenants specified in the interview. In addition, map the closest hospital (if there was none in Zone #1), the closest police station (if there was none in Zone #1).

All of these Zone #2 resources should be labeled in red according to the code for that resource in the Zone #1 instruction sheet. Only those which the tenants volunteered as having used from the interview should also be outlined in red (unless already outlined in orange because it is walked to).

Circled Areas

1. Outline in blue each land parcel by category of residential land use as listed below. Label each outlined parcel with the designated code. Write in red and outline in blue those commercial resources which also have resedences in the same structure.

Code

A
B
C
(specify on map)

Residential Land Use Category

1-2 story residence
3-5 story residence
6 + story residence
other residential (e.g., nursing home, public housing, hotel, motel)

2. Code and outline in green each land parcel categorized as "open space" in the list below. Label each outlined parcel with the designated code; e.g. "S₃" for Park.

Open Space Land Use Category	Code
Open land (demolition and cleared)	S_1
Vacant Lots	S_2
Parks	S_3

3. Label specifically the industrial use and outline in yellow each of the following two types of land parcels:

Industrial Land Use Category	Code
Factory	I_1
Warehouse and Storage	I_2

Labeled Areas

Complete Zone #1 by adding the following resources in red according to the designated code.

The coded words in the right hand column below correspond with categories on the grid recording sheet. However, we need more specific information on the map itself. For example, write "library" on the map rather than "cultural". On the grid recording sheet, "library" will then be tallied under the category "cultural".

RESOURCES		CODE
Bakery		Ba
Bank		Bk
Bar		Br
Beauty Shop		Bt
Barber shop		BB
Church/Synagogue		CH
Clothing		CL
Cultural (library, theater, (not movie) museum)		CT
Check Cashing		CC
Doctor's Office (dentist, podiatrist, psychiatrist etc.)		DR
Drugstore		DG
Drycleaner		CN
Food Specialty (butcher, fish, cheese, etc.)		BU
Fun (pool room, movie, bowling)		FN
Friend/Relative		FL
Gas Station		GS
General Store (dept. variety, 5&10)		ST

Appendix A-3

Grocery Store (NOT supermarket)	GC
Hospital	HO
Laundry/Laundromat	LD
Liquor Store	LQ
Miscellaneous Commercial	MC
Motel/Hotel	MH
Office Buildings	OF
Public Buildings (city hall, court house, fire station, etc.)	PB
Public Housing	PH
Police Station	PS
Post Office	PO
Repair/Service Shop	RE
Restaurant/Drive-In, Luncheonette	ET
Relative/Friend	RL
Vacant Storefronts, houses, lot	VC
Social Service ie: directed to elderly like drop-in, legal aid, YMCA, Golden Years, Welfare etc.	SS
Supermarket	SU
Transit Stop	TR

Note: There will be some resources that are not delineated on the code

sheet, and therefore do not need to be mapped explicitly. If you run across

any commercial facilities, for example, which do not fit into any of the coded

categories, label them "miscellaneous commercial".

(4)   Third Site Visit (Accessibility Mapping)

Tools Needed: map; new overlay; purple marker; slope measurement device

The third site visit, then, is the final mapping. The purpose of this visit

is to obtain slope measurements in areas of more than 5%, and to locate barriers

and public transportation stops in the actual Zone 1.

*** need definition
** need definition

*need to define 10%=10% of what?

**need definition
***

Accessibility Factor

BARRIERS

Target Building	BG
Cliffs	CF
Fence	FC — line
Highway	HG — line, area
Industry	IN — area, point
No Sidewalk	NA — line
***OPEN LAND- (zoned for commercial)	OL — area
**Open space public	OP — area
Other Barriers	OT — line, point
Playground	PG — area
Parking Lot	PK — point, area
Parks	PP — area
Stair	SA — area or line
*Slope (10%)	SL — line
Traffic light	TL — point
Uneven sidewalk or street	US — line
Waterbody	WB — point or area, line
Walklight	WL — point
Zone #1	ZN — area
Street pattern	II — line
School	SH — area or point

Appendix A-3

Record the location of the following on a new overlay in the actual Zone I:

(W) - walk light for pedestrian street crossing

(L) - traffic light

(T) - public transporation stop

B1, B2, B3 - barriers to pedestrian access, i.e.:

* percent of slope over 5%
* stairs other than those leading to buildings, including those leading to public transporation stops
* uneven sidewalk conditions
* railroad tracks
* water bodies
* major highway located at ground level
* cliffs
* other barriers (specify)

Provide legend to your codes as in examples.

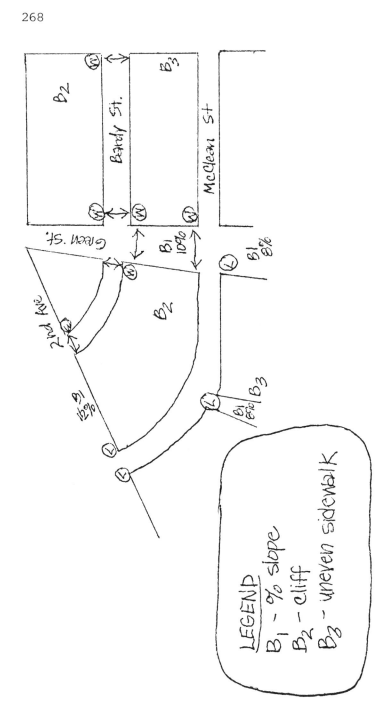

LEGEND
B1 - % slope
B2 - cliff
B3 - uneven sidewalk

Appendix A-3

(5) Grid Recording

After completion of the third site visit, transfer all of the color-coded

and located information onto the larger site area map.

Next, overlay the grided mylar in the way that it covers the greatest per-

centage of the located resources. Once you have found this position, outline the

mylar with a pencil all the way around.

Every grid cell you see with information inside now needs to be recorded on

the grid recording sheet, identifying the grid cell by the row number first,

column number second. Record quantities as demonstrated under "grid recording

sheet" explanation.

(6) Return to M.I.T.:

* large site area map(s) completely recopied from original
* tracing paper
* city map(s), as marked with dot legend
* grid recording sheets

Mailing address:

HEW Design Evaluation--Social Uses of Housing for the Elderly
Department of Architecture
77 Massachusetts Avenue, M.I.T
Room 3-433
Cambridge, Massachusetts   02139

Environmental Mapping – Zone 1   Appendix A-4
Deck #518

Col.	Item	Extended Label	Label
1-3	Site Identification	Site Identification 518:01-03	SITEID
4	Location identification	Location Identification 518:04	LOCIDEN
	Zone 1 Land Usage (%)		
5-6	Industrial	Industrial Land Usage 518:05-06	INDUSTRY
7-9	Residential *	Residential Land Usage 518:07-09	RESIDENT
10-11	Mixed residential and commercial	Mixed Residential & Commercial 518:10-11	RESICOMM
12-13	Commercial	Commercial Land Usage 518:12-13	COMMERCE
14-15	Total open **	Total Open Land Usage 518:14-15	OPENTOT
16-17	Open land(farm land, undeveloped,unforested)	Undeveloped Open Land 518:16-17	UNDVELOP
18-19	Public land (public ownership: park, play-ground, roadside rest)	Public Ownership Land 518:18-19	PUBLIC
20-21	Other (swamp, forrest, cemetary,etc.)	Other Open Land Usage 518:20-21	OTHEROEN
22-23	Other (river, lake, etc.)	Other Land Usage 518:22-23	OTHERUSE
24-25	Don'tknow, not labelled	Unknown Land Usage 518:24-25	UNKNOUSE

00	None
03	1-4%
05-95	5-95%(coded in intervals of 5)
99	Don't know

Barriers

26	Railroad	Railroad Barrier 518:26	RAILBAR
27	Highway, interstate	Highway Barrier 518:27	HIWAYBAR

* Includes residential parking on PH sites
** Includes all open land (open, parks, playgrounds) on PH sites
Design Evaluation Project - Data File 1974

Appendix A-4

Deck #518
Environmental Mapping – Zone 1

Col.	Item	Extended Label	Label
28	Wide street	Wide Street Barrier 518:28	STREET
29	River	River Barrier 518:29	RIVERBAR
30	Swamp	Swamp Barrier 518:30	SWAMPBAR
31	Cliff, sharp drop	Cliff Barrier 518:31	CLIFFBAR
	0 None		
	1-7 Code as counted		
	8 8 or more		
	9 N.A.		
	Facilities		
32	Barber or beauty shop	Barber, Beauty Shop 518:32	HAIRCARE
33	Clothing store	Clothing Store 518:33	CLOTHING
34	Doctor (any kind), dentist, clinic, medical building, (not hospital—coded separately)	Medical Office, Clinic 518:34	MEDICAL
35	Bank (not loan or check cash)	Bank 518:35	BANK
36	Drug store	Drug Store 518:36	DRUG
37	Grocery	Grocery Store 518:37	GROCERY
38	Supermarket	Supermarket 518:38	SUPERMKT
39	Church	Church 518:39	CHURCH
40	Social agencies (with services for elderly: drop-in center, Golden Years, Y's, etc)	Social Service For Elderly 518:40	SOCSERVE
41	Schools (any age)	Schools 518:41	SCHOOLS

Appendix A-4

Deck #518
Environmental Mapping – Zone 1

Col.	Item	Extended Label	Label
42-43	Vacancies (buildings only, not lots)	Building Vacancy 518:42-43	VACANT
44	Bars	Bars 518:44	BARS
45	Hospitals	Hospital 518:45	HOSPITAL
46	Restaurant, snacks	Food Service, Eatery 518:46	SERVFOOD
47	Police station	Police Station 518:47	POLICE
48	Booz (liquor store)	Liquor Store 518:48	LIQUOR
49	Repairs	Repair Store 518:49	REPAIRS
	0-7 as counted		
	8 8 or more facilities		
	9 NA, can't determine		

Zone 1 Notes and Measurements

Col.	Item	Extended Label	Label
58	Explanatory note abt.map Zone 1	Ex Zone 1 Ex 518:58	EXPLAIN
	0 absent		
	1 present		
59-62	Area in thousands of sq. feet	Zone 1 Area 518:59-62	AREAZONE
63-66	Total public housing area (site and other PH)in thousands of sq. feet	Zone 1 PH Area 518:63-66	AREAPH
67-70	Difference between Zone1 and PH area in thousands of sq. feet	Difference Zone 1 & PH Area 518:67-70	NONPH
71-73	Streets in hundreds of linear feet	Linear Footage Zone 1 Streets 518:71-73	LENTHSTR
74-76	Scale-MIT maps	Scale of MIT Maps 518:74-76	MITSCALE
78-80	Deck number	Deck Identification 518:78-80	DECK518

Appendix A-5

ENVIRONMENTAL MAPPING - NEIGHBORHOOD
RESOURCES AND USE

Preliminary Data Analysis Plan

Per Site

* frequency of use of resources
* frequency of occurrence of resources
  (base map data?)
* deviation among tenants in paths used and
  density of paths
* deviation among tenants in how far they
  walk
* boundary of resource utilization areas
* separate by resource category for mode
  and frequency
* relationship between tenants having access
  to a car vs. those not and their resource
  utilization
* how people get to friends
* proximity to major thoroughfare and
  correlation with crime perception
* how many people use each resource
* what resources are there and not being
  used
* equating physical distance as the crow
  flies and what distance people are
  actually travelling

Across Sites

* deviation among tenants walking distances
  (extremes in sites walked far, not walked
  far)
* comparison of resource area boundaries
  (smallest vs. largest)
* comparison of sites where people walk
  only close by (closest walking distance
  and average walking distance)
* by resource category for mode and
  frequency of category usage
* classification of sites by urban-rural
  and comparison of distances travelled by
  modes (walk vs. ride)
* types of resources used in urban vs.
  rural - scattered site vs. dense high-
  rise neighborhood use
* comparison of usage frequencies among
  resources located in Zone 1 and those
  outside Zone 1

Design Evaluation Project, MIT National
Survey 1974.

Appendix A-6

PREPARATION OF MAPPED DATA FOR THE COMPUTER

I   Overview

Information about resource locations, barriers, pathways, and
street intersections from the sixty site area maps will be
systematically entered on gridded trace by means of coordinate
system (Part I). Pathways and barriers will be keypunched
(Part II). When this is complete, information will be fed into
the computer using the "magic tablet" of the Architecture
Machine (Part III).

II   Brief Background

The Environmental Mapping component of the Design Evaluation
Project deals with analyzing neighborhood resources (commercial
and non-commercial entities where people go to satisfy day to
day needs). We are looking at types of resources, distance of
these from the site, the frequency of visits, and the mode of
transportation used. Our purposes are threefold: we wish to
develop this methodological instrument so that it may be used
by other researchers, we wish to compile and analyze this data
for the sites in our national sample, and lastly, if possible,
we would like to come up with some siting guidelines based on
neighborhood resources.

III Objective

To enable production of a graphic computer printout which
will show: resources available in the neighborhood, the
street patern, objects and terrain characteristics which
influence accessibility, and pathways taken by residents
to friends or relatives, resources and pleasure walks.

IV   Definitions

A.   Resource

     Any commercial, social, medical facility available for
     public use.

B.   Pathway

     Route walked by elderly resident to resource, friend/
     relative, or for pleasure.

C.   Accessibility Factor (Barrier)

     Any physical object or characteristic of terrain that
     could influence the route walked by elderly residents
     (psychological barriers are not included).

PROGRAM DOCUMENTATION

COMPUTER ANALYSIS SECTION
DESIGN EVALUATION PROJECT

We are dealing with a series of programs and utilities intended to accomplish our goals on the equipment we have available to us on the Design Evaluation Project. Basically, this consists of the Architecture Machine in Building 9 and the Information Processing Center in Building 39. While it would, of course, be preferrable to do everything with the same machinery, it does not work out that way. The IPC has Calcomp plotters, considerable dependability and availability, and the capability to handle large quantities of data easily. Thus, we are using those facilities for most of the work — the graphic output programs and the analysis programs. The architecture machine, however, has one thing the IPC lacks, and that is the necessary graphic input capability. That requires dedication of a small computer and associated graphic devices. So the Architecture Machine is used for digitizing the large site maps prepared by the Design Evaluation Project personnel.

To this point we have: 1) written the input program for the Architecture Machine and begun to collect data with it, 2) written the graphics output program for the IPC computers, tested it, and begun to run off preliminary plots. The analysis programs have yet to be specified and written. That will be accomplished in the course of this coming semester.

Graphic Input Program — Architecture Machine:

This program is to convert a large site map of individual points into a list of those named points along with their associated x- and y-coordinates (measured from the focus of the site, in feet). The final result is a paper tape of this data to be used as input to other programs.

Environment:

The Architecture Machine program is an interactive program. It makes use of a large Summagraphics tablet and an ARDS graphic display unit attached to a dedicated INTERDATA 7/32 computer. The program which handles the digitizing is written in Fortran. It consists of a short main routine — BRANDT.FORTRAN — and a shorter subroutine — NEWSIT.FORTRAN. The load module is BRANDT.LM. All are stored in the directory BRANDT.S.

Programming and Operation:

The subroutine handles the initialization of a new site. When a new site is indicated, or the program has just begun, a message asking for the site number is displayed on the ARDS screen. The operator then enters the number on the ARDS keyboard, and it is checked for syntax. Then the scale (feet/inch) is requested, entered, and checked in a similar manner. Finally, the origin for the site (the center or front door of the housing development) is requested by the program. To enter this, the operator must place a sensitive pen on the tablet at the point to be entered as the origin. The subroutine is then exited.

In the main routine, the program asks for a location name to be entered on the ARDS keyboard, and accepts the response. The response SI or SITE indicates that a new site is wanted (and the subroutine is called again to initialize for the new site). The response DO or DONE indicates that the operator is through, and the program ends. Any other response is accepted as a point name. A message is then displayed asking for the location of the point. Again, the operator must place the pen on the tablet to enter the point. The program contains, at this point: the site number; the scale; the point name; the location of the point, in hundredths of inches; and the location of the origin, in hundredths of inches. (The output from the tablet is x-y-coordinates, measured from an arbitrary point around the center of the tablet.) The coordinates of the point are recalculated be subtracting the coordinates of the operator-specified origin, dividing by 100 (divisions per inch), and multiplying by the scale (feet per inch). The resulting x and y values represent feet distant from the center of the site. The site number, point name, and new x and y values are written onto an output file.

Control:

At every juncture during the program at which the operator has entered information, it is assumed he may have made a mistake. To counteract this, the data just entered is always displayed on the ARDS, and a Y mustbe entered if the data is correct. Any other response forces a step backwards so that the data can be reentered. While this slows the operation, it prevents many errors.

Special Subroutines:

The access to the ARDS and the Summagraphics tablet uses inhouse routines. The ARDS is accessed by the subroutine ASK. It displays messages and, if requested, will wait until an entry has been returned through the keyboard. The Summagraphics subroutine is TABLET. When called, this will immediately return coordinates according to the position of the pen. It also returns a flag indicating whether the pen is touching the surface. Since the data is invalid until this situation occurs, the call is repeated continuously until the pen is placed on the tablet.

Output:

When all the data has been entered, and the program is finished, the output file is transferred to a paper tape using a simple utility. This tape is the transfer medium between the Architecture Machine and the IPC as no online transfer is available.

Input Preparation for the IBM 370/168

There are 3 types of data to be entered onto files for the 370 processing: the locations taken from the site map using the Architecture Machine program; pathways determined and coded by the Design Evaluation Project personnel; and interview data collected by various agencies in different formats.

All data sets referred to in conjunction with the 370 are disk files prefaced by the project and programmer numbers. Thus, when I refer to LOCUS.DATA, the system catalog knows it by the complete name U.M12060.P13885.LOCUS.DATA. On the TSO terminals, the logon identifies the prefix, so LOCUS.DATA is sufficient.

All Fortran load modules for this project are stored in the module library U.M12060.P13885.MAIN.LOAD.

Locations:

The locations are on the paper tape created by the program above. This tape is entered directly onto a 370 disk file via a TSO terminal equipped with a paper tape reader. However, it requires two manipulations before it is ready for processing. First, the duplicates must available on the 370. The two operations are done in one job using a 3-file system. The new input being added to the data is stored on LOCUS.DATA. A copy of the existing data is stored on LOCUS1.DATA. The Both files are sorted together and stored on a temporary data set. The duplicates are eliminated from this data set and it is stored on LOCUS2.DATA. This is the complete file, ready for processing.

Pathways:

The pathways are punched onto cards. There are two types: "paths" contain site number, tenant number, destination, and names of points along the way; "objects" contain the site number and the list of points defining the object. This file also requires some manipulation. It is first copied onto PATH.DATA using a copy utility. The final column, to indicate whether a path is to be continued, must be converted to a numeric using the Fortran program PATHCHNG. And the records are sorted using the utility. Again, a 3-file system is used. New data — PATH.DATA — is fed to the PATHCHNG, then combined with the existing data — PATH1.DATA — for the sort. The sorted records are stored on PATH2.DATA.

Interviews:

The interview data is stored on a magnetic tape, at least until it is needed. It is stored in 80-column records in various formats. It will not be used until some analysis programs are written.

Graphic Output Program — IBM 370/168:

This program is intended to display the basic elements known to us about the areas near the elderly housing projects. A Calcomp plotter is used to plot the information for a particular site within a 28" x 28" square. It can plot the existing resources and intersections by point and name, and show other objects, barriers, and pathways taken by the residents. Various options regulating the amount and manner of display of different elements are detailed in the accompanying input documentation.

Environment:

The graphic output program is a Fortran program named BRANDT stored on the library MAIN.LOAD. It includes 5 subroutines: LOCATE, PTHFIL, PTHPLT, POINT, and OBJCTS. The source is stored on the file GRAFIC.FORT. The program is run on the IBM 370/168 in a time-sharing mode and produces a listing and a magnetic tape. This tape controls a separate Calcomp plotter, which produces a plot on a 30" roll. (Ballpoint on white paper is used unless otherwise specified.)

Programming:

The program is centered around two common blocks. One contains up to 500 locations, meaning arrays for the x-coordinates, y-coordinates, and names. Because the name may exceed 4 characters, an 8-byte location is required for each. The other common contains up to 1000 individual path segments. Each segment includes the start and end points, and the number of times it is traversed.

The first two subroutines are concerned with storing data in the commons, the last three with displaying it.

The main routine first takes care of some standard plotter initialization and other set-up tasks. It then reads a record from the job stream input. It prints out the site and the scale. It then evaluates each control switch in turn and prints a description of the option chosen. The following calls are made, unless the options indicate that a call is unnecessary:

LOCATE reads in the locations. The arrays in the common are first filled with zeroes. Records are read from the LOCUS2.DATA file until the relevant site number is found. Records are then read sequentially and stored in succeeding locations in the arrays — name and x and y values (the first point is always designated 'II ',0,0). The coordinates are summed separately to determine to what extent the map is off-center. When a new site is encountered, the average is calculated and subtracted from each point to re-center the plot empirically. The number of points is printed, and the subroutine is exited.

PTHFIL reads in the pathways. The arrays in the path common are filled with zeroes. Records are read from PATH2.DATA until the relevant site is encountered. Paths are then read sequentially and tested for acceptability. If "no paths" has been specified, all paths are bypassed. If only specific tenants are to be accepted, the tenant number is checked against the list of tenants specified. If only specific resource types are to be plotted, the resource designation is checked against the list of acceptable resources. If either test fails, the path is bypassed. (If the path continues over more than one record, the entire path is discarded.) If the path is accepted, the first point is assumed to be 'II '. Each point is combined with the succeeding one to form a segment. The arrays are searched to find out if that segment has already been included. If so, the number of uses is incremented. If not, the path segment is added to the arrays, and the uses set to one. If the path is continued to the next record, the last point is combined with the first of the next record to form a path segment, and processing is continued. When a path delimiter (* in column 15) is discovered, the subroutine is exited.

FTHPLT plots the path segments. It proceeds sequentially through the path arrays, plotting each segment separately. It draws one line between the endpoints. If multiple stroking has been specified, it draws additional lines parallel to the first, .01 inches apart, alternating sides, until the number of paths has been reached. (A maximum of 10 lines is allowed.) This gives the appearance of a much thicker line, in proportion to the amount of use. If annotation is requested, the number of uses is plotted above the line, regardless of whether single or multiple lines have been used. The direction and magnitude of x- and y-offsets for multiple stroking and annotation are determined by: 1) conversion of the angle of the line to its perpendicular and 2) a reverse application of the Pythagorean Theorem (we know the hypoteneuse = .01). A list of the segments and frequencies is printed along with missing points. When the end of the data is reached, the subroutine is exited.

POINT plots the point symbols, except the origin, which is plotted in LOCATE. The intersections are +'s. Resources are o's. If all resources or intersections are to be plotted, the points from the location common are used. If only those appearing on the pathways are to be plotted, the points from the path common are used, and the location common is searched to find the associated coordinates. If the name indicates that the point is of the object category, the point is ignored altogether. If not, the beginning of the name is checked to see if it is an intersection or a resource. Intersections begin with 'II '. Others are resources. If only one type is to be plotted, the others are ignored. If the point is accepted, the proper symbol is assigned and plotted.

NAMEPT is an entry within POINT. It uses basically the same processing, but at the end, instead of the symbol, the name itself is plotted slightly above and to the right of the point.

OBJCTS plots additional objects on the site. It is used for two purposes. First, to show barriers and other objects of interest (not resources). These can be single points, linear objects, or solid objects. Single points are shown by a simple symbol - superimposed 'X' and 'O', and the name of the point, linear objects by connecting two or more of these points, and solid objects by connectig back to the first point. The second purpose is to show the general street system, as a series of linear objects connecting intersections. The file PATH2.DATA is read, beginning where PTHFIL left off. If only streets ('II') or only the other items are to be plotted, the first point of the record is checked. If irrelevant, the next record is read. The first point is plotted (symbol and name). Each successive point is plotted, and connected to the previous one. If the object requires more than one record, the remainder is treated as a separate, but connected object. A list of objects and/or streets is plotted along with any missing points. When a new site or the object delimiter (** in column 15-16) is encountered, the subroutine is exited.

Back in the main routine, the first note (site number and scale) is plotted. If additional notes have been specified, that exact number are read from the job stream input and plotted in the lower right corner. The program goes back to the beginning and reads the next specification card, and begins all over again. When it reaches the end of the input, it closes the plot and ends.

Special Subroutines:

Calcomp subroutines are avalable on this system from the library SYS5.SUBR.LIBRARY. This program uses only PLOT, SYMBOL, and NUMBER. See IFC documents for detailed descriptions. The Fortran function ATAN(X) is used to determine angles from endpoints.

Operation:

The program is run from TSO, using the userid BRANDT. This gives access to all the files mentioned, as well as others used to manipulate them. The Job Control Language used to run the program is stored in CALCOMP.CNTL. The input should be edited to perform the required tasks (see input documentation for details). Care should be taken not to destroy the final line of the job, which writes the specifications for the plot. The job can then be entered with the command 'subx calcomp'.

A listing will usually be available in 15-30 minutes, and the plot in 45-90 minutes.

BRANDT ANDERSSON
January, 1976

BEHAVIOR MAPPING - Definition. Behavior mapping is a term used to describe methods of observing and recording the way people behave in or use spaces. The procedure has 5 elements:

1. A graphic rendering of the area(s) to be observed;

2. A clear definition of the human behaviors to be observed, counted, described or diagrammed;

3. A schedule of repeated times during which the observation and recording will take place;

4. A systematic procedure which is followed in observing;

5. A coding and counting system which minimizes the effort required in recording observations.

An example of behavior mapping relates to common spaces in Elderly Housing, where the primary question posed was the extent of Informal (not Programmed) use of these spaces.

A. Community Rooms

1. How do elderly tenants informally use community rooms?

2. How active are community rooms in elderly housing?

   a. Behaviors (number and variety)
   b. Circulation (Peripheral, Internal, Transient)

3. What is the proportion of tenants who occupy community rooms over daytime hours?

4. What do elderly tenants do in community rooms?

   a. alone
   b. in pairs
   c. in clusters
   d. by sex (in relation to tenant mix)

B. Entry foyers, areas and entry lobbies (same questions as A 1-4).

   a. How does size of entry area affect intensity (% of tenants) who occupy rather than pass through?

C. How do the spatial relations of entry areas and community rooms affect the informal uses of community rooms?

1. Does visibility of community room and its activities from entry area attract entry area users?

2. Does closeness of community room to entry area affect frequency of use (entering) community room?

3. When a corridor separates a community room from an entry area, does this distance discourage informal exploration and use of community room?

4. Does exploration and uniform use of community room from entry hall depend on length of corridor?

Appendix B-1.

5. Does exploration and uniform use of
   community room from entry hall depend
   on how visible community room is
   down corridor from entry area?

6. Does exploration and informal use of
   community room depend upon such
   intervening excuse-activities as mail
   boxes in corridor between entry and
   community room?

INTERIOR: MAIN FLOOR SPATIAL TYPOLOGY I.

Mid and High Rise Structures. Spatial Typ - ology I is specifically concerned with community rooms, entrance lobby and the connecting area between them in elderly housing.

Definitions:

1. Entrance Lobby or Area (Main) - that space into which the main door opens and defined by existing walls.

2. Main Community Room - the largest non-lobby social space (for purposes of this segment, on the main floor, only).

3. Connecting Spaces - corridors or any other areas which connect the entry area directly or indirectly to the main community room.

4. Elevator Landing - main floor - the space immediately surrounding the elevator(s) opening(s) on the main floor.

5. Mail Area - the area in which tenants have access to their mail boxes.

How to Select Buildings to be Studied: The three variables used in the development of the building spatial typology I were: a) visibility, from the Entry to Elevator Pathway into the main community room; b) the length of the corridor, from the Entry to Elevator Pathway access point to the main community room; c) the existence of a mail box area within the corridor (where one exists) which lead to the main community room.

Appendix B-1.

THE 5 BUILDING TYPES TO BE STUDIED

TYPE*   CRITERIA

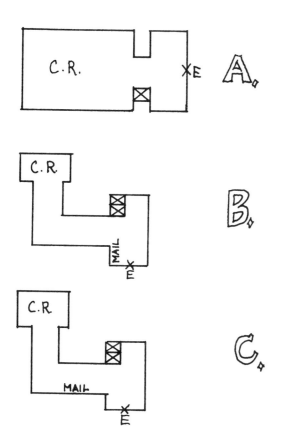

1. $\geq$30% visibility into community room
    from any point along E-E Pathway
2. No connecting (e.g., corridor) space,
    i.e.: $\geq$2'
3. No intervening mail area

1. No visibility into community room from
    any point along E-E Pathway
2. Connecting space or corridor $\geq$50' in
    length from lobby to community room
3. No intervening mail area.

1. No visibility into community room from
    any point along E-E Pathway
2. Connecting space or corridor $\geq$50'
    in length.
3. Intervening mail area

TYPE

CRITERIA

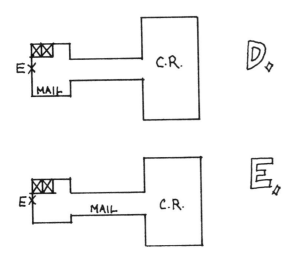

1. ≤30% visibility into community room
2. Connecting space or corridor
   2'<L<50'
3. No intervening mail area

1. ≤30% visibility into community room
2. Connecting space or corridor
   2'<L<50'
3. Intervening mail area

* the diagrams shown are similified examples
of <u>possible</u> arrangements of spaces that follow
the rules for selecting one particular
building type. Either the location of the
entry or of the elevators may be different
for the building to still qualify.

Directions for computing % of visibility of community room from the entry to elevator pathway:

1. Find the point on the E-E Pathway which affords the largest view of the main community room.

2. Draw the angle of view afforded by that point into the community room; assume all doors open.

3. Compute the total square footage of the community room included in the viewed angle.

4. Compute the total main community room use in square footage.

5. Determine the percentage the view footage is of the total area.

$$\text{Visibility} = \frac{\text{View of Area}}{\text{TCR Area}} \times 100$$

Behavior Mapping: Preparation, etc.

In order to do behavior mapping, it is necessary to have floor plans of ground and typical floor plans, (and sometimes site plans as well).

The scale of these plans should be 1/8" = 1', and should clearly show floor layout without any numbers or verbiage which might cover floor area.

Since the main entry floor with its community room, main entrance, is our focus, it is this area of the building which is most important to have in a useable form. In most cases, this necessitates getting the whole main floor "cleaned up" of any unnecessary labels, numbers, etc., and in a reproduceable form. Once clear, easily legible copies have been made of the main floor, it is a simple matter to cut them up into 8-1/2 x 11 sizes, being careful to include the salient, previously designated areas all on one page (in some cases, it might be necessary to use a slightly large size copy).

Once the area to be studied has been delineated and is in a useable form and size, it is suggested that registration marks be added via two x's spaced across one side of the plan by which future overlaid information can be matched up.

Order of Tasks:

1. Review floor plans of elderly housing and select a site which meets typology criteria.

2. Go to the site and compare actual spaces with the floor plan.

3. Prepare simplified floor plan of areas to be studied.

4. Label those rooms on your base map to establish a room ID code that will go on every sheet of trace used to record that room.

5. For each room you plan to map, go through the following procedure:

   A. Do Overlay #1

      1. Label site and room ID
      2. Draw registration marks that correspond to those on the base map and pin or tape overlay to base map at registration marks
      3. Label views and draw arrows from vantage points as explained in Overlay #1

   B. Do Overlay #2

      1. Label site and room ID
      2. Draw registration marks and pin to base map
      3. Label fixed features as explained in Overlay #2

   C. Do Overlay #3

      1. Label site and room ID
      2. Draw registration marks and pin
      3. Draw in and label furniture according to Overlay #3

   REPEAT A-C for each room you plan to map

6. Set up a schedule of observation blocks according to plan.

It is important to know how typical the uses of a room or an area are in the day to day life of a building. One or two observation blocks are, therefore, not enough evidence of typical use. Time Sampling is one method used to schedule observations of spatial behavior.

A typical schedule for visiting and observing will:

a) select specific days of the week on which to visit,

b) select the same blocks of hours on those days to visit.

Sample Schedule for Observation Block

	Mon.	Tues.	Wed.	Thurs.	Fri.	Sat.	Sun.
AM 10-11		X	X				X
PM 2-3			X	X			
5-6	X					X	

Site_____

Room_____

Observer name_____

Each of the above days and hours should receive a minimum of 3-4 data recording sessions. Resulting information should reveal, for example, that activities in the lobby area at the site are different at 10-11 AM on Sunday than on Tuesday and Wednesday (when mail is delivered), or that there is (or is not) consistent types of use of a community room between 2-3 PM on week-day afternoons.

Draw registration marks:

You have made reproductions of the floor plans for the areas to be studied according to the instructions. Each area will appear on a separate sheet approximately notebook size. Provide the following information about each area to be studied.

1. Views through windows and doors (from any point in the room), using an arrow from vantage point to outside the room then describe what you see in writing (see suggested list below). For each window, measure (in inches) from the floor to the window sill and the vertical window dimension. Specify dimension on each overlay, e.g., 34"/48".

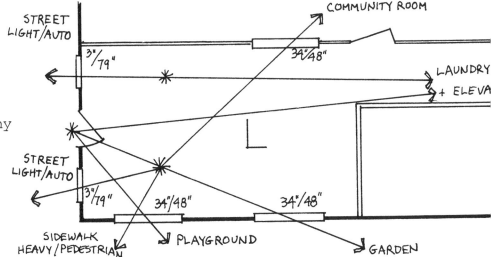

$$\frac{\text{floor to window}}{\text{vertical window dimension}} = \frac{34"}{48"}$$

List of possible views:
STREET -- Heavy/light; auto/pedestrian
SIDEWALK -- Heavy/light
OUTDOOR PARKING LOT
PLAYGROUND
ON-SITE SITTING AREAS
FENCES
GARDEN
RESIDENCES

Site_____

Rm. I.D._____

Label a new sheet of trace with the site and
room ID, lay it over the base map, and mark
all built-in or semi-permanent features of
the space as shown below (this overlay shows
locations of things more permanent than
furniture, but less permanent than walls...
see Overlay #3 for furniture). Where
applicable, use the following code. If
you encounter an object not mentioned here,
make up a code for it and be sure to
write a definition of your code in the
margin of that overlay.

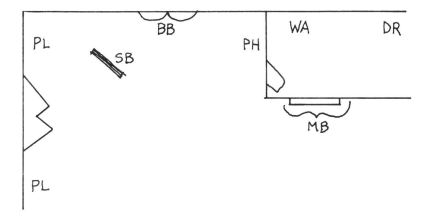

FIXED FEATURE CODES:

MB   mailboxes for tenants
USMB   U.S. mailbox for depositing mail
BB   bulletin board
WF   water fountain
PL   large plants or planters
ASH   built-in ashtrays
DIR   wall-mounted building directory
        (listing residents)
SB   free-standing blackboard or sign
        board (as opposed to a wall-
        mounted blackboard or bulletin
        board)
PH   pay phones
VM   vending machines
WA   washer
DR   dryer
GB   garbage chute

Site _____

Room I.D. _____

Appendix B-1.

Draw registration marks!

We are interested in the following issues in behavior mapping:

1. Type of activities - notation of activities as observed in a visual sweep of the room/space.

2. Circulation - notation of movement patterns within and between rooms/spaces.

(Specific procedures for mapping these follow).

The following 5 episodes constitute a single observation block.

Episode 1= First Sweep (S_1)
Episode 2= Second Sweep (S_2)
Episode 3= Circulation mapping (C)   = ONE OBSERVATION BLOCK
Episode 4= Third Sweep (S_3)
Episode 5= Fourth Sweep (S_4)

Each behavior mapping episode will be done on a separate numbered (coded) sheet of tracing paper laid over the furniture overlay and the base map for the room being mapped.

Fill in the information in the corner on each sheet of tracing paper as shown below:

Name of room _____

Date and day of week_____   Sheet

Time of day _____   ID

Check appropriate box:

☐   ☐   ☐   ☐   ☐
S_1 S_2 C S_3 S_4

Note observer location on each sheet with an X. Choose a location within the room/space with the best vantage point, if possible.

You will record all persons present in the
room during each observation episode. Remain
in the same position in the room during each
episode, but you may relocate yourself
between episodes. Mark you position with an
X on the beginning of each observation
episode.

Each episode consists of a single complete
visual sweep around the room.

EXAMPLE: a) O to mark the exact location
of person (if sitting down,
draw circle over the appropriate piece of furniture)

b) use ♂ (female   symbols to
♀ (male)   indicate sex
and orientation

EXAMPLE: ♂⚥O male and female facing one
another

c) inside or near each circle, code
the behavior(s) observed at
that moment using the following
letters:

T - talking
G - game playing
D - game watching
E - eating or drinking
R - reading
S - sleeping
C - doing crafts or making
something

W - writing
V - watching TV
M - moving furniture
K - walking or wheeling
A - greeting or acknowl-
edging

When other types of behavior are observed,
please specify.

Do not go back to pick up new people and
events. As you scan, record where an
individual is and what he/she is doing in
accordance with the codes above for behaviors.

Immediately after completing the first
observation episode, replace Tracing 1 with
a fresh trace making sure to draw registration
marks and fill in sheet I.D. before
beginning the second sweep.

d) if the person is in a wheelchair or
using a walker or cane, use the
following code:

wheelchair

walker/cane

The circulation mapping is the Third episode in an observation block. It immediately follows the first two behavior sweeps (S_1, S_2) and is immediably followed by two more behavior sweeps (S_3, S_4). The circulation episode should cover a 15 minute time interval.

You will record all persons moving about the room/space in which you are located. (We are interested only in single direct movements and not in following an individual's path). Remain in the same position in the room during the entire episode. On a separate piece of paper, begin coding movements according to the following directions:

1. Place already completed furniture trace over the base map. Place the gridded transparency over the furniture trace and base map. Line grids up to major exits and entrances into the room/space appear in separate grids, as much as possible. Registration marks on gridded transparency must correspond to those already on base map and furniture overlay. Become familiar with locations of furniture and physical features on the grid.

2. On a piece of 8-1/2 x 11 paper, set up a circulation recording sheet as shown on the attached sample form. Write your name, site, room, date, time and weather conditions on recording form. Begin to code the circulation movements in the room/space by recording each single movement of a person from the grid where the movement either stops, changes direction or is no longer visible. Place movement notation and sex of individual in appropriate column.

EXAMPLE: If a male moves from grid 2B to the mailbox (3C), stops to open and read his mail, and then moves back to grid 2B, code this as two separate movements

M	F	
✓		2B-3C
	✓	3C-2B

If the person enters the room/space from another room or an unobservable location, precede the grid notation where he enters with an arrow; if he exits to another room, an unobservable space, follow the grid notation at this location with an arrow.

EXAMPLE: If a female enters the lobby from the elevator (6A), goes to the mailbox (3C) to check her mail, and then leaves the building through the front entrance (3D), it is coded as follows:

```
M      F
 ───────────────────
       ──→ 6A-3C

       3C-3D ──→
```

movements in black. Movements that have been coded as entering or exiting with arrows are drawn as dotted lines from the exit or entrance grid out to the unobservable spaces or other room (see example).

3. Do NOT record any stationary behavior during this entire 15 minute circulation mapping. At the end of the 15 minute circulation observation, do Behavior Sweeps 3 and 4 to complete the observation block.

4. You are now ready to draw circulation lines from the information recorded during the 15 minute interval. Place trace overlay on top of grid and base map. Be sure to line up registration marks. Draw registration marks on overlay. From information taken from circulation recording sheet, fill in sheet I.D., note observer location with an X on the overlay. Proceed with drawing on this overlay the movements from the center of originating grid to the center of terminating grid. Draw Female movements in red; male

Appendix B-2

Design Evaluation Peoject, MIT, Cambridge, MA 1976

Tenant Interview
SPATIAL ANALYSIS

Apartment Number _____
Building _____
Date _____
Interviewer _____

1. How long have you lived here?

   1 _____ more than two years
   2 _____ 6 months to 2 years
   3 _____ less than 6 months
   4 _____ one month or less

2. Did you live in this neighborhood before you moved here?

   1 _____ yes   Where? _____
   2 _____ no

2.1 Can you describe to me where you lived before?
    (Probe for dwelling type and number of rooms)

    _____
    _____

2.2 Why did you decide to move into this building?

    _____

3. About how many people in this building did you know
   by name when you first moved in?

   1. _____ none
   2 _____ few
   3 _____ many

4. About how many new people in the building do you now know
   by name?

   1 _____ none
   2 _____ few

Is there a tenants' club in this building?

1 ___ yes
2 ___ no (go to Q. 6)

[IF YES, ASK:]

A. Do you belong to that club?

1 ___ yes   Why not? _____
2 ___ no   _____

B. How often does it meet?

1 ___ every week
2 ___ every two weeks
3 ___ once a month
4 ___ whenever called

C. How often do you attend?

1 ___ almost always
2 ___ occasionally, sometimes
3 ___ rarely } → Why not more often? _____
4 ___ never   }   _____

6. What other groups or activities do you regularly participate in here? And where do they meet?

Activities   Where

1 ___ beano, bingo   1 _____
2 ___ arts & crafts   2 _____
3 ___ card playing group   3 _____
4 ___ men's club   4 _____
5 ___ diet club or exercise   5 _____
      group   6 _____
6 ___ other (list) _____
      _____

7 ___ none

7. Do you participate in any activities or organizations outside of the building?

1 ___ yes   List: _____
2 ___ no   _____

(If Yes)

7.1 How do you get there? (mode of transportation) _____

Appendix B-2

8. Would you say then that most of your activities happen within the building or away from it?

1 _____ within
2 _____ outside, away from
3 _____ about equal
4 _____ does not engage in activity outside of apartment

9. How many people do you think live in this building?

_____

10. Have you ever lived in a building this size before?

1 _____ yes   If yes, what type? _____
2 _____ no

11. Do you think that there are too many people, too few, or just the right number in this building?

1 _____ too many
2 _____ too few
3 _____ just the right number
4 _____ NA, DK

Why do you think that? _____

12. What do you think is the ideal number of people for an apartment building like this one?

_____

12.1 Which would you prefer: to live in a building with all older people or to live in a building with people of all ages?

1 _____ all older
2 _____ all ages
3 _____ no opinion
4 _____ NA,DK

13. Is there anyone here who visits you in your apartment?

14. Would you rather visit in other's apartments or have people visit you in your apartment?

1 ___ other's apartments
2 ___ own apartment
3 ___ both
4 ___ neither
5 ___ NA, DK

15. Can you usually recognize when someone in the building is just a visitor and doesn't live here?

1 ___ yes, most of the time
2 ___ sometimes
3 ___ no, it's hard to tell the difference
4 ___ never notice
5 ___ NA,DK

16. People call different rooms by different names. Now I would like to ask you about the names you use for the rooms and areas outside of your apartment. (Describe) LABEL ROOM NAMES ON GROUND FLOOR PLAN AND TYPICAL FLOOR PLAN ATTACHED AT END.

17. Are there any hours of the day or night when you cannot use any of those rooms?

1 ___ yes ——⟶ What are the rooms and the hours? _____
2 ___ no   _____
                                                 _____

18. Are there any rules or understandings that you have about what people can or cannot do in any places?

1 ___ yes ——⟶ What are those rules? _____
2 ___ no   _____
3 ___ DK

[Probe: sitting, sleeping, drinking]

19. Can you tell me what happens here at night? What do people usually do and where does it happen?

_____

_____

_____

20. About how often do you go out of this building in good weather?

1 _____ every day
2 _____ several times a week
3 _____ once a week
4 _____ once every 2 weeks
5 _____ once a month
6 _____ never
7 _____ other _____

SHARED ZONE

General Information

21. Is there a particularly good place in the building to meet new acquaintances? PROBE.

_____

_____

22. Do you ever feel the need just to get out of your apartment?

1 _____ yes ⟶ Why do you feel that need? _____

2 _____ no   _____

23. How many times last week did you get together with others somewhere in the building other than in your apartment?

1 _____ more than once a day
2 _____ once a day
3 _____ several times last week
4 _____ once a week
5 _____ not at all

25. Are there places on your own floor or other floors
where people do get together? [PROBE FOR USE OF
UPSTAIRS LOUNGES.]

1 _____ yes
2 _____ no (go to Q. 26)

[IF YES] where are these places? _____

_____

_____

What do people do when they get together in these places?

_____

_____

When do they usually get together in these places?

1 _____ morning
2 _____ afternoon
3 _____ evening

When you use that space, do you ever feel that you might
be bothering others in nearby apartments?

1 _____ yes   Comments _____
2 _____ no   _____

Does it bother anyone that there are people using that
space?

1 _____ yes   Comments _____
2 _____ no   _____

Appendix B-2

Ease of Social Contact

26. Where are you most likely to run into others:

1 _____ coming in or going out of the building
2 _____ passing by social spaces
3 _____ going to get mail

28. Where are you least likely to run into others?

1 _____ coming in or out of the building
2 _____ passing by social spaces
3 _____ going to get mail

29. Yesterday, did you pass by/go into the following:
    (fill in spaces according to specific building)

	Pass by	Go in
a.	_____	_____
b.	_____	_____
c.	_____	_____
d.	_____	_____
e.	_____	_____

31. Can you tell if there is something going on in the
    (fill in 3 rooms in specific building) without going in?

a. _____

1 _____ yes
2 _____ no

[IF *NO* : do you usually go into _____ to find out?

1 _____ yes
2 _____ no
3 _____ sometimes

[IF YES- if you do see or hear someone you know in the
    when passing by, do you usually go in?

1 _____ yes
2 _____ no
3 _____ sometimes

b. _____

1 _____ yes
2 _____ no

[IF *NO* : do you usually go into _____ to find out?

1 _____ yes
2 _____ no
3 _____ sometimes

[IF YES- if you do see or hear someone you know in the
    when passing by, do you usually go in?

[IF *NO* : do you usually go into _____ to find out?

_____ 1 yes
_____ 2 no
_____ 3 sometimes

[IF YES- if you do see or hear someone you know in the when passing by, do you usually go in?

_____ 1 yes
_____ 2 no
_____ 3 sometimes

_____

32. Generally, about how often would you say you go into any of the social rooms in the building?

_____ 1 every day/night, 5 or more times a week
_____ 2 several times a week, 2-4 days/week
_____ 3 once a week
_____ 4 2-3 times a month
_____ 5 once a month
_____ 6 rarely, less than once a month
_____ 7 never (go to Q. 34)

33. Do you make a special trip to go to any social rooms here, or do you usually just stop in when you are on your way somewhere else?

_____ 1 usually special trip
_____ 2 usually on the way somewhere else
_____ 3 both about equally
_____ 4 don't know
_____ 5 other. SPECIFY

_____

Ease of Access to Apartment

"Now I want you to think about the trip from the front door of the building to your apartment."

34. Do you find it is too long a trip?

_____ 1 yes ———→ Why is it uncomfortable? _____
_____ 2 no
_____ 3 no opinion

34.1 (For those who live on the first floor): Do you ever use the elevator?

_____

_____

35. Now what about the trip from the front door to the elevator -- do you find that too long or inconvenient?

1 ___ yes ——⟩ Why is it uncomfortable? _____
2 ___ no
3 ___ no opinion

36. Now what about the ride in the elevator -- do you find that too long or uncomfortable?

1 ___ yes ——⟩ Why is it uncomfortable? _____
2 ___ no
3 ___ no opinion

37. What about your trip from the elevator on your floor to your apartment door -- do you find that too long or uncomfortable?

1 ___ yes ——⟩ Why is it uncomfortable? _____
2 ___ no
3 ___ no opinion

38. Have you ever lived in a building before that had an elevator?

1 ___ yes ——⟩ [IF YES] how would you compare that elevator
2 ___ no   ride to this ride? _____

_____
_____

39. Do elevators make you feel uncomfortable?

1 ___ yes   Comments _____
2 ___ no
_____
_____

39.1 Do you think it is easy for strangers to get into the building?

_____

Security and Privacy of Access Route to Apartment   Appendix B-2

40. Do you think that the location of the elevator makes it
easier for strangers to get up to the apartment floors
once they are in?

Comments: _____

1 ____ yes
2 ____ no
3 ____ no opinion

41. Do you ever see people on your apartment floor who you
don't recognize or who don't seem to live here?

Does that make you feel uncomfortable?   1 ____ yes
                                                 2 ____ no

42. Do you ever see people you don't recognize when riding in
the elevator?

Does that make you feel uncomfortable?   1 ____ yes
                                                 2 ____ no

Offensive Surveillance and Unwanted Social Contact

43. Do you feel uncomfortable passing by certain places in
the building where people are sitting around and
talking?

                          Specify places:
1 ____ yes
2 ____ no   _____
3 ____ no opinion   _____

4 ____ NA(does not happen)

45. Can you tell me what path you take and what stops you make
along the way when coming into the building?

Appendix B-2

46. Is that the same route you use when you leave the building?

```
1 ___ yes          ⌐
2 ___ no - [TRACE ROUTE ON FLOOR PLAN]
3 ___ most of the time
```

47. Do you ever use any door other than the main entrance when you leave the building?

```
1 ___ yes, often          ⌐ What door? _____
2 ___ yes, sometimes      |
3 ___ yes, but rarely     ⌐ _____
4 ___ no
```

48. Are there any places in the building where you <u>always</u> see the <u>same</u> people?

```
1 ___ yes ——→ Where? _____
2 ___ no              _____
```

Privacy of Shared Spaces

49. Are there any areas that you think are too exposed to neighborhood view?

```
1 ___ yes
2 ___ no
3 ___ no opinion
4 ___ not applicable

[IF YES:] Which rooms are those and why do you feel
          they are too exposed/public? _____
          _____
```

49.1 Are there any areas in the building that you think are not private enough?
_____

how they are dressed?

1 ___ yes
2 ___ no
3 ___ no opinion
4 ___ not applicable

[IF YES:] Where are those places? _____

_____

[IF NO:] Would you like such a place?

1 ___ yes
2 ___ no
3 ___ no opinion
4 ___ not applicable

51. Do you feel uncomfortable in using the social spaces if there are people present who you don't know?

1 ___ yes
2 ___ no
3 ___ no opinion

Openness of Facilities to Surrounding Community

52. Are there ever activities in the community room to which people from the neighborhood are invited along with the people who live here? (i.e., meals program)

1 ___ yes
2 ___ no
3 ___ don't know

[IF YES:] Do you ever attend those activities?

1 ___ yes
2 ___ no
3 ___ NA

[IF YES:] Does there seem to be enough room to accommodate all the people who attend those activites?

1 ___ yes
2 ___ no
3 ___ DK, can't judge

53. Are people from the neighborhood allowed to use the community room for their own meetings and activities?

1 ___ yes
2 ___ no
3 ___ don't know

[IF YES] Do you think that it is a good idea that they use this building for their own meetings?

Comments: _____

1 ___ yes
2 ___ no
3 ___ no opinion

_____

54. What do you think about this neighborhood? Does it seem friendly to you?

_____
_____
_____

Now I want to ask you some questions about your floor.

Residential zone

55. About how many people on this entire floor do you know by name?

Specific number _____

56. Do you happen to know how many people live on this floor?

Specific number _____

57. Would you say that this number of people per floor is too few, too many, or about the right number?

1 ___ too few
2 ___ too many
3 ___ about right number
4 ___ no opinion

58. Do you feel that you know the people better on your side of the elevator/building?

1 ___ yes
2 ___ no
3 ___ about the same

Appendix B-2

59. When you are riding up to your apartment on the elevator and the doors open, how do you tell if you are on the right floor? (Probe for recognition of features of elevator lobby, not signals inside the elevator.)

_____

_____

60. Have you ever gotten off on the wrong floor?

1 _____ yes, once or rarely
2 _____ yes, sometimes
3 _____ yes, frequently
4 _____ no, never
5 _____ NA

61. When you get out of the elevator on your floor, do you ever feel as if you are closed up inside the building or don't know where the front is?

1 _____ yes, often
2 _____ yes, sometimes
3 _____ no
4 _____ no opinion
5 _____ NA

[IF YES:] Why do you get that feeling?

_____

_____

62. Now I am going to give you two words and I want you to tell me which one of these two words best describes a certain part of the building.

A. How would you describe the lobby and hallways of this floor?

1 _____ like a private home   or _____ like a public building
2 _____ hard   or _____ soft
3 _____ simple   or _____ complex

Why?

_____

_____

B. How would you describe the inside of the main floor (the social spaces)? As

1 _____ like a private home   or _____ like a public building
2 _____ hard   or _____ soft
3 _____ simple   or _____ complex

Why? _____

_____

C. How would you describe the way the building looks from the outside?

1 _____ like a private home   or _____ like a public building
2 _____ hard   or _____ soft
3 _____ simple   or _____ complex

Why? _____

_____

63. In your opinion, is your hallway (on own floor):

A. too long?
1 _____ yes
2 _____ no
3 _____ no opinion

B. too dark?
1 _____ yes
2 _____ no
3 _____ no opinion

C. too narrow?
1 _____ yes
2 _____ no
3 _____ no opinion

64. Do you think that it is easy for a person in the hallway to hear what is going on in other people's apartments?

1 _____ yes
2 _____ no
3 _____ no opinion
4 _____ mind own business

64.1 When you are in your apartment, can you hear what is going on in the apartments next to you?

1 _____ yes
2 _____ no
3 _____ no opinion
4 _____ mind own business

Appendix B-2

65. Would you like sitting areas along your hallway?

1 ____ yes
2 ____ no
3 ____ no opinion

66. Would you mind passing these places if other people were sitting there?

1 ____ yes
2 ____ no
3 ____ no opinion

67. Do you find it easy to tell the difference between your apartment door and others?

1 ____ yes   How? _____
2 ____ no
3 ____ no opinion

Is it any different? (INTERVIEWER COMMENT) _____
_____

68. When you open your apartment door, do you think that it is too easy for someone in the hallway to see all the way inside?

1 ____ yes   Does that bother you? ____ yes   ____ no
2 ____ no
3 ____ no opinion

70. People prefer the comfort of their own apartments for certain activities, for others they like to go to a lounge on their own apartment floor, for some activities they choose to go to the social spaces on the ground floor. I am going to list several activities and I would like you to tell me which location you prefer for each.
[REPEAT THREE LOCATIONS FOR EACH ACTIVITY.]

	ground floor	lounge on apt. floor	own apartment	no opinion
A. reading book or magazine				
B. playing cards with a few friends				
C. giving small birthday party for friend				
D. hanging out and chatting with people				
E. sitting and watching others				

71. Would you say that most of your friends in this building live on this floor, or do most of them live on other floors in the building?

1 ____ most on this floor
2 ____ most on other floors
3 ____ about equal for both
4 ____ most live outside this building
5 ____ no opinion

Appendix B-2

Apartments with balconies   Appendix B-2

72. How often do you use your balcony in nice weather?

     1 _____ often
     2 _____ sometimes
     3 _____ rarely
     4 _____ never

73. What do you usually do when you use the balcony?

     _____

     _____

74. If you had a choice, would you prefer the balcony, a
     larger living room, (IF ONE BEDROOM) a larger bedroom,
     (IF EFFICIENCY) or a separate bedroom?

     1 _____ balcony
     2 _____ larger living room
     3 _____ larger bedroom
     4 _____ separate bedroom
     5 _____ larger kitchen

Selected Responses (Percent)
Tenant Interview - Spatial Analysis
Design Evaluation Project - Cambridge, MA 1976.

Question	Building		
26. Where are you most likely to run into others?	A	B	C
1) coming/going in building	7	26	38
2) passing by social space	3	15	24
3) going to get mail	90	48	29
4) laundry	0	7	-
5) NA, DK	0	-	9
(N)	(20)	(27)	(21)

32. Generally, about how often go into any of social rooms in building?			
1) every day/night	45	27	24
* 2) more than once/mo.	40	20	14
3) once/mo. or less	15	33	42
(N)	(20)	(27)	(21)

* categories collapsed

22. Feel need to get out of apartment?
(Percent) (by unit size and occupants)

	0 BR building			1BR 1 occupant building			2 occupants building		
	A	B	C	A	B	C	A	B	C
Yes	40	18	76	0	0	9	30	7	0
No	20	52	14	0	0	0	10	23	0

(N)

Behaviors in Shared Spaces
Time and Setting Sample

	Site A	Site B
Tenants on Site (N)	220	245
Mean tenants observed, informal activities*	11	6
Percent of tenants	5%	2.5%
Mean tenants observed, formal activities	18	23**
Percent of tenants	8%	9%
Mean number behavior settings	2	4
Observed attendance, tenants association meeting	42	70

Observed Behavior Setting Types

Informal

Solo: sitting or standing
    watching out window
    watching interior activity
   *passing through, looking in
    reading
    playing game

Social: talking, one other
    talking, group
    playing cards
    playing pool
    standing or walking
      interaction

Formal

Tenants club
Church service
Bingo game
** Noon meal program
birthday party

*Approximately 20 observation periods per site.

Source: Design Evaluation Project, MIT 1976.

PHOTODOCUMENTATION.

General Instructions

Recommended film - B&W 35mm Tri-X

Alternative - slides or color prints

A. Plan initial photo sequence from floor plan.

B. Mark on floor plan with arrows, location and direction from which shots to be taken.

C. Inform manager and tenants that "you will be photographing commonly used spaces inside their building". If a tenant appears face front in any shot, ask for signed release on use of photo (use standard release form). Photographs showing people using various spaces or objects are more informative than shots of empty spaces. Wherever possible include people in the photos.

D. Suggested order of shots (carefully note, within numbered arrows on floor plan, any deviations from this order):

1. Immediate exterior of main entry to the building, focusing on main entry, preferably with entering or exiting tenant in shot.

2. Immediate interior of main entry, as tenant would see straight ahead on passing through door(s).

3-6[+] Left to right shots from entry, as tenant would scan environment on entering the building (Take as many shots as necessary).

6[+] Pathway: between main entry and elevator landing. Who and what is a tenant likely to see in traversing this path, i.e., gatherings; mailboxes; corridor to community room; bulletin boards.

10[+] Lobby area: develop and note on floor plan, a left to right scan.

14[+][*] Elevator landing: what does a tenant see as he leaves the elevator or when he is waiting for it?

16[+] Community Room: at entrance to community room, do a left to right scan with photographs of what is visible at that point. Then stand in middle of room, or best vantage point and shoot a panoramic sequence - note on floor plan.

[*] Be generous with these shots to cover all potential design and person interaction issues.

Site _____   APARTMENT UNIT QUESTIONNAIRE
Apt. No. _____
No. of Bedrooms _____

Now I would like to ask you a few questions about your
apartment unit and how you have furnished it.

1. Let's start with the size of the apartment.
    How well does it suit your needs?

        a.____ too large
        b.____ just fine
        c.____ too small
        d.____ NA, DK

2. Did you give away any furniture when you moved in here?
    NOTE HOW MANY OF EACH ITEM.

        a.___ bedroom bureaus
        b.___ bed (___twin or ___double)
        c.___ night tables
        d.___ dining table
        e.___ dining room chairs
        f.___ china cabinet
        g.___ easy chairs
        h.___ couch or sofa
        i.___ end tables
        j.___ bookshelves or display cases
        k.___ other (specify)
        l.___ NO

3. Were there any pieces that you would particularly liked
    to have kept had you had more space?

        a.___ bedroom bureaus
        b.___ bed (___twin or ___double)
        c.___ night tables
        d.___ dining table
        e.___ dining room chairs
        f.___ china cabinet
        g.___ easy chairs
        h.___ couch or sofa
        i.___ end tables
        j.___ bookshelves or display cases
        k.___ other (specify)
        l.___ NO

4. What furniture have you bought or been given for this
    apartment?

        a.___ TV
        b.___ stereo
        c.___ bed (___twin or ___double)
        d.___ dressers or bureaus

Appendix C-1

4. Continued

e. ___ couch
f. ___ chairs
g. ___ end tables
h. ___ dining room set
i. ___ other (specify)
j. ___ NONE

IF THEY DID GET NEW FURNITURE, ASK: Why did you want
this furniture for the apartment? PROBES: APT. FELT
TOO LARGE WITHOUT IT or WANTED NEW FURNITURE FOR A
NEW APT.

_____

_____

_____

5. Are you planning to get any more furniture?

a. ___ yes
b. ___ no
c. ___ don't know

IF YES, what are you planning to get and why?

_____

_____

_____

Where will you put it? HAVE RESPONDENT SHOW YOU AND MARK
IT ON THE FLOOR PLAN.

6. Do you re-arrange your furniture often?

a. ___ yes, frequently (___weekly or ___monthly)
b. ___ yes, sometimes (yearly)
c. ___ yes, rarely
d. ___ no, never

IF YES, do you re-arrange some pieces of furniture more
than others? NOTE WHICH ONES.

_____

_____

Appendix C-1

7. Do you have a favorite piece of furniture like a chair
   or table which you use frequently? NOTE WHICH PIECE.
   Why did you put it where it is now?

   _____

   _____

   _____

8. Do you have any visitors or do you entertain anyone in
   your apartment?

   a.___ yes
   b.___ no

   IF YES, how many do you entertain at a time?

   _____

   _____

   IF YEG, how often do you have visitors?

   a.___ every day
   b.___ several times a week
   c.___ once a week
   d.___ 1,2 or 3 times a month
   e.___ infrequently

   IF YES, do you have any folding chairs or tables which
   you use while entertaining or playing cards or in some
   other activity?

   a.___ yes
   b.___ no

   IF YES, where do you set it up? _____

   _____

9. FOR EFFICIENCY APTS., Do you feel awkward if visitors
   have to walk by your bedroom area to get to the batnroom?

   a.___ yes
   b.___ no
   c.___ don't care,NA

   Comments _____

Appendix C-1

10 . Which do you prefer?

    a.___ eat-in kitchen
    b.___ a separate dining area (dining room)
    c.___ like it is here with the dining area as
        part of the living room
    d.___ don't know, don't care

11 . APTS. WITH CENTRALLY LOCATED ENTRANCES, Do you mind
seeing the kitchen when you enter?

    a.___ yes
    b.___ no
    c.___ don't know, don't care

Comments _____

_____

12. APTS. WITH SIDE ENTRANCES, Do you mind going through the
living room to get to the kitchen when you are coming
home with groceries?

    a.___ yes
    b.___ no
    c.___ don't care, don't know

Comments _____

_____

13. Do you have any final comments about your apartment unit?

_____

_____

_____

Appendix C-3

Sample Field Notes, Team Photo Review

Setting #35

E. Mrs. A. is her name, French, she lived in a three family home, 2nd floor. She made this move because of health, could no longer climb the stairs, but she constantly reiterates that she knew the people there, she misses them, they miss her. Seems resigned to the fact that she must live in elderly housing. She is "thrilled" with the apartment, that is quite obvious, but her standard reply is, "Well I don't want to complain." I was able to figure out, that this china cabinet and this seat to the left of the table which is just out of view on the slide are two very significant things, she sits in that chair, that is her favorite chair at the table, she can look at the TV but what is more she can look at the china cabinet, which she does.

Q. Is that yellow chair, the chair with the yellow pads her favorite?

E. No, the favorite is part of the dining room set, an ordinary straight-back chair. She is not one to lounge around, she sits in that chair and looks at that china cabinet. (There had been two of them). The one very important thing about this unit for Mrs. A is its lack of a dining room. She's the only respondent I had who when asked if she would like a larger bedroom or an eat-in kitchen responded that she would like a dining room because her entertainment and her sole purpose in life is being able to serve food to her family, when they come to visit. She has a considerable number of grandchildren and because of the size of the unit, and in her mind the necessity to serve food, they must come in groups, they can never come all at once. (I really think that if you were to take that china cabinet away and use that space to serve dinner she would probably go into a crying bout, because it is the only thing that makes her feel "important and useful"!). The unit is extremely neat, I almost get the impression that she never lives in it. To me that was a very significant thing. It is so neat and so sparse that it is as if she gets up in the morning, gets dressed, and sits down in that chair.

Q. She has to do some housework. Do you get any idea of how she spends her day in regard to tidying around that apartment?

E. I don't think she ever cleans it up, because I don't think she ever messes it up. She probably gets up immediately and makes the bed.

Q. Does she use that rocking chair?

E. Apparently. She did not say that she did.

Q. She watches TV?

E. She sits in that little chair.

Q. Does she watch TV?

E. Yes, she does watch TV because it was on when I got there. She watches TV from that same chair.

Q. You don't know really because you are a visitor, you don't know come night time that she doesn't move that green chair around with the doll in it.

E. I asked her two or three times about it and I'll tell you something - I'll bet you dollars to doughnuts that she doesn't move that chair. I don't think she moves a thing in that apartment. She is almost a guest in her own house(?). Here is another view of the bedroom, again every-thing absolutely in place, I've been to that apartment twice and it has never been any different. Nothing has ever been one inch to the right or left of where it was before. Here is the bathroom, I have wondered often in these units where the towels are. I don't know where they keep the towels, there is not a towel in sight, but she does have these rather pretty covered up soaps...stuffed swans.

Setting #09

E. This apartment is occupied by the G. sisters. It is one bedroom, side entry. This is coming into their living area,

Q. Had they lived together before they came here?

E. Yes, they have been living together for a long time.

Q. Were either married?

E. One was married, the younger one, R. The older sister was not andthey had been living separately until R's husband died. They have been living together for quite some time.

Q. Has the furniture now become collective or is it clear that each piece is someone's?

E. My impression is that it is collective. They didn't specifically say.

Q. Any consistency in where they sat?

E. That is J. and that is her perpetual sitting place, there is practically a dent in the cushion, she sits there all the time. She has a very bad case of arthritis and can't get out, has considerable amount of difficulty. She has been in this apartment all winter long, has not been out and the other sister, R., who is considerably less articulate, takes care of the shopping, cleaning up and apart-ment maintenance. R. sits in that orange chair, with the white foot stool in front of it, and those seem to be their places. I have been in this apartment three or four times, to take a check and to go back and photograph and a couple of other things like that and they are always in the same places. They are very active socially in terms of having people in their apartment, everybody on the floor that I interviewed knew the sisters. They seem to talk a lot to the other single women, who don't have any other friends, in other words they would say, "No, I don't know very many other people on this floor, but I know the sisters at the end.", "I go to mass with them" or "I talk to them". So they have a funny kind of social arrangement and the people come into their apartment for various reasons. Most of the times I went there they had two or three residents in the apartment.

Q. Where were they sitting?

E. They sat on the couch.

Q. They eat their meals where?

E. At this little round table right there. This is looking back towards the entry on the left. there is their eating table. Those are religious pictures, those three pictures hanging on the wall. That green chair is where I sat when I did the interview. That is another sort of sitting space. They had a lot of complaints about the kitchen. They are both quite short and they brought up the complaint of the cabinets being too high. And this is particularly a problem for J. with her limitations of movement. The first time I went there, the far right piece of countertop was covered with cosmetic bottles. So I presume that they cleaned it off for this photo session.

Q. Do you think they only cleaned them off for the photograph session?

E. Well, I was in there twice before the photo session and both times they had cosmetic bottles there. We came back for the photo session (they had received the letter ahead of time) and the bottles were not there.

Q. Did you ever see the cupboard doors open to see the extent to which they use the shelves.

E. One time she (J.) was showing me how she couldn't reach in, she reached into the one that is right above the stove and it had a few plates and cups on the bottom but nothing on the upper two shelves;

what they do is stack these plates here in the corner which is to the left hand of the counter. They store basic things above in the cabinets and this is what they use all the time. They can't reach up so they stack also on the top of the refrigerator. This is the bedroom, they had a lot of complaint about the bedroom as well. You can see it here (two single beds) on the far side of the room there is a chest and chair, under the window, in the corner that you can't see to the right, is a side chair. It looks like a living room piece like the ones with the round table, rather formal mahogany rosewood, which they used to put my coat on. They complained that it was very difficult to get to the beds, and in fact there is very little space between the bed and the face of the vanity, you can't open the drawers and stand in front with the drawers open, you have to stand in between the beds, in that little space. They didn't like that at all. This is looking back into the hallway. So that is the sisters.

REFERENCES

SELECTED REFERENCES

American Association of Homes for the Aging. Planning and Financing Facilities for the Elderly. Washington, DC: American Association of Homes for the Aging, 1978.

American Institute of Architects and Center on Aging and Human Development. Designing for the Elderly: Proceedings of 11th Annual Architectural Research Conference. Nashville, TN: 1975.

Bechtel, Robert B. Enclosing Behavior. Stroudsburg, PA: Dowden, Hutchinson & Ross, 1977.

Berk, Richard A. and Berk, Sarah F. Labor and Leisure at Home. Beverly Hills, CA: Sage Library of Social Research, Vol. 87, 1979.

Birren, James E. and Schaie, K. Warner, eds. Handbook of the Psychology of Aging. New York: Van Nostrand Reinhold, 1977.

Cantor, Marjorie H. "Neighbors and Friends: An Overlooked Resource in the Informal Support System." Research on Aging, Volume 1, No. 4, December, 1979, pp. 434-463.

Comptroller General of the US. Report to the Congress: Housing for the Elderly--Factors Which should be Evaluated Before Deciding on Low-or High-Rise Construction. Washington, DC: Department of HUD, 1975.

Davis, Sam, ed. The Form of Housing. New York: Van Nostrand Reinhold, 1977.

Donahue, Wilma T., Pepe, Penelope H. and Murray, Priscilla. Assisted Independent Living in Residential Congregate Housing- A Report of the Situation in the US, 1978. Washington, DC: International Center for Social Gerontology, 1978.

Donahue, Wilma T. and Pepe, Penelope. An Annotated International Bibliography on Assisted Independent Residential Living for Older People (A Form of Congregate Housing). Washington, DC: International Center for Social Gerontology, 1977.

Esser, Aristide and Greenbie, Barrie B., eds. Design for Communality and Privacy. New York: Plenum Press, 1978.

Francescato, Guido, Anderson, James R., Weidemann, Sue, and Chenoweth, Richard. Residents' Satisfaction in HUD-Assisted Housing: Design and Management Factors. Washington, DC: Supt. of Documents, 1979.

Gelwicks, Louis and Newcomer, Robert. Planning Housing Environments for the Elderly. Washington, DC: The National Council on the Aging, Inc., 1974.

Gelwicks, Louis E. "The Building Program: A List of Spaces is Not Enough." Concern, June-July, 1975.

Howell, Sandra. "Needed: Performance Specifications for Using Behavior Science." Industrialization Forum, Vol. 5, No. 5 (1974), pp. 25-29.

Howell, Sandra C. "How the Elderly Live: What We Know and Need to Know." in Environmental Context of Aging, eds. Thomas Byerts, Sandra Howell and Leon Pastalan. New York: Garland STPM Press, 1979.

Koncelik, Joseph A. Designing the Open Nursing Home. Stroudsburg, PA: Dowden, Hutchinson & Ross, 1976.

Lawton, M. Powell. Planning and Managing Housing for the Elderly. New York: John Wiley & Sons, 1975.

Lawton, M. Powell, Newcomer, Robert J. and Byerts, Thomas O., eds. Community Planning for an Aging Society. Stroudsburg, PA: Dowden, Hutchinson & Ross, 1976.

McClain, Jan. Housing the Elderly-Proceedings from the Regional Seminars and Workshops Held in Winnipeg, Vancouver, Toronto, Montreal andHalifax 1974-75. Ottawa, ONT: The Canadian Council on Social Development, 1976.

Nahemow, Lucille, Lawton, M. Powell and Howell, Sandra C. "Elderly People in Tall Buildings: A Nationwide Study." in Human Response to Tall Buildings, ed. Donald J. Conway. Stroudsburg, PA: Dowden, Hutchinson & Ross, 1977.

Rose, Edgar A. Housing for the Aged. Hampshire, England: Saxon House, 1978.

Riley, Matilda W. and Foner, A. Aging and Society, Volume 1: an Inventory of Research Findings. New York: Russell Sage Foundation, 1968.

Sherwood, Roger. Modern Housing Prototypes. Cambridge, MA: Harvard University Press, 1978.

US Dept. of HUD. Evaluation of the Effectiveness of Congregate Housing for the Elderly. Pamphlet 023-000-00378-3. Washington, DC: Superintendent of Documents, 1976.

US Dept. of HUD. How Well are We Housed?-4. The Elderly. Washington, DC: Superintendent of Documents, 1979.

US Dept. of HUD. Housing for the Elderly and Handicapped-The Experience of the Section 202 Program from 1959 to 1977. Washington, DC: Superintendent of Documents, 1979.

Wagner, Jon, ed. Images of Information. Beverly Hills, CA: Sage Publications, 1979.

Zeisel, John, Epp, Gayle and Demos, Stephen. Low Rise Housing for Older People. For Dept of HUD, Washington, DC: Superintendent of Documents, 1977.

INDEX